God's Love
LANGUAGE

God's Love
LANGUAGE

WALDON B. WRIGHT

Library of Congress Control Number: 2014907447

ISBN: 978-1-63821-063-4 (Paperback Edition)
ISBN: 978-1-63821-064-1 (Hardcover Edition)
ISBN: 978-1-63821-055-9 (E-book Edition)

Unless otherwise stated, all Scriptures are taken from the Kings James Version (KJV) of the Bible. Other Scripture quoted from versions other than the King James Version are as follows:

Scripture taken from Holy Bible, New International Version*, NIV* Copyright ©1973, 1978, 1984, 1995, 2011 by Biblica, Inc.*, Common English Bible (CEB) Copyright 2010, Contemporary English Version (CEV) Copyright © 1995, English Standard Version (ESV) Copyright © 2001, New English Translation (NET Bible) Copyright ©1996-2006, Good News Translation (GNT) Copyright © 1992, New Living Translation (NLT) Copyright 1996, 2004, Used by permission. All rights reserved worldwide.

Quotations and references are used from Ellen G White© Estate, Inc. Used by permission. All rights reserved. The author assumes full responsibility for the accuracy and interpretation of the Ellen White quotations cited in this book.

Quotations and references from Dr. Gary Chapman's book, The Five Love Languages, Moody Publishers, are also used by permission.

The author also assumes full responsibility for the accuracy and interpretation of other quotation and facts presented in this book.

Book Ordering Information

Phone Number: 315 288-7939 ext. 1000 or 347-901-4920
Email: info@globalsummithouse.com
Global Summit House
www.globalsummithouse.com

Printed in the United States of America

CONTENTS

DEDICATION

Primary

This book is dedicated to my most wonderful, loving, and amazing God who has successfully wooed me to become acquainted with Him, and who has given me wisdom and spiritual insight to write this inspiring and thought- provoking book.

Secondary

To my wonderful family: wife, Violet; sons: Pierre-Anthony, Jean-mark, and Andre-Paul. To all my siblings, relatives, in-laws, and friends. To all those who are genuinely seeking for truth and the spiritual Pearl of righteousness, as well as the triune God (who loves you with an everlasting love) and want you to lead a lifestyle of loving obedience to God and to practice His love language.

To all those who have met disappointments in life and feel like giving up. To all those who want to make a change in life for the better, but are not sure how to do it.

ABOUT THE AUTHOR

The author is an ordained elder and someone who has been involved in the leadership of the Church for over twenty-five 25) years in varying capacities and ministries including: stewardship, family life, personal evangelism, religious liberty, as well as business manager for many evangelistic crusades. He knows and understands firsthand the challenges and blessings of leadership in a Church that operates in a multinational, multicultural, multilingual, multi-religious, pluralistic and dynamic environment with a plethora of diverse political and economic systems. He has helped and witnessed numerous persons becoming followers of Jesus Christ and the joy they experience, and is acquainted with the challenges that many others face in choosing otherwise.

He is a graduate of the University of Technology (Utech) with a Diploma in Pharmacy; the University of the West Indies (UWI) with a Bachelor of Science (BSc.) degree (Management Studies); and the University of New Orleans (UNO) with a Master in Business Administration (MBA). At the time of preparing the manuscript of this book for reprinting he was pursuing doctoral studies at Northern Caribbean University (NCU).He has done several post-graduate courses from various institutions, locally and overseas, covering: financing, credit, business development and management. He lectured at both graduate and undergraduate levels at universities including NCU, UWI, UTech, and the University of the Commonwealth Caribbean (UCC), and made seminar presentations at seminars and conferences both locally and overseas. He worked in various management positions in financial (NGO and non- NGO) and non financial organizations for over twenty-five (25) years.

He is blessed by God as a multi-skilled business and Christian professional with experiences spanning the financial, educational, health and religious sectors, and has used these blessings to enrich the lives of others in Jamaica and overseas. He left the financial sector in 2011 in response to answer the call to join the team of Administrators at East Jamaica Conference as Treasurer in February 2011. He subsequently served as Director of Health and Stewardship Ministries and Trust Services, before serving as an Auditor since 2018.

He is happily married to Violet, Nursing Educator, and the union produced three sons: Pierre-Anthony, Jean-Mark, and Andre-Paul. He is a lover of God's people and His truth, young people, and is man of God. His mission is to embrace God's love language and to encourage others to do the same, and his vision is to live in readiness for the second coming of Jesus Christ.

Now under divine influence, personal conviction, a passion for writing and sharing his knowledge, this author combines his talents and skills, business acumen, spiritual gifts, rich and rewarding experience as a church leader, husband and father, to produce this master piece- God's Love Language. It is a love language that in the words of Pastor Everett Brown "is authentic and exclusively" God's, that God wants us to become acquainted with, love, speak, and share with others so that humans may enjoy the best relationships possible, that are good and beneficial, saving and eternal.

FOREWORD

When Waldon Wright invited me to write the foreword for his extraordinary appealing work, God's Love Language, I readily acceded to his request without reservation, having had the privilege of discussing with him his insatiable desire to document his ideas for a much wider audience.

The author brings to this project decades of practical experiences and knowledge as a critical thinker, successful professional and devout Christian. Wright's years of devoted service to the church as an ordained Elder, Conference Treasurer, and Director, coupled with the pivotal roles he has played over the years as husband and father has prepared him adequately to address both in scope and substance the matter under discussion.

God's Love Language is carefully arranged into seven (7) expertly organized easy to read Chapters. In the book the author expertly and methodically responds to the question: "Does God have a Love Language?" In just over 290 simple yet profound pages, Wright shares with his audience his concept of God and God's Love Language.

Having personally perused the manuscript which forms the foundation on which the book stands, I have discovered that God's Love Language, philosophically speaking, is much more than an analytical discussion about the Love of God. The author painstakingly and methodically marshalls his arguments to support his thesis that God's authentic and preferred method of communicating with mankind is by means of His Love Language.

Wright passionately began his work by taking a detailed look at the meaning of Language and Communication, including God's interest in language and communication. He then went on to systematically define Love and Love Language, including love as a choice, love as a principle, love's ultimate objective, kinds of love and love hierarchy. Wright deliberately posits his God-centered world view in the book as he attempts to substantiate his position by unequivocally articulating his definition and explanation of God and God's Love Language.

The author then segues into a rather fascinating section of the book by looking at what he describes as requirements, Blessings and Benefits of God's Love Language. Wright concluded his arguments in support of his thesis by looking at cause and effect, and challenges those who read the book to respond to God's Love Language.

This amazingly profound masterpiece is securely grounded in the Bible, the Word of God, but interestingly from a Seventh-day Adventist perspective, the book is timely, theologically sound and doctrinally authentic. I would without reservation recommend this book, not only for use by the public at large but one that the church in general should definitely utilize as a resource in its mission to promulgate the gospel.

Pastor Everett Brown
President, Jamaica Union Conference of Seventh-day Adventists
June 7, 2020

ACKNOWLEDGEMENTS

First I want to acknowledge God who gave me the thought, the compliant spirit, the perseverance, and the wisdom to write this book. Special thanks to my wife, Violet, for her objective and analytical support; my sister: Mrs. Shirnet Wellington (for reviewing the draft and providing invaluable feedback) and her husband, Pastor Leon Wellington, as well as to my brother, Dr. Wycliffe Wright and his wife Marie, for their kind consideration in providing a conducive writing environment, general support and encouragement, and assistance in reviewing the material. Thanks also to my brother, Dr. Lincoln Wright, for pointing me to very pertinent quotations from E. G. White, some of which have been included in this book.

Special thanks to Dr. Anidolee Chester, family friend, for providing critical and analytical feedback on the first completed draft manuscript. Thanks also to Dian Bailey, another family friend, for reviewing two consecutive manuscripts and for providing valuable written comments. Appreciation also goes to Pastor Everett Brown, President, Jamaica Union Conference, with whom I shared my desire to undertake this project, and who willingly gave of his time to assist me in my search for a publisher, and also for agreeing to do the foreword, as well as for his general words of encouragement. Like, Pastor Brown, Pastor Glen Samuels has also provided quality feedback and from a theological perspective. Thanks also to Kay Scott for proof reading the earlier draft manuscript. I am also very grateful for the sincere and effervescent teen-agers and young adults who met at our family home on weekends and read sections of the drafts and gave their honest feedback and encouragements.

Finally, I must also acknowledge my thankfulness to Mrs. Camile Morris-Robinson, who extended the invitation on behalf of her church board, to allow me to speak on the topic, which turned out to be the precursor for the book.

INTRODUCTION

Background and origin

Life can sometimes be truly amazing. You never always know today, what tomorrow will bring. Today, right now, you know for sure where you are, and what you are doing. But you cannot always prophetically say with honesty, correctness, and certainty, who are the people that will enter your life. Neither do you know with exactitude what they will ask you to do for them in the future or how your response will affect you. However, a favourable response to their asking or requests can sometimes change your life, in ways that you may never have dreamt.

Well, that happened to me! I was asked to speak on a specified topic that I never spoke on before at the divine service at a church one weekend. Up to the present time, I am not sure as to why I was asked to be the speaker, when there is a varsity of better speakers to choose from. However, with the unfolding of events, I have concluded that it was not by chance, or accident, but by divine providence. While I did various presentations and conducted numerous studies on different aspects of the topic, I never spoke directly to, or on that specific topic.

Nevertheless, I accepted the invitation, and did the presentation. It went well. Interestingly, since that presentation, I have had repeated reflections on that topic and realized just how germane and appealing it is. It arouses curiosity. It begs a question that a keen seeker searching for truth will want to get a satisfying answer to. It is so enthralling that at other speaking engagements, I have had the opportunity to mention it time and time again in communicating certain important truths. With the effluxion of time, I have had reason to think that the content should be shared with a wider audience.

Three months after making the presentation, I started to write a book on business entitled: "Ten Steps to Starting and Managing Your Own Business", which will soon be ready for publishing. After completing the draft of that book on business, an inspiration took hold of me. It went like this: "why not write a book on this topic first?" I have responded! Within less than nine (9) months since starting it, that same divine providence that directed me to speak that weekend, helped me to complete this book entitled: "God's Love Language", the same topic that I was asked to speak on that divinely appointed, foreordained weekend. That to me is truly amazing! Why? Simply put, if you had asked me then, at the conclusion of that weekend if I would be interested in writing this book, my answer would most likely have been no. So, now you are reading this book, as a result of someone asking me to speak on that weekend. Given this background, you may well appreciate, therefore, that this book is not only for you, the present reader, but for all the other persons that you will tell about it, and ask to get a copy, because it has touched and changed your life.

Intended target

This book is intended for all those persons who are seeking an answer to what is "God's Love Language", and are looking for a church that practices God's Love Language. These persons include: genuine seekers of truth, who want to obtain, caress and practice truth in their lives. Included also are all those parents who want to enrich their Christian experience, as well as that of their offspring, who they want to embrace enduring and life changing truths. Teens and young adults are also included in this intended target group. It is also a book for leaders, including church leaders, Bible workers and instructors. It's also for preachers of the gospel, evangelists and teachers.

Notwithstanding the above, this book is inclusive rather than exclusive, and is therefore intentionally directed also to those who have been disappointed (whether by design or default) by family, relatives, friends, church, the workplace, and society. It is for the victim, but also for the villain and perpetrator of vice. It is a book for those who need a second chance, as well as for those who are very confident and even overly self-confident. It is also for those who have tried everything in life, even witchcraft.

It is a book for all those who are members of the Church to which I belong, as well as those who would like to become members. By contrast, it is also for those who will have nothing do with such a church or any church for that matter. Finally, it is for all those readers who want to have a better relationship with God and their fellowmen, plus a guarantee on the best life, eternal life, in paradise unparalleled, Heaven and the earth made new.

Content and purpose

This book is a must read. Some are already suggesting that it is a best-seller. This is because it delves directly and comprehensively at the meat of the matter of what is "God's Love Language." This is done in a manner that will reaffirm the believer, challenge the objective and analytical minded, while helping many ignorant, doubters, skeptics, and agnostics to cross the line to believe and to appreciate that God is not a loser, and that those who are on His side are on the winning team. This treatise is complemented with a caressing and eye-opening content on love, language and communication of love. Additionally, it is mingled with fascination as it not only outlines the reasons for the nagging problems of life, of the home and family, of the church, of the society and the world at large, but it provides answers and solutions that will startle you. But it is a book of contrasts. This is because it speaks about life, but it is also a book about death. It outlines genuine truths,while it does not ignore deception and the counterfeit. It is big on communication among the living, but it discloses plots,decoy and apparent communication between the living and the dead. It deals with justice (what we deserve for what we did)but also with amazing, marvelous, matchless grace (what we receive for what we didn't deserve).

As you embark on this breathtaking reading journey, you will notice that some words, statements and sentences in this **first reprinted edition** *are presented in bold throughout the book. This is intended for emphasis mainly and allows for easy recognition, locating or recall by you, the reader. Additionally, this first reprinted copy reflects the advantages of editing and expands on the meaning of the word 'lifestyle' cited in Chapter 3. Bible texts quoted are also shown in italics. Finally, a bibliography is included in this edition (copy) using the Turabian/ Chicago style.*

Beginning with the first two sentences of that weekend presentation, but clearly expanding significantly on it, the seven chapters of this book provide spiritual meat and insight, logic and reason; challenges to scholars; mystique for the artist; analysis for the analyst; mingled with drama and intrigue and surprise for the literary minded person. Its plots are full of life and suspense, yet saturated with blessings and benefits for those who make a decision in favour of practicing God's Love Language. But the path on which it takes us also includes excuses and impact; responsibility and accountability; cause and effect, reward and consequences which are the two inescapable results of the exercise of our choice, the devastating consequences of ignoring God's Love Language, as well as the profundity of God's love and love language. In its pages are also carefully and comprehensively outlined the peppercorn price we (those who embrace God's Love Language) will be required to pay for the truly unbelievable, but really inexhaustible, infinite, pure and undefiled, incomparable benefits.

Ironically, it also speaks about a lawyer who sought explanation for the answer he gives in answering his own question. It speaks about the challenges that arise when human love languages are ignored. But it speaks in profusion of a triune God, His love, the incarnation, and the requirements of that human divine gift to all mankind. Contrastingly, it unearths aspects of the spirit world and of a king who tried to escape media attention to have a nocturnal secret meeting, in what may be called the plot of all plots or the drama of all dramas. It speaks about the **integrity** which is expected of leaders and shows the proportionality between **accountability** and **responsibility.** Then it closes with our response to God's love for us, and this includes the desired right response, behaviour and living in anticipation of an endless life of love and happiness.

Greatest benefit

You can never read this book from cover to cover and remain the same. This is because its peaks to body, mind, spirit, and soul. It will sharpen and enhance your understanding of love, love languages, cause and effect, as well as the need to avoid deception, and personal deficiencies. It serves to lift the thoughts from things mundane to things divine. This will add value to enrich the quality of your present life and the remainder of your years here on planet earth. You will gain direct leads and guidelines as to how to secure a life that is better than the one that now is. It provides a new way of thinking and reasoning, decision making and relationship building. Another noticeable benefit is that it will help you to weigh more carefully every decision and every choice, as our decision will determine our future here in this world and our chances of gaining access to the wider joy of greater service in the sinless world to come.

However, the **greatest benefit** that can be gained from reading this book, which is the goal of the author, is to discover God, the real author of "God's Love Language", and to establish, and maintain a genuine, saving, and preserving love relationship with our divine triune God so that you will lovingly and willingly embrace and practice His love language. Such a relationship will result in transformed lives, mutually beneficial relationships and readiness for resurrection or translation at the second coming of Jesus. This realization will exceed man's best expectation. It will be truly amazing to realize that one of these days, there will be no more sin, sadness, crime and violence, disease and death, and that we will be going to live with Jesus. It will be doubly amazing when you come to realize how it all started; someone whom you did not know, extended an invitation to this sinful human author, touched and transformed by God, to speak on "God's Love Language." But, in the final analysis, it will be worth it after all. Happy reading!

CHAPTER 1

LANGUAGE AND COMMUNICATION OF LOVE

ARE YOU LOVED and are you in love? How do you know? Can you honestly vouch for your answer? Do you truth fully know and understand, what is the meaning of love? Giving and receiving love can be a most wonderful reciprocal experience. My wife and I are a testimony to this, and we are also acquainted with some other really great lovers. As a result of communicating with, and learning from many of them for over thirty (30) years, we have observed that great lovers communicate their love in the language of love. They place great value and importance on the person, the main object of their love.

This placing of emphasis on the object of their love is what motivates them to want to learn and know more about the language and communication of love. Like the right hand and left hand which cannot clap without each other, language, and communication of love go together. Like great lovers, those who are not so good at giving and receiving love, will if they are prudent, want to know more and more about the language of love and how to communicate love. And God, the greatest lover of all, also has immense interest in them both: (i) the object of love, and (ii)the language and communication of love. Isaiah, the Old Testament prophet, cites this communication as "reasoning" as follows:

> "Come now, and let us reason together, saith the Lord."¹

Another Old Testament prophet, Jeremiah, captures this picture as a "wooing" or a "drawing" in these words:

"The Lord hath appeared of old unto me, saying, Yea, I have loved thee with an everlasting love: therefore with loving kindness have I drawn thee."[2]

God's interest in these matters, as recounted in these pages to follow, may surprise you beyond measure.

1.1 Communication

For love to be meaning fully felt, understood, and appreciated by the recipient, it must be communicated. This is true in my own marriage relationship, as well as those of many of my own siblings. But I have also witnessed it playing out in many situations including the workplace, church, in formal as well as in informal settings.

This communication is a process of reaching person(s), people, and beings with information, truths, ideas, facts, figures, in order to achieve one or more objectives. A good communication objective may be to have others understand us, share our joys or sorrows, sympathize and empathize with us, and love us. They may be to win the friendship of another person, or as varied to include gaining a place in an educational institution to pursue undergraduate or graduate study, gaining a nearly date for dental, medical, surgical or other health related appointment. Or your communication objective, may be quite different: it may be just to satisfy your curiosity to explore and to discover, to obtain employment, to get a salary increase, pass an important examination, gain a favourable decision from your soul mate for marriage, or the acquisition of very important and costly assets, get an appointment to preach a life changing sermon, or just to revive and have a revival and reformation of important social and spiritual relationships.

But some other persons, by contrast, may choose to embrace quite opposite and even abrasive objectives such as to dislike others, or to break-up the friendship of others. Despite this plethora of

---

[2]   Jeremiah 31:3.

possible communication objectives, if the communication objective is not right and just, and if the motive of the communication is not for genuine goodness, the main object of love will not be satisfied, or delightful.

The essence of true communication is shared understanding which provides a basis for love among human beings, including the sharing of ideals, values, norms and standards, dreams, feelings and emotions, secrets, plans, life's mission, goals and objectives, whether they be physical or health related, social, financial, mental or educational, cultural, and spiritual. This was absolutely true for me and my expected bride when we were courting, and it has always been so, and even more so, for my wife and me, after thirty (30) good years of married life. In addition, we have met many happily married couples who have shared the same sentiments.

Communication is great when a shared understanding takes place among varied interest groups: husbands and wives, parents and children, pastors and members, directors and shareholders, employer and employees, as well as within groups such as parents, siblings, employees, and the management team within an organization. This involves reciprocal listening, reasoning, and learning. The effect of good communication is that individuals in each group will feel good about themselves and could become more motivated to carry out their roles and accomplish individual, common or corporate goals. This motivation would ignite their lives as they pursue outstanding life goals and mission. This assumes, of course, appreciation of each other, existing skills set and core competences for the assigned tasks or roles, honesty, truthfulness, and goal congruence. In many instances however, the communication is not great, and keen observers are aware of its difficulty. The victims will become withdrawn, afraid to speak, or carry out tasks half-heartedly. In other cases, there may be resentment as well as physical, social, psychological and emotional symptoms. In other cases, it may be very difficult to identify.[3]

1.2 Language

Language is the vehicle that makes the communication possible. Like the various components of a vehicle, whether Lexus or BMW, language has various symbols that represent objects, concepts and ideas: soft and hard, material and immaterial, tangible and intangible, visible and invisible clues that must be known by the common users. If I speak English and you speak German, it is unlikely that we will be able to communicate with each other in a meaningful way, unless we have an interpreter. Yes, we may be talking a lot, but not satisfying each other's needs for shared understanding. We may even be excited, but that excitement will quickly dissipate into frustration and disappointment. So, it's better for two German speakers to get together and for two English speakers to get together. Either group will have a greater chance of accomplishing more because they share a common language.

Couples who speak different languages will have difficulties communicating love. Similarly children will have difficulties obeying parents, just like employees would have relating to employers if they speak different languages. So, where the language used in communication is different, there is the likelihood of much confusion, as occurred in the story of the Tower of Babel.[4] The Bible tells us that after the flood (which took place some 1656 years from Adam[5]), the whole earth was of one language, and one speech.

Can you imagine the immeasurable possibilities for the accomplishment of good and great things? But there was a problem. The people didn't like the idea of God telling them what to do, and the thoughts of the deluge of the Flood were still fresh in their minds. They just didn't like God's way and the content of His communication with them. Sadly, they had not yet fully appreciated the fact that their happiness, harmony and unity, and ongoing quality communication ***depended on their love for God and obedience to His commands***. So, they decided to build a tower to defy God and show the prowess of their architect and skills as well as the magnificent structural edifice - the work of their hands.

They believed that if God sent another flood, the building would be so strong and high (top may reach to heaven as in verse 4) that it would not affect them.

A decision to embark on such a slippery and ruinous course is clear evidence that the people who came after the Flood did not believe God. Neither did they find favour with His covenant, and His sign of the rainbow in the cloud, that He, God, gave them as a constant and on-going reminder that God would not again destroy the earth with a flood.[6] God decided that enough was enough! Moses in the Genesis account states that God sent the Flood because:

> *And God saw that the **wickedness** of man was great in the earth, and that every imagination of the **thoughts of his heart was only evil continually**. And it repented the LORD that he had made man on the earth, and it grieved him at his heart. And the LORD said, **I will destroy man whom I have created from the face of the earth**; both man, and beast, and the creeping thing, and the fowls of the air; for it repenteth me that I have made them.*[7]

Obviously and unfortunately (as emphasized in bold), the Antediluvians did not learn the important lesson God wanted them to learn: that man cannot win against God, and that it is a dangerous thing to "fly in the face of God," or to disobey God. So, here in Genesis Account, we see where **God confounded their language** that they may not understand one another's speech, and scattered them upon the face of the earth, and they left off building the city. [8]

Help me imagine the scene: one worker saying to another, "Bring me the cement" and the other worker returning with a

---

6   See Genesis 9: 11-13.
7   Genesis 6:5.
8   See Genesis 11:7-9.

bucket of sand. In another case, one worker says to the other: "Bring me the shovel or the spade", and to his amazement, his working colleague returns with a hammer. So, the situation only gets worse. There is perhaps shouting, misunderstanding, chaos, disunity and separation resulting in the discontinuation of the construction of the tower. Here is the interesting conclusion outlined below. [9]

> *"So the* **LORD** *scattered them abroad from thence upon the face of all the earth: and they left off to build the city"…* *"…and from thence did* **the LORD scatter them abroad** *upon the face of all the earth."*

As the Babel story illustrates, common language is vital for the building of relationships as well as for advancement in communication, construction, and human progress generally. Notwithstanding this reality, a departure from God's plan and commandments as well as His intended purpose for our lives will bring unnecessary disappointments and set backs.

1.3 God's interest in language and communication

The story of Babel (confusion) from which we get the word "Babylon" (spiritual Babylon) is a clear illustration that **God is interested in man's communication and the language used in that process of communication**. Because God is the author of both language and communication, He can intervene whenever He chooses to influence and or change the outcome of man's goals and objectives. God has chosen to intervene in many situations where man uses that communication to disobey and defy Him, the preexistent God, who was before man was created, while at the same time magnifying and idolizing his mortal, sinful self, instead of God.[10]

Communication started with God long before the creation of the human family (began with Adam and Eve) and was *intended to provide understanding, friendship and love, sharing of information and truths.* These are critically essential to any healthy and wholesome relationship. The Bible also tells of communication between God and Lucifer before the creation of the human family and before sin entered the human family.[11] These Biblical accounts give an overview of the origin of sin with Lucifer in Heaven before the creation of the human family. Moses gives an introduction of the creation of man (in the generic sense: man and woman as in Adam and Eve) as well as God's involvement in that creation. Read below what he records.

> *"And **God** said, Let **us** make man in **our** image, after **our** likeness: and let them have dominion over the fish of the sea, and over the fowl of the air, and over the cattle, and over all the earth, and over every creeping thing that creepeth upon the earth."*[12]

Notice here, the words in bold: "let **us** make man in **our** image, after **our** likeness". They reveal unselfish communication between the Godhead prior to man's creation, and this communication is about the creation of man, with an indication of the span of control given to our fore-parents.

God not only created man, but also taught him how to communicate as well as what language to use. This is demonstrated in the Genesis creation account, where God made both Adam and Eve and communicated with them. That communication also outlined the dominion that God gave to them. God's plan was that communication would continue in the earthly family; and the objective is that there would be shared understanding and reflection of the love and character of God in the human family. God set the example as follows.

---

[11] See Isaiah 14:12-17 and Ezekiel 28:12-17.

[12] Genesis 1:26.

> *"And **God blessed them**, and **God said unto them**, be fruitful, and multiply, and replenish the earth, and subdue it: and have dominion over the fish of the sea, and over the fowl of the air, and over every living thing that moveth upon the earth."*[13]

Although in the beginning there was oral communication, later followed by written communication starting with Moses, God expected that parents would spend much quality time communicating and teaching their children divine truths and principles including loving God.

> *And thou shalt **love the LORD** thy God **with all** thine heart, and with all thy soul, and with all thy might. And these **words**, which **I command thee** this day, shall be in thine heart: And thou shalt **teach them** diligently unto thy children, and shalt **talk of them** when thou sittest in thine house, and when thou walkest by the way, and when thou liest down, and when thou risest up. And thou **shalt bind them for a sign upon thine hand**, and they shall be as frontlets between thine eyes. And thou shalt **write them** upon the posts of thy house, and on thy gates.*[14]

This language/communication in the family, as outlined in this passage above emphasizes that God's intention is that our love for Him ought to be comprehensive and profound as it requires loving God with the entire being. (See Chapter 7 for more details on this, dealing with how we are to response to God). Clearly, the home is the starting point to lay a safe, solid, and secure, foundation for love to one another as well as love for God. It is in the home that the first lessons of love and obedience are to be imparted from, and by parents, to children. As children are taught to love

---

[13]   See Genesis 1:28.

[14]   Deut 6:5-9.

and obey their parents, they will find it a joy to love and obey God. And as parents correctly reflect in their words, preaching and living, love and reverence for God, the children will find it easier to emulate them and likewise show love and obedience to God in all things. God is very interested in this communication in the home and family. Propagating the communication of this principle of love and obedience in the home and family (especially to children) ought to include: the use of words, teaching, talking, binding (the words for a sign) and writing the words, whether stationery (sitting and lying down) or in motion(walking).[15] Some words that will be used incessantly include: "please", "thank you", "I am sorry", "it was my mistake", "please forgive me", "I love you", "you are beautiful", "you are sweet", "you are wonderful", "you are special". Some words that will be practiced more than they are spoken are:"respect","trust","faithful", "commitment", "truthful", integrity","honesty", "empathy", and "forgiveness".

These principles and methodologies are not to be restricted to the home. They are used by many students and scholars in preparing for examination because they are a rewarding way of learning important material. Lyman Briggs College, Michigan State University is a case in point, where its Student Advisory Council have worked together to make academic honesty a source of pride.[16] They are also used by many successful companies (such as Microsoft, Starbucks) around the world as they are universal in application.[17] "Failure of Enron, Lehman Brothers, and Sub Prime Crisis are the classic examples of failure to use honesty and moral integrity in making ethical decision and for them the end justified the means. However, on the other side, Tata and Infosys are the classic examples of honesty and moral integrity that is still

---

[15]   (See Deuteronomy 6:6-8.)
[16]   (See its posting (3-June-2012) on "Academic Honesty and Integrity" at http://www.lymanbriggs.msu.edu/current/honesty.cfm).
[17]   (See Sherri Smith, eHow Contributor's Article Online "What is a Value Statement" at http://www.ehow.com/about5063071value-statement.html).

preferred from employees and command a respectable and value based position in the world today."[18]

Similarly, God also expects His people, the family, and people generally to know Him through His Word and by the use of a combination of methodologies to familiarize themselves with His Words. Knowing Him through His Word can also be enhanced through a daily devotional life that includes daily study of His Word, an incessant life of prayer, and sharing His Word with others (evangelism and witnessing). This will prepare people from different walks of life to love God and to embrace His love language.

All will be well as long as God is at the centre of our language and communication. Tests and trials may come along our pathway, but God has promised to fight our battles.[19] However, once God is sidelined or omitted from the communication, untold problems of sin, deception, estrangements, mistrust, hiding, nakedness, blaming and accusation, pain and suffering will arise, as was in the case of Adam and Eve. But even after Adam sinned, God went in search of him to communicate forgiveness, love and hope and a future. Imagine yourself listening to God speaking to Adam as follows:

> And **the LORD God called unto Adam,** and said unto him, Where art thou? And he said, I **heard thy voice** in the garden, and I was afraid, because I was naked; and I hid myself. And he said, Who told thee that thou wast naked? Hast thou eaten of the tree, whereof I **commanded thee that thou shouldest not eat**? And the man said, The woman whom thou

---

[18] Articlesbase (Free Online Articles Directory): "Honesty and Moral Integrity: Missing Metric in Management Practices & Corporate Decisions" accessed May 28, 2010 @ http://www.articlesbase.com/strategic-planning-articles/honesty-and-moral-integrity-missing- metric-in-management-practices-corporate-decisions-2484379.html.

[19] See Exodus 14:14; Deuteronomy 1:30.

*gavest to be with me, she gave me of the tree, and I
did eat.*[20]

What was he afraid of? Sin made him afraid. Before he
sinned, he was not afraid. Sin will be expounded upon in more
detail later in this book in Chapters 2 and 3. But for now, sin is
disobeying God's commandments. He disobeyed God. But God
does not want us to disobey Him; that's why He wants us to know
and communicate His love language.

Here we get a bird's eye view of the reason for the entrance of
the problem of communication in the human family. Adam, the
first man, created sinless, discovered certain things after disobeying
one of God's clearest commands not to eat of the forbidden tree. He
discovered that he was "afraid", "naked", to the point where he "hid"
from God, His maker. When we understand God's love language,
we will not want to hide from Him. When communication has
broken down, the parties in a relationship will want to stay, or hide,
away from each other. But God will not hide or stay away from
us. As He did in Adam's case, He will come seeking after us. Why?
Because He loves us!

> *"Like as a father **pitieth** his children, so **the Lord
> pitieth** them that fear him. For he **knoweth our
> frame**; he **remembereth that we are dust**."*[21]

That's why God outlined the first promise of redemption in
the Genesis account, viz:

> *"And I will put enmity between you and the woman,
> and between your offspring and hers, he will crush
> your head and you will strike his heel."*[22]

---

[20]   Genesis 3:9-12.
[21]   Psalm 103:13-14.
[22]   Genesis 3:15, NIV.

Is this evidence of God's interest in the human family and in their language and communication? Most definitely! In this quotation in Genesis, God communicated to our fore-parents the plan of salvation, the great controversy between God and Satan, and the competing forces of obedience (God) and disobedience (Satan). In this conflict, Jesus would win, and the salvation of the human family would be made secure as the devil would be defeated.

The truth is that when the communication is turned away from the God of love as its central theme, it usually becomes self-centered. The result is that it leads to misunderstanding, pain, disobedience, confusion, disrespect, anger, maliciousness, jealousy, corruption, stubbornness, violence and murder as was first demonstrated by Cain (the first human son) in the murder of his brother, Abel,[23] and sadly, as many of us observe taking place in the home, school, church, workplace, community, society and the world. Our own experience reveals that communication void of God is also void of brotherly love (phileo).

Languages such as Hebrew, Greek (the main original languages of the Bible), Aramaic, French, Latin, Spanish, English, Chinese, to name a few, are different types of symbols used in communication. Most countries have a single or main language of communication, while some have more than one. What is essential also to note is that language, although being dynamic, is critical to communication and reflects the grouping of people into countries or nations. Persons who are multilingual tend to have special advantages in communication across language groups.

We must nevertheless, not forget that over time, God has intervened and continues to intervene in the affairs of man, men and kingdoms of the world. This is in an effort to get their attention, and to communicate through them His will for the carrying out of His plan for the salvation of mankind. His intervention through visions and dreams to Pharaoh, during the

---

[23]   See Genesis 4:1-11

time of Joseph saved the nation of Egypt from famine, as well the children of Israel from death, and fulfilled the prophecy of their sojourn into Egypt.[24] When Daniel's three friends were cast into the inferno in Babylon, God intervened by His physical presence in the inferno and rescued His three champions from what, humanly speaking, appeared to be an inevitable death. That intervention also paved the way for Nebuchadnezzar's repentance and turning to worship the true God of Heaven. These are just a few examples that communication knows no boundary or limitation when it comes to God intervening to rescue or save His people. When God chooses to do so, man with all his appearance and trappings of position, pride, power, and might, cannot limit God.

This process of communication may involve human beings, visions and dreams, prophetic visions, priests, the use of angels, the use of nature (as in earthquake, rain, flood, wind, storm) and the intervention of God himself. As mentioned above, it even involves heathen potentates such as Pharaoh, King Nebuchadnezzar, and Darius. What is God's motive in all of this? The answer: Love. God is love; that is His name and His character. He is seeking through His love and to get man's attention, including yours and mine, to have a loving and saving relationship with us that is eternal, to stop us from evil, and or self-destruction, and to woo us unto a path that leads to using His love language so that we may enjoy a life of love, peace and happiness. That is why God tenderly watches over us.

TENDERLY HE WATCHES OVER YOU[25]

Tenderly He watches over you, every step, every mile of the way; Like a mother watching over her baby, He is near you every hour of the day.

---

24   Read Genesis 41 - 47
25   Tenderly He Watches over You by Mary Lou, accessed at http://www. namethathymn.com/hymn-lyrics-detective-forum/index.php?

Long before time began you were part of His plan;
Let no fear cloud your brow, He will not forsake you now...

CHAPTER 2

LOVE AND LOVE LANGUAGE

2.1 What is love?

i) Different perspectives on love

LOVE MEANS DIFFERENT things to different people. A man's interpretation of love, in many cases, is different from a woman's understanding, as men and women are wired differently, not only by gender, but also emotionally. A married person's understanding of love will be different from that of someone engaged to be married, and different from someone who is not in love, or someone who experienced a failed love relationship. Even in a family, yours for example, you may find that the family members have different perceptions and opinions of love.

A person's definition, perspective, and appreciation of love is often or usually shaped or coloured, consciously or unconsciously, by many things. These include: one's experience of being in or out of love, gender, socialization, culture, age, family and or caste, ethnicity, education, marital status, employment, financial status and standing, pride, position and power (or the lack thereof), health, travel, political leaning, religious persuasion, and one's own choice.

You may have heard others say that love is an emotion, affection, a feeling, an attachment, as well as attraction between people. Here is an emotionally charged explanation of love, that you may also have heard or some variant of it: "Love is the feeling that you feel when you feel like you get the feeling that you feel that you have never felt before." This is a pun on words, but doesn't add much, if anything at all, to the real meaning of love. But to those who have an insatiable desire for the emotional side of life and or infatuation, it may mean much.

ii) Love as a choice

What then is a good definition for love? **Love** means "**to choose** always **to do the best that you can** for others, **even when they don't deserve** it, and **you don't feel like it**."[26] Before delving into this love definition, let's quickly define the words "choice" and "choose", noting that "choose" is a form of "choice". The Oxford Dictionary defines **choice** as "*an act of choosing between two or more possibilities*", and it defines **"choose"** as to "*pick out (someone or something) as being the **best or most appropriate** of two or more alternatives*"[27]

Both definitions (for choose and choice) imply available options and alternatives from which to make a selection. But, while choice is an act of choosing, **"love" or "choosing" is picking out the best or most appropriate from the available options or alternatives.** So, when we reach the place where we truly and honestly understand (the earlier the better) love, we are better able to appreciate that it involves choosing the persons we want to love, which ought to be far more important than how we choose our careers or professions from a range of available alternative careers or professions; even though to be consistent, we will want to choose the best careers or professions. But to love fellow human beings also includes a choosing to do the **best or the most appropriate** for them under different and trying circumstances.

That is why I had to be so very careful and intentional when I chose my wife. This is because, I needed to choose someone that

---

[26]   Cornerstone Connection (Youth Quarterly),
       1st Qtr, 1997, p. 21; Romans 13:10
[27]   Source: http://oxforddictionaries.com/definition/english/
       choice;http://oxforddictionaries.com/definition/english/choose

I could do the very best for, even if afterwards (i.e. after the choice was made) I didn't feel like it, as well as if she did me something that may have been sufficient reason for her not to deserve my love. Choosing my wife was, therefore, a very challenging yet joyful decision for me because there were so many factors to consider and I could not afford to make any major blunders. As one person stated: *"if you use to pray, pray three times as frequency daily when contemplating the choice of a soul mate and companion in marriage."* Thank God it has worked for me.

It must also be stated that love is not just about choosing a partner for life. It involves choosing different types of friends and relationships. More will be said on this under 'kinds of love and the love hierarchy' below in subsection 2.2. This love that is exercised in choosing a person for a relationship is a positive, action-packed verb (doing word). It involves thinking and reasoning, looking at the pros and the cons, which is part of what decision making involves. (More will be said about decision making in Chapter 4.) The love that is defined above transcends "feeling" and is, therefore, not dependent on it. Rightly understood, love is not a "zero-sum" game where one or some must lose for others to win, as in the Lotto and other forms of gambling. On the contrary, it is a "positive sum" game; yes, the kind of love game of life where all the participants can win, and which is opposite in meaning to the "zero-sum" game. This kind of love also reflects the concept of "goal congruence" also used in organizations where both employees and employers, like persons who love, can achieve their goals by working together as a team. It may also be termed "win-win" as in entrepreneurship where, by seeking to satisfy the needs (or goals) of customers (who receive quality product or service at a reasonable price) it enables the entrepreneur to make a profit and thereby achieve his/her profit motive or goal. As you will recognize as you read on, you will need to make a related choice concerning God's Love Language.

iii) Love as a principle

In addition to love being a choice and a choosing, it is also a principle. What then is a principle? The Oxford Dictionary defines **"principle"** as "a fundamental truth or proposition that serves as the foundation for a system of belief or behaviour or for a chain of reasoning"[28] For love to be truly love and for lovers to have meaningful love relationships, both must be governed by principles. True love is considered to be also a principle because it is based on a set of core values and beliefs that govern what takes place and what ought to take place in human relationships.

But, why are principles important generally and especially in love relationships? Because they are based on a set of core and shared values and a common belief system; they define the boundaries of acceptable human behaviour and clarify what is acceptable and what is not. They are important because of the variableness of human nature.

For this reason, if not for any other, the love principle cannot be any principle, but a divine principle. **Divine principles** are explained in more detail in the Chapter 3 (subsection 3.2 ii) d) on "Meaning of God and God's Love Language." Genuine lovers follow divine principles, because they reflect rectitude or uprightness as well as God's standard of what is virtuous and morally right, just and good, and they are unchangeable as God – their divine author. These principles provide for consistent and acceptable behaviour and conduct in human relationships, which is a result of what goes on in the mind (at the psychological and spiritual levels) of persons in relationship.[29]

In this context, we can understand that love is first a principled way of thinking followed by acting and that requires a selfless, Christ-centered maturity and a high level of self- assurance on the part of the giver and receiver of love. This kind of love is positive,

---

28   Source: http://oxforddictionaries.com/definition/english/principle.
29   Matthew 12:34; Luke 6:45

deliberate, intentional and intelligent, sure, secure, beneficial, irrefutable, optimistic, encouraging good behaviour, affirmative, and involves an informed decision- making process that seeks to knowingly do good to others. This occurs even when the recipient of love does not deserve it, and we the giver of love (because of our human failings and shortcomings), don't feel like doing good for others.

iv) Love's ultimate and best objective

We have so far defined love, both as a choice (choosing) and as a principle. We now need to define "ultimate" and "objective" in order to create an understanding of love's ultimate and best objective. "Ultimate" means 'the best achievable or imaginable of its kind', whereas "objective" means 'the desired or needed result (or outcome) to be achieved by a specific time' or 'an end that can be reasonably achieved within an expected time frame and with available resources.'[30] An objective may be considered to be a subset of a goal or purpose. Because love is passionate about the best, it is understandable that love's ultimate and best objective has to do with making the very best available as the desired or needed result within a reasonable time to the object of love mentioned in Chapter 1. As a person, it's normal for you to desire the best within a reasonable time. I know that you surely do.

In the two (2) citations below, two New Testament writers: Dr. Luke and John, respectively record perspectives on love to enhance our appreciation of love's ultimate and best objective.[31]

*"For the Son of man is come **to seek and to save** that which was lost."*

*"For **God so loved the world**, that **he gave his only begotten Son**, that **whosoever believeth** in him should **not perish**, but **have everlasting life**."*

These two amazing texts show clearly love's ultimate and best objective, viz: to seek, to save, and to give or grant eternal life to all those in the friendship or love relationship who believe, love and obey Jesus and His commandments (details provided later in Chapter 3 on God's love language), as an act of gratitude for what Jesus did for humanity: that is, dying a death of ignominy at Calvary.

Based on the definition for love given above, and to be consistently in harmony with its meaning, persons especially in relationships will want to point their friends to Jesus, who is the best friend to have. They will also want to introduce them to God's Love Language which is discussed at length in Chapter 3 of this book. Additionally they will also introduce them to its benefits which are outlined in Chapter 4. To do so is to select the best or most appropriate from all the available alternatives.

2.2 Kinds of love and the love hierarchy

The loving nature and character of God helps us to understand that **love is about relationship**, for God is eager to have a relationship with His creatures, His people, human beings - the crowning work of His creation. The Greek word "phileein" means to love. However, in order not to confuse God's love for us with any other love, it's important to understand that there are different kinds of love, and different kinds of relationships. The Greek language is quite helpful in this regard, as it has words that explain the different kinds of love. Five of these Greek words for the kinds of love are highlighted below, viz: Agape, Phileo, Eros, Storge, and Philia. These principles are also found in the Scriptures.

An easy way to remember them is to use the Acronym for the first letter in each of these words, as shown below.

A -Agape
P - Phileo
E - Eros
S - Storge
P -Philia

Let's explain the meaning of each of these five kinds of love.

i) Agape

Agape refers to God's (divine) unconditional love for humanity. Yes friend, this love is self-sacrificing, active and volitional (i.e. love by voluntary and conscious choice or will), and thoughtful. Notice how the Apostle John and the prophet Jeremiah sum it up respectively below.

*"Herein is **love**, not that we loved God, but that **he loved us, and sent his Son** to **be the propitiation** (expiation, sacrifice or atonement) **for our sins.**"*[32]

*"The LORD hath appeared of old unto me, saying, Yea, I have **loved** thee with an **everlasting love:** therefore with loving kindness have I drawn thee."*[33]

This kind of love sets the stage for us to seek to know, practice and never cease embracing God's **Love** Language.

---

[32]   1 John 4:10
[33]   Jeremiah 31:3

We (human beings) don't love naturally. But God does. Here we see that God proactively initiated volitional, everlasting love for mankind;

*"not that we loved God, **but He loved us**."*

Can you appreciate a love that knows no end, and that is given even though it's not deserved? We couldn't buy it because it is priceless or invaluable; and there is nothing we have done, is doing, or will do in the future to earn it. It cannot be earned, for it is a gift. Gifts are for free; we either accept or refuse them. This love is free (at no cost to us), but not cheap, as this love of God was demonstrated by self-sacrificing, giving of self (on the cross) to all humanity, for all humanity including: high and low, rich and poor, good and bad, bond or free, friend and foe. (Read carefully the paragraph below.) It is also used in the love chapter in the New Testament, in 1 Corinthians 13.

God wants us to understand the genuineness, the magnitude, and incomparable nature of His love for us and the kind of (vertical) relationship that He wants to have with us. That is why by His loving kindness, He draws us to Himself, in order for us to reciprocate love to Him and our fellowmen. Imagine this unimaginable and contrasting act of love scene: God - the Creator dying for His creatures; the superior dying for the subordinate, **the sinless one, died for the sinful one**; He, the selfless one died for the selfish ones! He, who is kind died for the unkind; He, who is patient, died for the impatient; He, who is meek and humble, died for the proud and arrogant; **He who is altogether lovely, died for the unlovely and abusers of mankind**. Yes, He, who is the resurrection and the life, died for the mortal and corrupt; and He, who is faithful and trustworthy, died for the unfaithful and untrustworthy. How comprehensive is the surpassing, exceeding and exceptional nature of God's (Agape) love for us, sinners, compared to our (human being's) love!

It may be difficult to conceive, grasp, and explain. But, as difficult as it may be for us to fully appreciate and even accept, it is nevertheless true. It is an historic fact that Jesus died a vicarious death for undeserving, ignorant, sinful mankind in **AD 31** on a cruel cross. It was His deliberate and missional decision to come and die for mankind when mankind had reached its lowest possible level and depth of sin, after the earth and mankind had been weakened by sin for approximately four thousand **(4,000)** years, and when the risk of rejection of that love must have been greatest. This verifies the authenticity and probity of God and His love, as is recorded by John and cited below.

> *"For **God so loved (agaped) the world**, that **he gave his only begotten Son**, that **whosoever believeth** in him should **not perish**, but **have everlasting life**."*[34]

God, the Father, gave Jesus, His Son, His one and only Son, to die for you and me, while we were yet sinners (breakers of God's law or from the Greek - "to miss the mark). What father do you know, in his right mind would offer his only son to die for a criminal, for indeed, each sinner is a criminal in the eyes of God? But that is exactly what God, the Father, did by offering His only Son, Jesus! And to compound the issue, the Father's one and only Son, Jesus, agreed, by accepting the bait: hook, line and sinker, to use common parlance, in going all the way to Calvary for you and me, undeserving sinners, and for the sins of undeserving human beings of the entire world, born and yet unborn. Yes, this is Agape love at its finest and optimal level; it cannot get any better.

Can you imagine how God, the Father, must have felt when Jesus, His one and only Son, went on the cross to die for the sins of the entire world? Can you empathize with Him, in terms of the emotion, the foreboding or trepidation, and the mental anguish? It must be difficult, humanly speaking, to grasp the magnitude of the expressions of love and apprehension on the Father's face? Yet, if you are a parent or a child caught up in a similar situation, you may be able to have a tip of the iceberg appreciation of what

---

[34]   John 3:16:

it feels like. One Friday night in June 2012, while watching the Hope Channel, I listened to Elizabeth Talbot, the only child of her parents, relate the story of her parents receiving an anonymous letter in which there was a threat to kidnap her, if her parents did not leave the country in which they were living the same day. Even though the parents were Christians, they had anxious moments.

In another case, my wife and I received the sad news of the sudden and untimely death of the only son of one of our very good Christian married couples and family friends. Their son was found death in his bed, in his apartment. The news almost broke their hearts. You may have had similar experience(s). It is never easy to lose a loved one. Yet, God permitted His only Son to die for us, and of course considering the risk that Jesus may sin, when He clothed His divinity with His humanity. One songster uses the expressions "mountains of love" and "oceans of grace" to describe God's amazing act at Calvary.

As an expression of appreciation, and in an attitude of gratitude, Alfred Ackley wrote the song, "All the way to Calvary". It was recorded by The Brooklyn Tabernacle Choir and Isaac Odeniran. It has been sung in many different places by many individuals and groups including The Brooklyn Tabernacle Choir, St. George's Cathedral, and the Clarks Sisters. A few lines of this beautiful, inspirational lyrics are provided herein below.

> *"All the way to Calvary, He went for me; He went for me,*
> *He went for me*
> *All the way to Calvary, He went for me;*
> *He died to set me free…*
> *Yes, my sins are gone. Now my soul is free,*
> *and in my heart's a song;*
> *I shall live eternally, Praise God! my sins are* ***GONE!***

Reader and friend, I do not know what your past life was like or what your present life is, but this I know for sure: "Jesus died for me, and has given me a new lease on life. I see the world differently because Jesus has given me hope, peace and joy, because

He has forgiven me of all my sins, which are many. He has given the blessed assurance and the promise that I can live with Him throughout eternity. That is why Agape means so much to me. I am a better husband, father, elder, and friend of God and lover of His people and His truth."

Additionally, the inclusive Good News (Gospel) is that He also died for you.

Ellen G. White stated that when Jesus died on the cross,

"He gave the best gift that God could offer, the gift of himself, his life."

Can we get a vision of the magnitude of God's love for us-sinners, and the value He places on us despite our selfish, slipping, sliding, sinful ways? The Bible correctly, and in an empowering way,states:

"But God commended his love toward us, in that, while we were yet sinners, Christ died for us." *...For if, when we were **enemies**, we were reconciled to God by the death of his Son, much more, being reconciled, we shall be saved by his life."*[35]

This is the Good News that there is hope for every sinner who believes and accepts Jesus as Lord of his/her life.

You may ask, why did Jesus agree to participate in this great but risky act of love? The Bible offers the following explanation:

a) To vindicate the character of God, the Father, who the devil had accused of being a dictator,tyrant.[36]

b) To reveal to mankind God's love and plan of Salvation.[37]

---

[35] Romans 5:8, 10.

[36] Isaiah 14:12-14, Ezekiel 28:1-17, Psalm 45:6-7, 40:6-8.

[37] Galatians 4:4-5, Isaiah 7:14, Luke 19:10.

c) To reveal the character of God in the life of His Son, Jesus, who came to earth to show mankind how they can be overcomers and how to live a sinless life.[38]

The more we understand this Agape love, the great controversy, and the role of Jesus in the Salvation of humanity and His sinless representation of His Father, the more we will want to know Him, love Him, obey him, and be like Him, and use His love language. Then, it will not be difficult to have the Phileo love described below.

ii) Phileo

Phileo means "brotherly love or friendship". It is the root word in Philadelphia, a city where one of the seven churches in the book of Revelation[39] was located. Philadelphia was known as "city of brotherly love." Phileo is a virtuous love which includes loyalty to friends, family, relatives, and community. This love shows kindness and respect for one another as human beings as a human response to the delightful Agape love shown to us by God and which works out in our lives. Whereas **Agape** love does what is right before God, **Phileo** love does what I want to do because I love you and care for your wellbeing. In addition, loving and caring for you is the best and right thing to do. We can, therefore, conclude that Phileo love is an outworking of God's Agape love.

Notice how the Apostle Peter puts this in perspective in the context of adding virtuous character qualities:

*"And to godliness **brotherly kindness**; and to brotherly kindness charity."*[40]

The apostle Peter is here helping us to understand that it is our godliness that leads to brotherly (phileo) kindness; and brotherly (phileo) kindness leads to (agape) charity or love. God wants us to love (agape) Him unconditionally (the first and great commandment) and then we will be able to exercise brotherly (phileo) love (the second commandment which is like unto the first). Therefore, our tender mercies, care, and concern for one another are part of, and rudimentary or foundational for our loving (agape) each other.

Look at both the Apostle John and the Apostle Paul contributions quoted below.

*"Beloved, **let** us (phileo) **love one another**: for (agape) **love** is of God; and every **one** that **love**th (agape) is born of God, and knoweth God."*[41]

> *"But as touching brotherly (phileo) love ye need not that I write unto you: for ye yourselves are taught of God to (agape) love one another."*

> **"Let brotherly love continue.***"*[42]

This is indeed God's ideal for the human family, that we would love one another continuously, not for reward, but because it's a very good thing to do. But to do this, requires a keen knowledge of God and acceptance of His Agape love. Agape, the self-sacrificing love of God, and Phileo, the tender mercy love of a brother, are therefore, interconnected. Phileo love may also be described as Christian love at its finest.[43] It requires equality and virtue. If Phileo love was practiced as it should be, our world would be so much better - less crime and violence, family feud, political overthrow and under-throws and seditions, murder and corruption.

iii) Eros

Eros is a special kind of love, intimate and passionate love, that God designed to happen between husbands and wives, heterogeneous couples, within the love and confines of marriage, as in the case where Adam knew his wife, Eve. Because this love involves passion and sex, persons who are not sanctified will abuse it; and some have abused it, and even entered into relationships that have no phileo love. Absalom, the third son of King David, had an affair with Tamar, his sister that involved rape. As the record shows, his action was driven by passion and lust, and not by either phileo or agape love. Where agape and phileo are absence in Eros love, one or both parties involved in that kind of love will be lustful and seek to gratify the lower debasing nature of man. This is an area of Satan's special target to pervert and destroy, turning love into lust which is rooted in self-centeredness, and physical attraction alone.

However, the Eros love of Scripture which is also based on principle, does not condone "shacking-up", "one-night" or "more nights stand", "concubinage" or "trial marriage" as are practiced by some in different circles and places. On the contrary, 'Eros' is intended for a higher and more worthy purpose. The reason for this is clearly outlined in the texts mentioned below (see footnotes), but may be summarized as follows:

a) The marriage relation is a symbol of the relationship between Christ (the Bridegroom)and His Church (the Bride). Therefore, illicit or illegitimate, flirtatious, and extramarital relationships will not, and cannot be used to represent the legitimate and pure relationship between Christ and His Bride.

b) Christ loves His bride, the Church, and does not desert, depart from, or divorce His Bride.

Although erotic, passionate, love making takes place outside of the sacred confines of marriage (pre-marital and extramarital relation), it is still **sin** in the eyes of God, because it breaks God's law, breaks human hearts, separates parents and children and often leaves permanent scars among family and relatives that emanate from and or are connected to those illegitimate relationships. Very often they turn out to be nothing more than hedonistic love. It is not the number of persons that are involved that makes an action right, neither, is it the frequency or duration of practice that determines whether an action or lack of action is right. Right doing, as in love and love relationships, must be based on the principles that are enunciated in God's moral law (love to God and love to man), and not on situational ethics or personal pleasure, position or economics.

And of course the Bible gives the basis for this in the books of Ephesians and Hebrews as outlined below.

> *Be ye therefore **followers of God**, as dear children; And **walk in** (agape) **love, as Christ also hath loved (agape) us, and hath given himself for us** an offering and a sacrifice to God for a sweet smelling savour. But fornication, and all uncleanness, or covetousness, let it not be once named among you, as becometh saints; Neither filthiness, nor foolish talking, nor jesting, which are not convenient: but rather giving of thanks. For this ye know, that **no whoremonger**, nor unclean person, nor covetous man, who is an idolater, hath any inheritance in the kingdom of Christ and of God. **Submitting yourselves one to another in the fear of God. Wives, submit yourselves unto your own husbands**, as unto the Lord. For the **husband is the head of the wife, even as Christ is the head of the church**: and he is the Saviour of the body. Therefore as the church is subject unto Christ, so let the wives be to their own husbands in everything. Husbands, **love your wives, even as Christ also loved the church, and gave himself for it; So ought men to love their wives as their own bodies**. He that loveth his wife loveth himself. For this cause shall a man leave his father and mother, and shall be joined unto his wife, and they two shall be one flesh.*[44]

---

[44]   Ephesians 5: 1-5, 22-25, 28, 31.

*"**Marriage is** honourable in all, and the bed undefiled: but whoremongers and adulterers God will judge."[45]*

"…Therefore take heed to your spirit, And let none deal treacherously with the wife of his youth."[46]

iv) Storge

Storge is the Greek word for natural affection such as the love of a parent for offspring. Because it is mainly used as a descriptor of relationships within the family, it is also referred to as familial love. However, it is a subset of phileo explained above, and is not as widely used or referred to as phileo.

v) Philia

Philia is a special love, affection, attraction or preference for a certain type of thing. It encompasses love for things such as a pizza, your car, house, or your pet dog, etc, which is and ought to be a long way from AGAPE or Phileo love. This kind of (Philia) love should not be confused with any of the other kinds of love, and should never under any circumstances be given a higher ranking than any of the other love. John the beloved disciple of Jesus, reminds us of the words of Jesus on this matter as follows.

"Love (phileo) not the world, neither the things that are in the world. If any man love the world, the (agape) love of the Father is not in him."[47]

Philia in many ways is also similar to hedonistic love.

For any of these relationships to be meaningful, it's important that the communication be appropriate and specific for the particular relationship. For example,certain communication between a husband and wife (Eros) would not be appropriate for a Philia relationship and vice versa.

vi) The love hierarchy

An excellent understanding of these five (5) kinds of love is based on a correct or right understanding of who God is, as the one who created both human beings and things. Human beings were created at a higher level than things. Accordingly, how we form relationship with God and His creatures should be different from how we love and relate to things. The love for things and our relationship with things should never be allowed to compete with, nor supersede our love for and relationship with God and secondarily for people. By God's grace, we should ensure that our love for things are subordinate and subservient to our love for God and His commandments. Speaking recently[48] as a product sample at the second Commencement Service at the Northern Caribbean University in Jamaica, Professor Bertram Melbourne, Howard University, made the pertinent point which is applicable here. He said that *"God made us to love people and use things. So we should never love things and use people."*

This love hierarchy may be illustrated by the following diagram.

The Love Hierarchy		
Hierarchy level	**Kinds of Love**	**Meaning**
First or Level 1	Agape	God's Unconditional Love
Second or Level 2	Phileo	Brotherly Love
	i) Eros Love	Love between married couples
	ii) Storge	Familial love and relationships within the family.
Third or Level 3	Philia	Love for Things

It is important to note that, even though some of these terms for love are not found in the Bible, these concepts of love as enunciated in the Bible, existed long before the emergence of philosophers such as Plato, and Socrates, who also wrote on the topic of love. So God is the greatest expert when it comes to love.

2.3 Love Language

i) Meaning of love language

I mentioned earlier that language is the vehicle that makes the communication or shared understanding possible in human relationships. What then is meant by love language? A love language is, therefore, the vehicle that people use to share love. It involves the way in which a person expresses, gives or receives love, or simply communicates love to another, and thereby makes a person in a relationship feel loved.

ii) Love languages

Dr. Gary Chapman, author of the book, The Five Love Languages, gives some insight into the subject of love languages. He believes that we humans have been wired to feel loved by means of one of five love languages. He outlines these five love languages, as follows:

- i)   Words of Affirmation
- ii)   Quality time
- iii) Receiving gifts
- iv)   Physical touch
- v)   Acts of service

Most persons have a primary love language and even a secondary love language. The primary love language is the language that is the most important to us in making us feel loved and is the most important way of communicating with the other person in a relationship, e.g. among husbands and wives, parents and children, siblings, co-workers, schoolmates, leaders and followers, church members, and so on. In using a person's love language and not your own, you are demonstrating love and respect for the persons and providing an opportunity to bring out the best in the person.[49] This is consistent with God's approach in dealing with us.

Consider this example! A brother, who knows that his sister loves gifts, brings home a cat for her birthday, as an expression of his Phileo and Storge love. But unknowing to him, he did not realize that although his sister loves gifts, cats are not included in that gift list, because cats trigger her asthma attack and she hates them with a venom. When he gives her the cat she gets upset, yells at him and in a disrespectful manner orders him to return the cat. He also gets upset, feels dejected and storms out of the house to return the cat.

What is the cause of the problem? The siblings have two different love languages unknown to each other. Her love language is receiving (certain) gifts, but no cats; her brother's is word of affirmation. Instead of affirming him by expressing appreciation for his consideration of getting a costly gift for her, albeit, not a gift in her love language, she chastises him, rather than giving him words of affirmation to build and reaffirm his self-concept. So here we find two loving siblings, one in an effort to do good for his sister ended up on the wrong side of her wrath, rather than bringing out the good in her and vice versa.

Could that, in principle, happen to you or has it happened to you? The truth is that it has happened to many persons who are honest and truthful enough to admit it. In fact, similar things have happened to many married couples, in some instances resulting in the break-up of the marriage, ending in divorce. Here is what may be considered as a typical example. The wife's love languages are quality time (primary) and words of affirmation (secondary),

---

49   Used by permission

while that of her husband is also word of affirmation. But as is often the case, they are in ignorance as to their love languages. Both went to a hotel for a holiday weekend. They both love each other and want to share their love. But her husband is "quick on the trigger." She gets annoyed as she wants him to spent time talking and sharing about life and reaffirming each other as a prelude and entering wedge. Nothing happened that night and the rest of the weekend as neither was able to communicate using each other's love language.

The **real truth** is that there can be no meaningful relationship (whether in the home and family even among husbands and wives, at work, school, or in the spiritual or church family) without effective communication. And there cannot be any effective communication in any meaningful relationship without the use of the love language of each person in the relationship. And **there cannot be any meaningful or quality love relationship where God is absent, and where His love language is knowingly ignored or rejected**. So we may conclude, from the above, that it is necessary to have an overlapping (or intersecting) of the love language of each person in the communication with that of God's Love Language; and it is **at this point of intersection** that persons in the relationship will have fulfilled lives.

iii) Human relationships and the interface with love language

Human relationships normally begin by the making of contacts, whether by personal face to face contact, telephone, fax, text message, email, Skype, ooVoo, Twitter, or Facebook, or by referral using one or more of these methods. As contacts are made and as the frequency increases, friendships develop. As friendship develops and grows, confidence in each other will emerge. As this confidence is exercised, it often leads to the creation of opportunity.

This opportunity stage may be considered the most risky stage, yet the most rewarding. This is because as people demonstrate trust in each other they leave themselves open and vulnerable, if the love (phileo) shared is not reciprocated. This arises because at this opportunity stage, persons in the relationship tend to lower their guards as they feel a sense of security in the relationship. But if the other person(s) in the relationship is/are true to each other and mean each other well, mutual trust, respect and love can prosper resulting in long lasting relationships. This also can set the stage for on-going and long-term Phileo/Storge love in families or other types of good social, career and religious bonding. It may also provide opportunities for the formation of marital relationships that is also characterized by Agape and Eros love.

As the diagrammatic representation of human relationships below tries to depict, space or accommodation for others is largest in the contact stage, then gradually decreases upwards to opportunity stage. This is because at the contact stage we meet and make many friends, from which as we go through the stages, we may choose a soul mate or marriage partner for life. The space in Opportunity becomes the smallest in the sense that at that stage there are some things that we will share only with our husband or wife to the exclusion of all others. And this is how, I believe, God intended it to be. Similarly, as we transition from the human relationship phileo level, to the object lesson of the spiritual agape love relationship, we must reach a place in our lives where we create an opportunity space for only ourselves and God to the exclusion of all others. At this point, we will be enthused to embrace God's Love Language, and we will also understand that the human marriage relation is a mystical (spiritual) symbol of the relationship between Christ and His Church. And that is why faithfulness in the love/ marriage relation is so important, because we are representing a God that is faithful. If we are to be faithful to God and His commandments, we must demonstrate faithfulness to our spouse and to the vows of the marriage.

The love language is very critical for making a smooth transition through the continuum from contact to opportunity. It is true also that love language does play a very vital role in providing the platform for shared love and understanding that acts as continuing glue for binding and bonding the relationship throughout the relationship stages in the years ahead.

Many **conflicts** between persons in relationships are, in part, as a **result of having different love language**s, and lack of appreciation for, and acceptance of this reality that persons in a relationship do have different love languages. If you are having marital problems, one of the possible reasons for the problems may be due to the fact that you do not know your spouse's love language and vice versa. And this in turn will arise from not complying with God's Love Language. Similarly, problems among parents and children, siblings, and in-laws, etc., may be due in part to misunderstanding from not knowing or caring to know the love language of the other person(s) in the relationship. This is played out constantly in many cases of conflicts in human relationships.

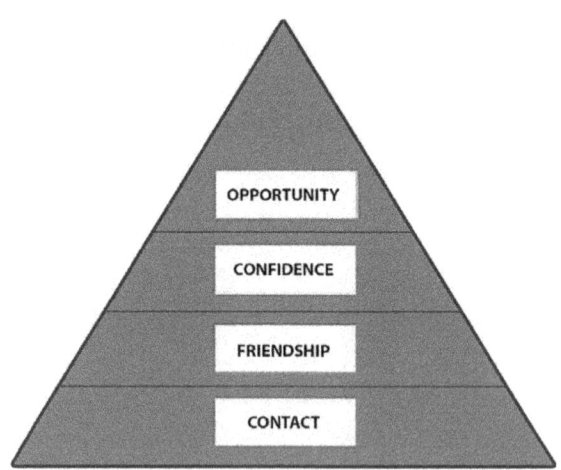

Diagrammatical Representation of Human Relationships

The song: "I love Thee I love Thee" that appears at the end of this chapter is a timely reminder that the real test of our love is what is displayed in our actions; what is visible, what others see, and how we treat those that we say in words from our lips that we love. Our ears hear what we say, but when our minds are not engaged it is because there is a breakdown in communication between tongue and mind, and there is a dichotomy between principle and conduct. But the song also provides the solution for happiness.

I LOVE THEE[50]

I love Thee, I love Thee, I love Thee, my Lord; I love Thee, my Savior, I love Thee, my God;
I love Thee, I love Thee, and that Thou dost know; But how much I love Thee my actions will show.

O Jesus, my Savior, with Thee I am blessed. My life and salvation, my joy and my rest.

Thy Name be my theme, and Thy love be my song; Thy grace shall inspire both my heart and my tongue.

---

[50] Source:http://www.cyberhymnal.org/htm/i/l/ilovethe.htm

CHAPTER 3

MEANING OF GOD
AND GOD'S LOVE LANGUAGE

THIS CHAPTER IS perhaps the most important of the seven chapters of this book. Your destiny may very well rest on your understanding of this chapter and what action(s) you will take after reading it. The earlier chapters assumed that some persons are familiar with, knowledgeable about, and accepting of God. For these persons this chapter is a timely refresher. However, for other persons who do not necessarily fall into that category, the first part (3.1) of this chapter should be of special interest to them.

While providing balance and objectivity, it is hoped that the information in this chapter relating to who is God and what is His love language will reaffirm believers while it will help some doubters and non-believers to cross over the line to believing in God and making Him a personal, reliable and trustworthy friend. It is also intended that it will present God in a way and light that God and the heavenly intelligences will approve of. For indeed, if we are accepting of God, it will be much easier to appreciate, value, and also accept and embrace His love language. Since the love language spoken about in this chapter is God's Love Language, what better way to start it than with the question: who is God!

3.1 Who is God?

i) Divine singularity and plurality

God is a divine being, who is singular, yet plural, and in this plurality is often referred to as the triune (three in one) God, the

Trinity (a word not used in the Bible), or the Godhead. Although this doctrine of the Godhead or Trinity (triple deities) is one of the fundamentals of Christianity, it mystifies and baffles many including scholars, and even kings such as Pharaoh of Egypt and Nebuchadnezzar of ancient Babylon. They just don't understand it, and some simply dismiss God, and claim that God does not exist, instead of admitting to the ignorance and limitations of their humanity. What a way to relate to reality we don't fully understand! The fact that I cannot fathom and explain some cancers, pain, and other baffling things in life, does not mean that they do not exist.

The real truth is this: finite, sinful man cannot explain an infinite, sinless, immortal, invisible, and only wise God- the Creator (see below) of all life and heaven and earth, who telleth the number of stars and calls them by name.[51] How can the created be more knowledgeable than the Creator?[52] Despite my graduate level training, vast management experience in various sectors, and international travel, I must admit my limitations when it comes to things of God. Some things I know, and others I just don't know. I humbly submit that I am willing to learn. This is part of what I believe wisdom teaches.[53] If I can learn from mortal specialists in their field about things that I have little or no knowledge of, why can't I learn from the immortal, Supreme lover and giver of life? King Nebuchadnezzar learned this reality of God only after he was driven by God from his position of king of Babylon, and from men and went to dwell with the beasts of the field, and ate grass as oxen do, for seven consecutive years. This was in fulfillment of the prophecy from God that God revealed to His prophet, Daniel. After this dramatic, mind boggling and eye-opening experience, the king had the following to say:

> *And **at the end of the days I Nebuchadnezzar** lifted up mine eyes unto heaven, and mine understanding*

---

[51]   See 1 Timothy 1:17 and Psalm 147:4-5.
[52]   Job 11:7; Ecclesiastes 3:11, 8:17; Romans 11:33.
[53]   Romans 11:33.

*returned unto me, and I **blessed the most High**, and I **praised and honoured him that liveth forever,** whose dominion is an everlasting dominion, and his kingdom is from generation to generation: And all the inhabitants of the earth are reputed as nothing: and he doeth according to his will in the army of heaven, and among the inhabitants of the earth: and none can stay his hand, or say unto him, What doest thou? At the same time my reason returned unto me;*[54]

The doctrine of the triune God means that there are three separate, distinct beings, all deities, (Father, Son as in Jesus, and Holy Ghost), who are one in purpose, nature and character, especially as is exemplified in the salvation of the humanity. The Bible, which refers to them as God in their plurality as in Genesis 1:26 when referring to their involvement in the creation of man, states: *"Let **us** make man in **our** image, after **our** likeness..."* also refers to God as one. So, we may speak of God in the plural - meaning all three: Father, Son,and Holy Ghost (whether or not their names are spelt out),or in the singular (or simply singly), referring to each separately. It is the context that helps us to understand who is intended, whether God in their plurality or singularity. Two examples are given below and in context: the first from the Old Testament and the second from the New Testament.

*"**Hear** therefore, O Israel, and **observe** to do it; that it may be well with thee, and that ye may increase mightily, as the Lord God of thy fathers hath promised thee, in the land that floweth with milk and honey. **Hear, O Israel: The Lord our God is ONE Lord:***

---

[54]   Daniel 4:34-36. Read the full story in Daniel 4; Read also Chapters 2 & See also below at 3.1(iii), the "The three O's of the God head..."

*And thou shalt **love the Lord thy God with all thine** heart, and with all thy soul, and with all thy might."*[55]

"And one of the scribes came, and having heard them reasoning together, and perceiving that he had answered them well, asked him, Which is the first commandment of all?

*And **Jesus** answered him, The first of all the commandments is, **Hear, O Israel; The Lord our God is ONE Lord:** And thou shalt **love the Lord thy God** with all thy heart, and with all thy soul, and with all thy mind, and with all thy strength: this is the first commandment."*[56]

These revelations make it very explicit that an important aspect of the **first commandment** is to accept the reality that the Lord thy God, OUR God, is ONE God, and the conjoining requirement and obligation is that we are to love the said Lord thy (our) God. The first speaker is Moses, (who was recounting to the Israelites what God had disclosed to him) and the second is Jesus. This Moses had many face to face contacts and communication with God. Some of these contacts and communication include the following:

i)   The experience of the burning bush.[57]

ii)   At the giving and writing of the ten (10)commandments by God upon Mount Sinai.[58]

iii)   In the desert of Zin where there was no water and God asked him to speak to the rock and it would give forth water for the people to drink.[59]

---

[55]   Deuteronomy 6:3-5.

[56]   Mark 12:28-30.

[57]   Exodus 3:3-5.

[58]   Exodus 19, 31:17-18; Deuteronomy 9:9-11.

[59]   Numbers 20:1-8.

While in Egypt during the ten (10) plagues before appearing before Pharaoh to deliver God's directives.[60]

Events leading up to the crossing of the Red Sea.[61]

This same Moses, who is now in Heaven, was present at the Mount of Transfiguration with Jesus, Elias, the Apostles Peter, James, and John.[62] John's testimony is that this same Jesus, "the only begotten Son, who is in the bosom of the Father, He has declared Him (the Father)" and who is also referred to as the 'Word'."[63] Jesus in whom dwells "all the fullness of the Godhead" and who came from and went back to heaven, when He spoke about the promise of the Holy Spirit, confirmed the reality of the Godhead. This is what He said as recorded in the New Testament Gospel of John.

> *"And I will pray the Father, and He will give you another*
> ***Helper**, that He may abide with you forever*
> *—**the Spirit of truth**"*[64]

The Helper referred to in the text is the Holy Spirit of God who is also the Spirit of Truth. Note also that the Greek word for *"another"* used in the text is *"allos"* which means *"another of the same kind."* Jesus was our Helper while on earth. After He ascended, His Father sent the Holy Spirit of Truth, who is not inferior in kind or dignity to the Son, so that His people on earth would not be comfortless.

Before Jesus' ascension to heaven, He reassured His disciples that He had all authority both in heaven and on earth. He commanded them to make disciples of all nations; again a reassurance of the universal nature of His mission of salvation which placed a premium on every single human and the need for

---

[60]   Exodus 3 to 15.
[61]   Exodus 12- 14.
[62]   See Deuteronomy 34:4-7; Matthew 17:1-3.
[63]   John 1:18, 1:1.
[64]   John 14:16-17.

the Gospel to be taken to each one. And because the Godhead is central to the Good News of salvation, Jesus commanded His disciples then (but also applicable to those in the future) to make disciples of every nation (Gospel Commission). Then having done that, they were to baptize them in the name of the Father, Son and Holy Ghost and also to teach them to observe all things that He had commanded them.

The Apostle Paul also confirms Jesus' revelation on this subject of the Trinity or Godhead. This is how he states his confirmation in the New Testament book of 2 Corinthians."

*The **grace** of the Lord Jesus Christ, and the **love** of God (the Father), and the **communion** of the Holy Spirit be with you all."*[65]

This quotation reveals both the unity of the Trinity and the cooperative roles played by each member of the Godhead.

However, the communication and focus on the Trinity or Triune God did not stop there. Another important and unique emphasis took place at the baptism of Jesus when the speaker at the spectacular and significant event was God, the Father. Jesus had just been baptized in the river Jordan. As he came up from the water, the heavens were opened to Him, and He saw the Spirit of God descending and like a dove alighted upon Him. Then suddenly there was a voice from heaven which said: *"This is My beloved Son, in whom I am well pleased."*[66] So all three deities were represented. All three divine beings are also identified as bearing record in heaven[67] (and as being one).

As the triune God, Godhead or Trinity, they are self- existent, pre-existent beings, unlike human beings who are created beings and mortal in tenure. They existed before all things existed and are pre-eminent beings, and by them do all things exist.[68] The triune God is the creator and sustainer of life, maker of heaven, earth,

---

[65] 2 Corinthians 13:14.
[66] Matthews 3:3-17.
[67] 1 John 5:7.
[68] Genesis 1:1-6, 26; John 1:1-3, 10, 17:1, 5; Colossians 1:16-17.

and the worlds, as referred to below respectively in the accounts in Genesis, Hebrews and Psalms.[69] The triune God also gave dominion to man, as the texts below also clearly reveal.

*In the beginning God **created** the heaven and the earth.*

*And **God said**, Let **us** make man in **our** image, after **our** likeness: and let them have dominion over the fish of the sea, and over the fowl of the air, and over the cattle, and over all the earth, and over every creeping thing that creepeth upon the earth. So God **created** man in his own image, in the image of God created he him; male and female created he them. And **God blessed** them, and God **said** unto them, Be fruitful, and multiply, and replenish the earth, and subdue it: and have dominion over the fish of the sea, and over the fowl of the air, and over every living thing that moveth upon the earth.*

*God, who at sundry times and in divers manners **spake** in time past unto the fathers by the prophets, **2** Hath in these last days **spoken** unto us by his Son, whom he hath appointed heir of all things, by whom also he **made the worlds;***

*Through faith we understand that the **worlds were framed** by the word of God, so that things which are seen were not made of things which do appear.*

*By the **word of the Lord were the heavens made**; and all the host of them by the breath of his mouth. He **gathereth the waters** of the sea together as a*

---

[69]   Genesis 1:1, 26-28 and in Hebrews 1:1-2; 11:3, and Psalm 33:6-12.

*heap: he **layeth up the depth** in storehouses. Let all the earth fear the Lord: let all the inhabitants of the world stand in awe of him. For **he spake and it was done; he commanded, and it stood fast.** The Lord **bringeth the counsel of the heathen to nought**: he maketh the devices of the people of none effect. The counsel of the Lord standeth forever, the thoughts of his heart to all generations. Blessed is the nation whose God is the Lord; and the people whom he hath chosen for his own inheritance.*

These texts reveal glimpses of the awesomeness, power, and might of God. How *powerful* are His *Words*! He *spoke* the world into existence. God creates, makes, speaks, blesses, frames, gathers, lays, commands, and bringeth things into existence. How in comparable is God? These acts of God,which reveal that there is none like Him, provide the basis and reason for all the earth, and indeed all the inhabitants of the world to stand in awe of Him. Another reason is that His counsel is immutable and stands for ever,[70] while He brings the counsel of the heathen to nought (e.g. where are Babylon and Sodom and Gomorrah today?). Because of the immutability of God's counsel and His unchanging nature, God cannot lie.[71] Finally, those nations who make this God their Lord are blessed.

Additionally, there is Biblical evidence that **each member of the Godhead is God**. As many to most persons accept the fact that there is a God, as in God-the Father, but not the others, some biblical evidence are provided herein that both Jesus is God and the Holy Spirit is God. God, the Father, referred to Jesus as God as follows:[72]

---

[70] Hebrews 6:17-18.
[71] Titus 1:2; Hebrews 6:17-18.
[72] Hebrews 1:8.

> *"But unto the **Son** he saith, Thy throne, **O God**, is forever and ever: a sceptre of righteousness is the sceptre of thy kingdom."*

The following texts show clearly where the Apostle Peter referred to the Holy Spirit as God, and the context justifies the claim and conclusion.[73]

> [3] *But Peter said, Ananias, why hath Satan filled thine heart to **lie to the Holy Ghost**, and to keep back part of the price of the land?*
>
> [4] *Whiles it remained, was it not thine own? and after it was sold, was it not in thine own power? why hast thou conceived this thing in thine heart?* ***thou hast not lied unto men, but unto God.***

Humanity, especially during the time while Jesus was on earth, recognized and accepted God as being able to forgive sins. Jesus was frequently accused primarily by the Jews for forgiving persons of their sins. He was frequently charged with blasphemy, for in forgiving people of their sins, they claimed that He was making himself equal with God. This was plain ignorance and stubbornness on their part. Jesus is God, and every one of His forgiving action was evidence that as God, He forgives sins.

But all three are involved in the forgiving business. This is because forgiveness is necessary for our salvation. John tells us that if we confess our sins, He is faithful and just to forgive us of our sins and to cleanse us of all unrighteousness. Then Jesus also tells us in the Lord's prayer that God, the Father forgives us of our sins, but obtaining forgiveness from His Father is conditional upon us forgiving others. Then Jesus tells us that there is only one sin that the Holy Spirit of God does not forgive and that is the sin against the Holy Spirit, which is also called the unpardonable sin.

---

[73]   *Acts* 5:3-4.

Each member of the Godhead is also referred to individually in numerous places in the Bible. While they are one in purpose and work cooperatively for the salvation of man and for their own glory, **they also have distinctive roles.**

God is referred to as the Father (commonly noted as the first member of the Godhead - a word used three times in the King James Version (KJV) of the Bible,[74] depending on the context.) He gave Jesus, His Son, for the salvation of mankind.

He also pardons iniquity and is involved in the Judgment as the Ancient of Days.[75]

Jesus is referred to as the Son, the Son of God, the Pearl of great price, the Lamb of God, the Lamb slain from the foundation of the world, Incarnate, Lord, Emmanuel, among others (the second member of the Godhead), who literally, physically and visibly, came and died for us (the incarnation - God becoming man and remaining in the form of a man to fulfill His salvific mission), in the context of His humanity and His role in the plan of salvation. Jesus is also a friend that sticketh closer than a good and faithful brother. He is the Bread of Life, the Living Water, the Door, the great Physician, the Way, the Truth, and the Life. Most of all, He is our Saviour- your Saviour and mine. He is also referred to as the main active person in, or through whom, creation was accomplished, and also as the Head of the Church. See the reference quotations below.[76]

> *For by him were **all things created, that are in heaven, and that are in earth**, visible and invisible, whether they be thrones, or dominions, or principalities, or powers: all things were created by him, and for him: And **he is before all things, and by him all things consist.** And he is the head of the body, the church:*

---

[74]   Acts 17:29; Romans 1:20; Colossians 2:9.
[75]   Micah 7:18; Daniel 7:22.
[76]   Colossians 1:16-18 and Ephesians 5:22-23.

> *Wives, submit yourselves unto your own husbands, as*
> *unto the Lord. For the husband is the head of the*
> *wife, even as **Christ is the head of the church:** and*
> *he is the saviour of the body.*

He also intercedes for us before His Father in Heaven.[77]

The Holy Spirit, often referred to as the third member of the Godhead, is the **Spirit of truth**, the Comforter, and **the one who leads or guides us into all truth** and **to accept Jesus.**[78] He inspires the prophets and He brings about the new birth.[79] He is the one who **reproves** the world of **sin**, and of **righteousness**, and of **judgment.**[80] So, the Holy Spirit points out sin (missing the mark of right doing and righteousness, as well as transgression of the law of God) in our lives, but He does not stop there. He directs us to the opposite: right doing or righteousness, such that we can choose by God's help to stop missing the mark and stop breaking God's commandments.

You see friend, we cannot be saved without the aid of the Holy Spirit and we will be in deep trouble if we neglect, refuse, reject the Holy Spirit who Jesus promised and made available to us from His Father. But the Holy Spirit goes even further to inform us that He respects our choice; so, whatever choice we make, we must be aware and assured that we will have to face the upcoming Judgment. The Apostle Paul reminds us of this reality in Romans 14:10 and also in 2 Corinthians 5:10, respectively cited below.

> *"But why dost thou judge thy brother? or why dost*
> *thou set at nought thy brother? for we shall all stand*
> *before the **judgment seat of Christ.**"*

---

[77]   1 John 2:1, 2.

[78]   John 14.

[79]   2 Peter 1:21; John 3:3-8.

[80]   John 16:8-11.

*"For we must all appear before the **judgment seat of Christ; that every one may receive the things done in his body, according to** that he hath done, whether it be good or bad."*

The wise man, Solomon, son of King David, also echoes very clearly the same message for all people of all ages and countries, in Ecclesiastes 12:14, given below as follows:

*"14 For **God shall bring every work into judgment**, with every secret thing, whether it be good, or whether it be evil."*

Let's look at God and the Judgment before returning to examine the three O's of Deity and the God head.

ii) God and the Judgment

What is this judgment and why shall God bring every work into judgment with every secret thing? The judgment is God's act of judging beings to determine who will be saved, granted entry into Heaven (God's paradise) and have eternal life in contrast to those who will not be saved and, therefore, will not be granted eternal life. All three members of the Godhead (Father, Son, and Holy Ghost) as well as records of individual deeds and the moral law of God play important roles in the Judgment. Jesus at His second coming comes with rewards *"to give every man according as his work shall be;"*[81] so the judgment is to decide who is to get what reward either for Heaven or for hell, based on persons' attitude toward God and His law as well as on the records of each person's life. This is part of the process of vindicating the character of God as just before the entire universe.

Like the earthly judicial system but immensely superior to

---

[81] Revelation 22:12; Matthew 16:27.

it, the heavenly court which is flawless, also places great emphasis on records and record-keeping. Consequently, God has a tamper-proof, crash-proof, error-free, virus-proof, water and fire-proof, age and rust-resistant, and missile-proof, **record keeping** and **record retrieval** system in heaven. This dual purpose system (record keeping and record retrieval) referred to as books in the Bible, records all our works, deeds, and things received and done by us (whether in or outside of our bodies), good or bad. And this record system is far superior to the best state of the art record storage and retrieval system presently existing anywhere in the world or that will be produced in the future by the greatest experts in the field.

This heavenly judgment will require our records to be called and presented before Jesus, the ultimate presiding Judge of all ages. And everyone will have to appear before God to give an answer in the Judgment,[82] including our response to God and His love language. He is interceding for us before His Father in Heaven.[83] That is, in the end, we will discover that we are ultimately accountable to God and will have to give an account for all our actions. Here are a few of the references from John, the revelator; the psalmist, David; and Dr. Luke:[84]

> *"And I saw the dead, small and great, stand before God; and the **books** were opened: and another **book was opened, which is the book of life**: and the dead were judged out of **those things which were written in the books**, according to their works."*

> *"And whosoever was not found written in the **book of life** was cast into the **lake of fire.**"*

> *"And there shall in no wise enter into it anything that defileth, neither whatsoever worketh abomination,*

---

[82]   2 Corinthians 5:10.
[83]   1 John 2:1, 2.
[84]   *Revelation 20:12, 15, 21:27, 22:19; Psalm 87:4-6; Luke 12:7.*

*or maketh a lie: but they which are written in the Lamb's **book of life**.* "

*"And if any man shall take away from the words of the book of this prophecy, God shall take away his part out of **the book of life**, and out of the holy city, and from the things which are written in this book."*

*I will make mention of Rahab and Babylon to them that know me: behold Philistia, and Tyre, with Ethiopia; **this man was born there**. And of Zion it shall be said, This and that man was born in her: and the highest himself shall establish her. The **Lord shall count**, when **he writeth** up the people, that **this man was born here**. Selah.*

*"But even the very **hairs** of your head are all **numbered**. Fear not therefore: ye are of more value than many sparrows."*

The apostle Paul (formerly Saul, who was converted after being knocked down on the Damascus Road while on his way to persecute the Christians) spoke about this Judgment in the books of Romans and Second Corinthians.[85] He had a personal miniature, firsthand bird's eye view experience recorded in Acts Chapter 9. He was struck with blindness resulting from the very bright light that shone around him at midday on his journey to persecute and lock away the Christians (followers of Jesus). It was that experience that helped him to realize that He was fighting against Jesus, who He was persecuting in the form of His disciples.

Remember that this Apostle Paul was a very scholarly and brilliant Jew of no mean order. He was a churchgoer, like so many other Church goers that are steeped in the error of tradition and pride,

---

[85]   Romans 14:10 and 2 Corinthians 5:10.

and a highly placed member in the Sanhedrin. He was educated at the feet of the eminent **Gamaliel**, a leader of the Sanhedrin, and the leading Jewish teacher of his day. He knew firsthand the risk he exposed himself to in his attempt, albeit ignorant, to silence the **faithful** followers of Jesus who embraced God's Love Language. This is evidence that ignorance is no excuse for sin and wrong. This is also evidence that education,scholarship, communication and language skills, church attendance, church membership and high position in the church, and mental and or academic brilliance, do not make a person immune from persecuting the faithful possessors of the truth as it is in Jesus, and from fighting against the truth. Sincerity and passion in doing that which is wrong, do not make wrong right. They can be very meaningless, unless a person has a genuine relationship with God.

King Solomon also learned a similar important lesson from his vast experience that embraced being son of an outstanding and faithful king, to being king himself. He had just about everything that one could want at his disposal: pride, power, possession, money and mammon, winsome personality, women, access, connections and networking (to say the least), knowledge and understanding of the meaning of Judgment. Despite all that knowledge and experience, he did not serve God consistently and faithfully, nor always embraced His love language, but vacillated between right and wrong. (How many do the same today?) He became involved in pagan worship and relationships with strange women contrary to the clear commandment of God.(This shows the far-reaching negative impact that the misdemeanor or transgressions of leaders can, and do, have on a nation and its citizens.) As a result of his unfaithfulness to God, the kingdom of Israel was divided with ten (10) tribes going to his servant, Jeroboam.[86]

You see, reader and friend, we **cannot be saved without the aid of the Holy Spirit *who guides us into all truth,*** including embracing God's Love Language (not some truths that we like,

---

[86]   See 1Kings 11.

while we reject those that we do not like or which do not conform with our preference, taste, and lifestyle or do not resonate with our personality). We will be in deep trouble with our eternal salvation and God if we neglect, negate, refuse or reject the Holy Spirit, who Jesus promised and made available to us from His Father.

The Holy Spirit is interested in our salvation and will help, and has helped, all genuine persons who want to practice God's Love Language. He will help us to successfully prepare for the Judgment now going on in heaven and which will conclude just before the imminent second coming of Jesus. He is unlike humans who, very often condemn others for their sins, but do the same sins that they condemn in others, while they wish that they are not exposed. Humans will not always point us to do what is right when we are caught in the act of wrong doing. They are inclined to say that we were doing wrong all along, but just got caught. And they do not always point out:

a) the possible consequences of our sinful actions from early, from the first sign of infraction (breaking of a law, regulation or contract of some kind) becomes evident;
b) our need of accountability and that we will have to face the certain imminent, impending, Judgment.

But the Holy Spirit does. A rejection of the Holy Spirit means rejection of the only connection between man and the Holy Spirit of God or the other Comforter, whom Jesus said before His ascension, that He would make available to us, after His ascension to Heaven.

Without the presence of the Holy Spirit in the life (yours or mine), we will not choose God and His love language. That is why we are admonished to *"grieve not the Holy Spirit of God, whereby ye are sealed unto the day of redemption."* So without the Holy Spirit's in one's life, there will be no knowledge (or I will refuse to admit) that I have sinned, and I will relish no desire for right doing and righteousness. So the idea or thought of the Judgment will be far-fetched and even meaningless to such a person. Therefore, such a person will relish no desire for repentance and for establishing or reestablishing a relationship with Jesus, the one who paid the penalty for all my sins on the cruel cross of Calvary with His own life. Then, and at this point, I will be very susceptible to the wooing of the devil, and to committing the unpardonable sin, which is the sin against the Holy Ghost.

The story of Pharaoh, king of Egypt, during the time of Moses, the servant and prophet of God, is a classical case in point, but it is sad story of a rejection of the pleading of the Holy Spirit of God in his life. The Exodus account relates that he was most defiant and disdainful of God, so much so that he repeatedly hardened his heart against God and the truths that Moses related to him about God, the great "I AM THAT I AM"[87] (the God who has an eternal presence: the past, present, and future area like to God. He sees the future as we see the presence). He repeatedly denied the request to let God's people go. His revolting and stubborn yet ignorant response was:[88]

> "Who is the Lord, that I should obey his voice to let Israel go? I know not the Lord, neither will I let Israel go."

Pharaoh's arrogance, stubbornness, deceptiveness, and bigotry in dealing with Moses and God, resulted in him committing the unpardonable sin as well as in the outpouring of God's wrath and judgment on him, the Egyptians, and on the land of Egypt. The judgment of God was also manifested in the outpouring of the ten (10) plagues, including the killing of the first born among man and beast from the lowest civilian to the king, and finally in the drowning of Pharaoh and his army in the Red Sea. And God's people Israel who Pharaoh did everything to enslave and to deny liberation, were eventually liberated from the clutches of the Egyptian bondage. Read the entire story in Exodus 5 to 13:16.

---

[87] Exodus 3:14.
[88] *Exodus 5:2.*

Once again, **this shows that man cannot win against God** by ignoring Him and His love language. It also shows how bad and wrong decisions of leaders can have tragic effect on the economy and people of the country they lead.

The Book of Acts also records the manifestation of the judgment in the lives of a husband and wife, Ananias and Sapphira, who died for lying unto God, the Holy Spirit. Cited below is a sectional clipping.[89]

> *But Peter said, Ananias, why hath Satan filled thine heart to* **lie to the Holy Ghost**, *and to keep back part of the price of the land?*

> *Whiles it remained, was it not thine own? and after it was sold, was it not in thine own power? why hast thou conceived this thing in thine heart?* ***thou hast not lied unto men, but unto God.***

> *"Then Peter said unto her, How is it that* ***ye have agreed together to tempt the Spirit of the Lord?*** *behold, the feet of them which have buried thy husband are at the door, and shall carry thee out.*

God expects us to keep our word especially when dealing with Him. This is because God is faithful or trustworthy and He wants us to develop and practice His character traits of faithfulness (trustworthiness), truthfulness and honesty in all our relationships: divine/human (vertical), and human/human (horizontal). To God, being trustworthy is far more important than being 'smart' and successful (the accomplishment of a goal, whether good or bad). Not everyone who is successful is faithful or trustworthy. Because God is trustworthy, He will help us to develop this character in our lives. When we do, we can have a meaningful, symbiotically trustworthy relationship with Him; so,

---

[89]   Acts 5:3-4, 9.

there will be no need to be fearful of God and His Judgment. Like God, we are to let our words be our bond. This is of paramount importance in any genuine and faithful relationship.

Ananias and Sapphira got into trouble with God on this point. They trifled with, and lied to God the Holy Spirit, who knows our hearts and intentions. They voluntarily agreed to sell their property and give a portion of the money to the young Church. They didn't have to, if they didn't want to. But they decided to do so. And nothing was wrong with that decision as they could decide to give whatever amount they wanted to the Church. What was wrong, however, is that after agreeing to give a specified amount, they quietly decided to give a smaller amount without disclosure or confessing the change to the lower amount to God, or to the Apostle Peter or the Church. They kept back a part of the price of the land that they had promised and vowed to give, without making confession of the change or their change of hearts. They wanted the praise of men for their giving. But their giving was a lie, and both husband and wife agreed to it, none seemingly being able to dissuade the other from their misleading and dishonest path. But, unknown to the givers, God, the Holy Spirit, revealed their hoax and deception to the Apostle Peter. As a result, both of them lost their lives, even though they came to the Church at different times.

The point is that **an agreement made between ourselves and God** (even in private) **is a binding commitment that we are not at liberty to change** "willi nilli" or "glibly" without risking our life and eternal salvation. Similarly, it is therefore, a dangerous thing to make an agreement with God (even in private) to embrace and practice His love language and then go on to change our mind (whether with or without bragging and ostentation), thereby giving a false and misleading impression to others including God's people, believing that God doesn't know or that we can fool Him. **Our vows with God** (including marriage vows) **must always be taken seriously.** But the fact that God is fair and just also in Judgment (where all will receive their just reward) is another reason to love Him and to want to know more about Him.

iii) The three O's of the Godhead and additional reasons to trust, love, and obey God

The triune God is Omnipotent,[90] Omnipresent, and Omniscient (the three O's). Omnipotent means that God is all powerful. Omnipresent means that God is all present or present everywhere, while Omniscient means that God is all knowing, or the source of all knowledge. The Greek word translated as **"Omnipotent"** is *pantokrator,* which means "**all-ruling**" or (more frequently translated) "**Almighty.**" By stating that God is "Almighty," according to the Bible, we are reaffirming our belief in His authority and rulership over all creation.

E. G. White made a comment on Daniel 10:13 which is verily applicable in this context of God's omnipotence.

Day by day the conflict between good and evil is going on. Why is it that those who have had many opportunities and advantages do not realize the intensity of their work? They should be intelligent in regard to this. ***God is the Ruler. By His supreme power He holds in check and controls earthly potentates.*** *Through His agencies He does the work which was ordained before the foundation of the world.*[91]

Regarding God's **omnipresence,** King David helps us to understand this matter by asking and answering his own questions.[92]

Question: *"Where can I go from Your Spirit? Or where can I flee from Your presence?"*

Answer: *"If I ascend into heaven, You are there; if I make my bed in hell [the grave], behold, You are there. If I take the wings of the morning, and dwell in the uttermost parts of the sea, even there Your hand shall lead me, and Your right hand shall hold me."*

---

90   Rev. 19:6.
91   E. G. White Estate: Letter 201, 1899; used by permission.
92   Psalm 139:7-10.

David also helps us with God's characteristic of **omniscient**. God as omniscient, means that God **sees all** things, and **nothing can be hidden from His knowledge—not even** the secret intentions of the heart.[93] He is the beginning and the end, and hence the Greek words the "Alpha" (first letter of the Greek Alphabet) and the "Omega" (last letter of the Greek Alphabet) are used in connection with God. He, God, goes even further in this matter, as outlined in His Word that He, **understands our own intentions better than we do!**[94] Sadly, Ananias and Sapphira, died apparently before learning this about God or from ignoring it. The apostle Paul also states that *"there is no creature hidden from His sight, but all things are naked and open to the eyes of Him to whom we must give account."*[95]

The better my/our **understanding** and acceptance of who God is**, the greater** will be my/our chances or the probability of praising and thanking God and obeying Him. Here are some additional reasons why we should thank and obey God:

i)   For giving us the power to be like Him.[96]
ii)   For the promise and the **power to supply all our needs**.[97]
iii)   For **His power to protect, sustain, deliver and save us**.[98]

But my **greatest reason** for thanking and obeying God is **for the gift of our Saviour,** Jesus, the second member of the Godhead, and for being nailed to, and dying on, the cross at Calvary to save me.

But the triune God is also invincible, immortal, sinless, holy, just, perfect, yet loving, merciful, good, kind, forgiving and saving,

---

[93]   Psalm 44:21.
[94]   See Jeremiah 17:9-10; Hebrews 4:12.
[95]   Hebrews 4:13.
[96]   John 1:12, 17:3; Phil. 4:13; 1 Cor. 10:31.
[97]   Phil. 4:19.
[98]   John 3:16; Psa. 37:4.

and the only true and wise God. It is God's **omnipotence** that enables us to make meaningful accomplishments in the several priority areas of our lives including: family, health/physical, academic/educational, career, financial, social/ relationship, and religious/spiritual. Similarly, it is through His **omnipotence** that we can embrace His love language. The apostle Paul affirms this as follows:

> *"For in him we live, and move, and have our being; as certain also of your own poets have said, For we are also his offspring."*[99]

Then the disciple, Matthew, conjoins with the following, in which he states that in God's eyes we are of greater value than the birds of the air. As a result, we should not lead a life of fear or worry, but one in which we trust God.

Therefore I say unto you, Take no thought for your life, what ye shall eat, or what ye shall drink; nor yet for your body, what shall ye put on. Is not the life more than meat, and the body than raiment?

> *Behold the fowls of the air: for they sow not, neither do they reap, nor gather into ; yet your heavenly Father needeth them. Are ye not much better than they? Which of you by taking thought can add one cubit unto his stature? And why take ye thought for raiment? Consider the lilies of the field, how they grow; they toil not, neither do they spin: And yet I say unto you, That even Solomon in all his glory was not arrayed like one of these. Wherefore, if God so clothe the grass of the field, which today is, and tomorrow is cast into the oven, shall he not much more clothe you, O ye of little faith? Therefore take no thought, saying, What shall we eat? or, What shall we drink? or, Wherewithal shall we be clothed? (For after all*

---

[99]   Acts 17:28.

these things do the Gentiles seek:) for your heavenly Father knoweth that ye have need of all these things. **But seek ye first the kingdom of God, and his righteousness; and all these things shall be added unto you***. Take therefore no thought for the morrow: for the morrow shall take thought for the things of itself. Sufficient unto the day is the evil there of.*[100]

It is **through God's omnipotence** that the world was created and is sustained and it is through His omnipotence that there will be a new heaven and a new earth. It is through His Omnipresence and Omnipotence that we are protected from evil and made secure. And it is through His Omniscience that He reveals to us His love language.

3.2 God's Love Language

This important subsection covers the definition of God's Love Language, the Components of, and summary of, God's Love Language, Endorsement of God's Love Language, Attitude towards God and His Love Language, Challenges, Divine Solution and the Question of Trustworthiness.

i) God's Love Language - A lifestyle

Thus far we've looked at Language and Communication of Love (including God's interest in language and communication), Love and Love Language, and Who is God? The question that remains to be answered is: what exactly is God's Love Language? The answer is simple yet profound!

God's Love Language is "a lifestyle of loving obedience to God and His moral law or ten commandments." This **"lifestyle........."** is God's Love Language as it is the vehicle that

---

[100]   Matthew 6:25-31.

God wants us to use to demonstrate, communicate, and share our love for, and obedience to, Him. When we truly love God we will also understand that His love language also requires sharing, and communicating His (Agape) love to our fellowmen. A prudent husband who truly loves his wife will demonstrate his love for her by using **her** love language and **not his,** both in his actions and mannerisms. When this happens she will feel respected, loved and secure. Similarly, a lifestyle and lifetime demonstration of loving obedience to God and His ten commandments provides the evidence for God to be respected, assured, and secure that we love Him and are willing to surrender our all to Him. This is because in using God's Love Language and not your (our) own, you (we) are demonstrating love and respect for God and providing an opportunity to bring out the best in God for us. **King Solomon calls this the whole duty of man.**[101] John, the Revelator, confirms this demonstration and opportunity as follows:[102]

> *"Blessed are **they that do His commandments** that they may **have right to the tree of life,** and may in **enter through the gates into the city** (of God)."*

This text reveals that the opportunity (and rewards) for using God's Love Language includes "blessed" (happiness and blessings) here on earth as well as entrance "through the gates into the city"and "right to the tree of life" in heaven.

Because God is the greatest, sinless lover of all times, He may be rightfully called the Supreme lover. Accordingly, He expects us to honestly and truthfully return (or reciprocate) this love, and obey Him in thought, word and action, and with all our heart, soul, mind and strength).[103] God's Love Language exists so that we will know how to communicate our love for, and to, Him in the language that He approves. He is even more particular about

---

[101]   Ecclesiastes 12:13.
[102]   Revelation 22:14, Mark 12:30.
[103]   John 14:15; Isaiah 1:18.

His love language (and rightly so) than human beings are about human love languages (discussed in Chapter 2). Through His love language, He wants to build the best possible loving relationship with us that is both saving and eternal.

Notice that it is He who is eager and wants to build this love relationship with us (and usually not the reverse), which is typical of His nature and character. He "draws" or "woos" us to Him with His everlasting love,[104] (just as how He went in search of Adam after Adam had sinned). This is just like how the Holy Spirit of God translates our prayers into heavenly language by making intercession for us with groaning which cannot be uttered.[105] This makes a lot of sense to me, because now I can better appreciate why God, the Father, so loved the world that He was willing to give His only begotten Son. Jesus, went all the way to Calvary, that whosoever believes in Him should not perish but have everlasting life. ["Only begotten" translates the Greek word "monogenes" which, in reference to Jesus, means "the only one of its kind or class, unique in kind." So, Jesus, is uniquely God's Son in the sense that He shares the same divine nature.]

Now I can have the best possible reason for living, and not just any kind of living, but a quality life of loving obedience to God. The reason is that God sent not His Son into the world to condemn the world, but that the world through Him might be saved.[106] Now I can better understand the many stories of love relationships in the Bible between God and His people, and why they are a testimony to the fact that **God has eternal interest in having a permanent love relationship with us. Yes, a permanent love relationship with us!**

Shawn Brace in his Article on "Speaking God's Love Language" writes

---

[104] Jeremiah 31:3.
[105] Romans 8:26.
[106] John 3:16-17.

More than any song we could sing or testimony we could share, **God's primary love language is that which is reflected in our lives.** *What* **brings joy to God's heart** *more than anything else* **is a life that has been touched by Calvary's love.** *When* **a person is truly motivated by that love, his actions** *will be* **the greatest praise God could ever receive.**[107]

What is it that, if reflected in our lives, brings joy to God's heart? The answer is a lifestyle of loving obedience to God and His ten commandments.

But **what does a lifestyle of loving obedience to God** and His moral law or commandments **mean in practical terms,** in everyday living and *what does it involve?* First and foremost, it must mean an understanding of the components of this phrase: "a lifestyle of loving obedience to God and His moral law or ten commandments". It also means an understanding of the prerequisites for using God's Love Language. This is like how the preparation before the marriage of two persons is important. It is also like how the preparation for an important exam will often determine whether the student will pass or fail the exam. So too are the prerequisites for embracing God's Love Language vitally important.

These prerequisites include: Requirements to satisfy, Man's (man used here in the generic sense) whole duty in developing a love for God's Love Language, as well as other important things to know. However, our understanding of God's Love Language would not be complete without spending some time to examine the Blessings and benefits of using God's Love Language (Chapter 4), the Common Excuses many put forward for not complying with God's Love Language (Chapter 5), the Consequences of

---

[107] Shawn Brace's Online Article in the Adventist Review captioned "Speaking God's Love Language" posted at http://www.adventistreview.org/ Accessed May 2012.

knowingly ignoring God's Love Language (Chapter 6), and finally, Our response to His love language (Chapter 7).

ii) The components and summary of God's Love Language

The components of God's Love Language which are discussed under this subsection are: Meaning of lifestyle, Loving obedience, God, God's moral law or commandments. The subsection concludes with a summary of God's Love Language.

a) Meaning of lifestyle

Lifestyle is a term that is used to refer to the way of life or style of living of a person (steward) or group (stewards) which reflects the presence or absence of principles, values, standards, norms, and attitudes. Pastor James Daniel speaking at a Stewardship Rally held in 2013 in Kingston, Jamaica, stated that "lifestyle" affects "every area of your life." This is rightly so because God is interested in every area and aspect of our lives. God knows more than we do, that our **lifestyle** which, is developed over time and has to do with what is practiced, is influenced by many factors including: family and socialization, education, religion, culture, and choice. Therefore, He wants assurance that every area and aspect of our lives are expressing our love for Him.

My favourite definition of lifestyle is the one by Larry Lewis, Health and Wellness Life Coach, as stated in *The Beginner's Guide To A Healthy Lifestyle,* cited herein below as follows:

'The aggregation of decisions made by individuals which affect their health, and over which they more or less have control."

For me, this is a very profound definition because it can be applied to God's Love Language for at least four main reasons.

i)   It relates lifestyle to the aggregation (sum or total) of decisions; meaning not one, two, or a few, but the total of all decisions made over time. Embracing God's Love

Language requires the reader to make a decision. See Chapter 4 for more on decision making.

ii) The decisions are made by individuals, human beings, male and female alike, who were made by a God who loves them both so much that He died to save them. Decisions are not made by things or inanimate objects, which cannot see, hear, feel, touch, and reason by themselves and on their own. God loves and died for people (and not things) with whom He can reason as outlined in Isaiah 1:18. God's Love Language is for human beings who need to make a decision to speak and caress it.

iii) Decisions affect the health of the decision maker, either for good or bad. And of course, health includes spiritual health. God wants us to embrace His Love Language as a lifestyle that positively enhances our spiritual health. God's Love language is designed to help us to do that.

iv) The question of control. Human beings love to have control. The decisions that we make affect our health: mental and emotional, physical, social, and spiritual. But the good news is that we have some control and can choose to make decisions that will have positive effects or outcomes. Similarly, choosing God's Love Language will affect all our faculties, so choose wisely as to how you relate to it. God's Love Language is also about surrender and subordination of our-selves and our own love language to God in favour of God's Love Language.

A lifestyle of loving obedience to God and His commandments must result from, not just a "head" or "**theoretical**" knowledge of God, but more importantly, from an **"experiential"** knowledge of God that develops over time. It's like being on a continuum, moving through time from past to present to future in our relationship with Jesus. Even though there may have been times, or will be time, when we go through fluctuations and transitions in our spirituality, we should seek/choose to return and remain on the continuum with Jesus. The lifestyle is not a "one-off" thing nor a "one-time" event. Neither is it a "one-night stand" connection with Jesus, but an on-going process, one in which we will seek to renew and recommit ourselves to God on an on-going basis. Follow the three (3) illustrative examples below.

First: Persons who are very concerned and conscious about the value of quality health know that they eat to live, and not live to eat. Understandably, they daily repeat the activity of balanced dieting (nutrition). They also exercise, drink enough water, have adequate exposure to sunlight, practice temperance, get enough of fresh air and rest and also trust in God. They know that if they want to be and remain healthy, their **lifestyle** must involve doing these things repeatedly.

Second: Happily married couples know that they cannot take their marriage for granted. They know that in order to keep their marriage going: happy, healthy and blessed, requires a lifestyle that involves among other things - repeated exercise of love (giving and receiving), communication (for shared understanding), compassion, caring, empathy, and mutual respect (for each other's individuality, rights, preferences and tastes, and so forth) mutual trust, commitment, and forgiveness. Spouses that I know, who are happily married for many years, tell me that they had to repeat these exercises, and not take them for granted. They developed a lifestyle that included doing all those things and more, in order to remain in the marriage, keeping it alive with flame and spark.

Third: Finally, prudent business persons can readily identify with the reality of going into business normally for the long haul. We refer to this as a "going concern." This is for the specific objective of increasing the value of shareholder wealth or value to the owners. If the business objective is to be realized, they know that they must consistently follow or practice certain business principles. Such business principles involve choices to ensure among other things: the results of profitability, liquidity, solvency and financial self-sustainability.

In each of the three (3) illustrations mentioned above, it has to be understood, first and foremost, that **lifestyle** is at its best when the people involved make their own free choices. Secondly, we may also use the fundamental accounting concept of "consistency" to emphasize the other point about being consistent. For the accountant, "consistency" means that once a business has chosen a particular method (e.g. method of depreciation) for the accounting treatment of an item (example a fixed or non-current asset), it will enter all similar transactions that follow in exactly the same manner. A business can choose to change its method, but it should not be done without much consideration. Where the change will have material effect (for example on the profit calculation of the business), the effect of the change should be stated or disclosed. **The point is** that, likewise, an individual can change from a non-Christian lifestyle to a Christian lifestyle. However, it should be done after much consideration. An individual should satisfy him/her self that the benefits of such a change will outweigh the cost involved; so that once the individual makes a disclosure regarding the change and its material benefits, he or she will want to remain in it for the long haul. This emphasis is being stated because it is important to remember that God's Love Language is about eternal love relationships.

The lifestyle of a Christian is very real and can be quite rewarding. I remember very vividly the story of a gentleman I know very well who is an example of what a lifestyle of loving obedience to God and His commandments is all about. When as a young teenager his mother gave him the option to decide on the high school of his choice, he chose a Christian school. He eventually became head-boy at the school. He successfully moved on to college, undergraduate and graduate schools. While at college his peers teased and taunted him to join them in drinking, smoking, and womanizing. But, he consistently refused. At some of the places that he applied for employment, he was informed that the jobs were his, but he had to work on the Sabbath (Saturday). But, he gracefully turned them down. At one of his postgraduate work places, he was informed that he will not get certain promotion, unless he attends Board meetings on the Sabbath; but he confidently stated that he is unable to work on the Sabbath. He remained faithful to his Christian beliefs, and to God, who is the centre and central theme of God's Love language. By remaining consistent and true to his Christian values and principles, he was able to represent his employers and Church at various functions overseas and is happy serving God. Today, he is happily married and is the father of three sons; and he and his family are rejoicing, serving the Lord. Yes, you too, can have similar faithful experience if you caress God's Love Language.

b) Loving obedience

The relationship that God wants to have with us, human beings, is one that involves both love and obedience to Him and His commandments, despite and in spite of the challenges that may be involved. And because followers of Jesus are called Christians (stewards or disciples), the lifestyle of the Christian must of necessity require **love** and **obedience**, or loving obedience. Rightly understood, both go hand in hand and help us to develop a righteous character; but love must come first. Joe A. Webb, principal contributor of Adult Teachers Sabbath School Bible Study Guide captioned "Evangelism and Witnessing", writes the following in Lesson 10 entitled "A Love Response":

> *Love and obedience are inseparable as long as they occur in that order. True love for God will always result in obedience to His revealed will,* but obedience will not necessarily lead to love (although it can)." "Our love for God must be rooted in His love for us. God existed before we did, and He has loved us supremely from the creation of

*humankind. **Love** can **only come** as a **result of,** and in **response to, love.**[108]*

On the same matter of obedience, Carsten Johnsen, concludes:

"Obedience is the highest praise man can offer to God."[109]

It was Samuel, the seer, judge, prophet and priest of God who said to king Saul, first king of Ancient Israel, in 1 Samuel 15:22b,

*"Hath **the Lord** as great delight in burnt offerings and sacrifices, **as in obeying the voice of the Lord**? Behold, **to obey is better that sacrifice**, and to hearken than the fat of rams?"*

Obedience, in the context of human relations (horizontal relationship) and divine-human relations (vertical relationship), means **the act of yielding to explicit instructions or orders from another, usually one superior in rank, position, or authority.** Synonyms for obedience are "surrender", and "subservience". Now we can better understand Jesus' statement in the Gospel of St. John. He said: *"If ye love me, keep my commandments."*[110] The conditional and operative word here is **"if",** and Jesus is saying that only love can be the true motivation for obedience, and willing obedience.

If I truly **love** my wife, I will not cheat on her. I will seek to please her, as long as pleasing her does not cause me to disobey God or compromise my relationship with Him. Likewise, if I truly love my children (and I surely do), I will not abuse them. So, if **I truly**

---

[108] Cited from Adult Teachers Sabbath School Bible Study Guide (April- May-June 2012 Edition), Topic: "Evangelism and Witnessing, Lesson 10 - A Love Response (page 114) by Joe A. Webb, Publisher: Inter- American Division Publishing Association, Doral Florida.

[109] Carsten Johnsen, The Maligned God, published by The Untold Story Publishers (1980).

[110] John 14:15.

love Jesus Christ, I **will gladly obey Him** for He is not an abuser. It is that straight forward, and the Word of God makes it easy to understand why the Holy Spirit helps us to correctly practice love and obedience for God and His commandments.[111]

Joe A. Webb's writing is about willing obedience that flows from love; but he also makes the point cited above that "*obedience will not necessarily lead to love (although it can)."* We know that forced obedience does not normally nor naturally lead to love. So let's quickly distinguish between willing obedience and forced obedience.

Willing obedience is the exercise of the choice to obey clear, reasonable, and legitimate instructions or orders, free from threats, force, intimidation, violence or punishment. Forced obedience is the opposite; it is a decision made under coercion or duress to comply with instruction(s) as a result of threat(s), intimidation, violence or punishment. When a former coworker of mine handed over her car keys to a gunman who pointed a gun in her face; that was forced obedience. She handed over the keys out of fear for her life (as her life was more valuable than the car).

In the 1970's, close to 1,000 persons/members of the Peoples Temple settlement died at Jonestown, Guyana, as a result of being fed a poison-laced drink. One source said that

> *at one level, the deaths at Jonestown can be viewed as the product of obedience, of people complying with the orders of a leader and reacting to the threat of force. In the Peoples Temple, whatever Jim Jones commanded, the members did. When he gathered the community at the pavilion and the poison was brought out, the populace was surrounded by armed guards who were trusted lieutenants of Jones. There are reports that some people did not drink voluntarily*

---

[111] John 14:16.

but had the poison forced down their throats or injected (Winfrey, 1979).[112]

This is neither the command nor the kind of obedience that Jesus referred to in His word; and this is not the kind of circumstances nor obedience that Jesus expects regarding obedience to God and His commandments.

c) God

This is the same God who is the originator of the Commandments and the same triune God that was discussed in subsection 3.1 above. God, the Father, wrote the commandments with His own fingers upon tables of stone and delivered them unto Moses. Jesus died to repair the broken relationship between God and man as a result of sin, the transgression of God's law. The Holy Spirit leads us into all truth and to appreciate the fact that God's law is the truth, relevant and binding.

Our God is not a figment of man's imagination. He is not dependent on mankind for anything as He is not a product of man. He doesn't need our praise or our gifts to be God. He does not need to obey man to maintain His integrity. On the contrary, we need Him to have and enjoy the best life possible. It is in man's best interest to get to become acquainted with God and to love and obey Him. Our present and future happiness depends on having a lifestyle of loving obedience to God and His commandments.

d) God's moral law or commandments

The following questions will be addressed under this sub-heading.

---

[112] Neal Osherow: Making Sense of the Nonsensical: An Analysis of Jonestown, Source at http://www.guyana.org/features/jonestown.html

    i)   Does God have a moral law or Ten Commandments? And if so, what it is or what are they, and where can hey be found?

    ii)   Why are these commandments important or what are their purposes?

    iii)   How can I know for sure if they are binding upon all people of all nations around the world?

God does have a moral law or commandments. This moral law is called the Ten Commandments of God. They are also referred to, among other names, as 'tables of testimony' and 'tables of stone', 'the writing', 'the writing of God', 'the Decalogue', 'the law of God', 'the commandments of Lord', the 'commandments of the Lord your God', 'His commandments', 'the royal law', 'the great commandment in the law and the second great commandment in the law', 'words of the covenant', the 'law of liberty', and the 'perfect law of liberty'.[113]

The Ten Commandments are a set of **divine principles,** designed, written, and given by God to help human beings identify what is right in contrast to what is wrong as they seek to develop and practice the best possible love relationship between themselves and with God. Although the term 'moral law' is not used in the Bible, it is nevertheless used to refer to the Ten Commandments of God which embrace concepts of 'right and wrong', 'honest', 'good,' 'honourable', 'ethical', 'just', and 'principled' behaviour and conduct. Although the Ten Commandments are a set of rules, they are much more than a set of rules. This is because they are moral principles, and in actuality a transcript, or mirror image, of God's character. God is described in the Scriptures as 'holy', 'just', and 'good'. These same adjectives are also used to describe the Ten Commandments law of God. So we need to be very careful as to how we relate to God's Ten Commandments, as they are not an

---

[113]   Exodus 31:18, 32:16; 34:28; Deuteronomy 10:4; James 1:25, 2:12; James 2:8.

enemy of mankind. Additionally, as part of God's Love Language, they are an essential vehicle which is needed for expressing, giving, receiving, and communicating love, thereby making a person in a relationship feeling loved.

God's Ten Commandments are found en bloc in Exodus 20:17. However, they are found in summary form, individually, and in aliquot in different passages throughout the holy book, the Bible.[114] "The number **'ten'** in the commandments in Scripture indicates **fullness or completeness**. Thus, the Ten Commandments represent God's entire ethical standard given to mankind."[115] So, these commandments are complete; nothing needs to be added. Take a little time to read or reread this passage in Exodus mentioned above.

They may be summarized as follows.

i) Forbid worship of other gods apart from the true God
ii) All forms of image worship is forbidden
iii) Taking God's name in vain is not permitted
iv) Remember the Sabbath Day of the Lord, thy God, to keep it holy.
v) Respect for parents
vi) No killing is allowed (as human life is important and sacrosanct).
vii) Adultery is disallowed
viii) No stealing is permitted
ix) Don't bear false witness against your neighbour
x) Don't covet anything from your neighbour

There is a summary of the law of God which I found some years ago, but can't recall the source, which I love very much and which shows the first four on one table and the remaining six

---

[114] Sampling of texts: Mark 2:28-34; Matthew 22:37-40; Romans 13:8-10; 1 John 5:3.
[115] God's Law For Modern Man by Brian Schwertley; source: http://www.reformedonline.com/view/reformedonline/law.htm

on the second table. It is simple, yet very profound. This I have included herein below. Colours are supplied for ease of recognition and contrast.

THE LAW OF GOD SUMMARIZED	
TABLE A - LOVE TO GOD WORSHIP GOD	TABLE B - LOVE TO MAN RESPECT OTHERS
1. Supreme and only	5. Parents
2. Directly and spiritually	6. Life
3. Reverently	7. Home and family
4. Reguraly and weekly	8. Honour and reputation
	9. Property
	10. Rights

The Ten Commandments were **written by God Himself, with His very own fingers** upon tables of stone on two (2) different occasions. First, God wrote them on the tables of stone upon Mount Sinai and gave them to Moses. The second writing was to replace the first tables of stones which were broken by Moses in his disappointment when the children of Israel made and worshipped the golden calf.[116] The writing on tables of stones clearly implies how unchangeable and enduring they are. God did not permit His servant and prophet, Moses, to write them as they are eternally important. Moses may make a mistake if he was the one to write them, but God doesn't make mistakes.

These ten moral precepts were given by our God of love, out of His love for us.[117] The first four, written on the first table of stone (shown as Table A above), deals with man's love for God (*Agape*), whereas the last six commandments on the second table (shown as Table B above) deal with love for man (*phileo*). Whereas the first four commandments define our relationship with God (vertical) and the basis for worshipping Him, the last six (6) define our relationship with our fellowmen (horizontal) including respect for them.

It is so **ironical** that the fourth and only commandment that **begins with** the word "**remember**" (see elaboration below) is the one that so many in the world forget, forsake, ignore, secularize and commercialize and in some instances even blatantly reject. In other instances, they even seek to ridicule, persecute and imprison those who seek to uphold it.[118] Oh, how many are ignorant of this enduring Biblical truth; and how the **devil allures and deceives** so many in the world to side against God on this all important matter of the fourth commandment![119] Yet, it is the only one that reminds man of His Maker, the One in whom we live and move and have our being. It is the only one that provides the basis for which man ought to worship and reverent God, the fact that God is our Creator, and extends to provide the basis for which children ought to obey their parents in the Lord. Yet, it is the only commandment that carries a reminder from God. In this very commandment, God requires of man the need to spend quality time with Him. (See more on this below.)

Yes reader, the fourth commandment **is the only commandment of the ten (10) that identifies who is their source as well as what is the seal of God.** A seal is a mark or stamp of authority, and evidence of authenticity. God's seal is reflected in His law, in the fourth commandment, as it contains the three (3) distinguishing features of a seal, viz: name, title and function, and domain or territory over which the one in authority rules. Applying these to the fourth commandment, we have His name: God; His title and function: Creator **God**; His domain or territory over which He rules: heaven and the earth, as He made them. If this fourth commandment of the ten (10) is scrapped we would not know who is their source or author. Let's look at the particular text (Exodus 20:8-11) cited below, one more time from two sources: NIV and CEV, respectively.

---

[118]   Ezekiel 22:25-27.
[119]   Exodus 20:8-11; Acts 17:26-26.

Remember the Sabbath day by keeping it holy.
Six days you shall labor and do all your work, but
the seventh day is a Sabbath to the Lord your
God. On it you shall not do any work, *neither*
you, nor your son or daughter, nor your manservant
or maidservant, nor your animals, nor the alien
within your gates. For in six days **the Lord made**
the heavens and the earth, the sea, and all that is in
them, but **he rested on the seventh day. Therefore**
the Lord blessed the Sabbath day and made it
holy. *(NIV 1984)*

Remember that the Sabbath Day belongs to me. You
have six days when you can do your work, but **the**
seventh day of each week belongs to me, your God.
No one is to work on that day — *not you, your*
children, your slaves, your animals, or the foreigners
who live in your towns. In six days I made the sky,
the earth, the oceans, and everything in them, but **on**
the seventh day I rested. That's why I made the
Sabbath a special day that belongs to me. *(CEV)*

This fourth commandment is the only one of the ten
that requires the weekly observance of the seventh-day of the
week (or Saturday) from sunset Friday evening to sunset Sabbath
(Saturday) evening as the day of rest, worship, and ministry in
harmony with the teaching and practice of Jesus.[120] This same Jesus,
who made the Sabbath for man (and not man for the Sabbath) is
Lord of the Sabbath. **The Sabbath**, which came to us from the
very first week of God's creation, as **a sign of our redemption,**
our sanctification, and mark of our ownership by God, is to be
observed and remembered by all as God's memorial of creation.

---

[120]   What we believe: Being mindful of his word, Chapter
        20 - What we believe about the Sabbath, Inter-American
        Division Publishing Association, Florida 33172,USA.

It was created before there was a Jew and is to be reserved as God's holy time by all human beings. The Bible tells us that God blessed the Sabbath, rested on it, and set it aside for holy use.

This is speaking about quality time on God's holy day that **God wants us to reserve for getting together with, and spending with Him, out of our loving obedience to Him and for our blessing of enhanced relationship with Him**. Notice that from Chapter 2, sub-section 2.3 above, Dr. Gary Chapman identifies quality time as one of the five love languages. To use Chapman's idea, the observing of the seventh-day Sabbath (consisting of twenty-four (24) hours), therefore, may be considered as a secondary love language of God. I cannot think of any other experience that is better or greater than spending time (quantity time which leads to quality time) with God. **If you have not been observing God's holy time, why not start doing so today! You will be obeying and pleasing God when you do.** But, if you don't (when you know otherwise), you will be placing your own love language above that of God's and that will sadden the heart of God and rob you of blessings God desires to give to the loving and obedient. If you were ignorant of this in the past, God winked at, but now that you know, He requires you to repent and start on the path of loving obedience to Him and His commands.[121]

If mankind truly loves God, the first four commandments would be obeyed, especially the fourth as Jesus requests.[122] Consequently, there would not be a single idolater, agnostic, infidel, or atheist in our world. False worship, including image and idol worship would either end or be at an all-time low. Likewise, swearing and misrepresentation of God's name and character would not occur and we would be looking forward passionately for a meeting with Him every week as a constant memorial of His creative wonders. To the extent that these are done, the stage would be set for fabulous interpersonal relationships around the globe,

---

[121] Acts 17:29-31.
[122] John 14:15, 21,15:14.

based on the last six commandments, which specifically outline how God expects us to relate to our fellowmen.

Greater emphasis should also be given to the fifth commandment, which is the first of the last six (of those on the second table), as it provides the basis on which children ought to obey and respect their parents. It would definitely serve to strengthen the family ties and reflect the reality that this is the first commandment with a promise. This commandment is shown below as follows:

> *"Honour thy father and thy mother: that thy days may be long upon the land which the Lord thy God giveth thee."*[123]

For, like God, parents are the "creators" of their children in the sense that they brought children into the world. In this regard, parents should earn the respect of their child/children to the extent that they rightly represent God to their offspring. The remaining five of the last six(6) commandments on the second table relate specifically to how God expects people to relate to one another, loving *(phileo)* each other as a result of loving God and accepting His *(agape)* love within clearly defined boundaries. They define acceptable behaviour and relationships and also outline those that God don't accept. However, because there is a lot of "lip" service taking place,the world is the way it is, despite all the technological advance.

The prophet, Isaiah, describes this hypocritical lip service as follows in the prophetic book of Isaiah as shown below.

> *"Therefore the Lord said: "Inasmuch as these people draw near with their mouths And honor **Me** with their **lips**, But have **removed** their **hearts far from***

---

[123] *Exodus 20:12.*

Me, And their fear toward **Me** *is taught by the commandment of* **men,** "[124]

We speak of our age as being post-modern with much modernization. But have we seen post-modern moral and spiritual improvements in the way we live? You know the answer and you didn't have to look far to find it! Why? The above text gives a very clear and pointed answer. But it can also be plainly stated that the reason for the concerns of moral decadence in our world, is because individuals and nations have substituted and elevated their own love language for, and above, God's Love Language. It is impossible to lead a lifestyle of loving obedience to God and His commandments and to simultaneously have the heart (mind and seat of intelligence) far removed from God. You see, friend, placing the commandment of slipping, variable, sinful mankind, above God's commandments is to set up a counterfeit love language. When we sow to the wind, we must reap the whirlwind.[125]

While homicide is still illegal in many countries, manslaughter and murder are still a major problem around the world. And war seems to legalize killing; but not so in God's book, which still states: *"Thou shalt not kill."* Because we cannot create life, we should not illegally and immorally take the life of anyone. For in so doing, there is permanent dislocation and damage not only to the victim(s), but also to families, relatives and friends and economies. 9/11 still leaves very fresh sordid scars and memories in the minds of many in and outside of the United States of America. Therefore, the Ten Commandments of God are meant for persons of all walks of life around the globe to respect the life of others.

Adultery and fornication, 'one night-stand" and the other names by which they are called, are still rampant and continue to contribute to the pain and heartaches within and outside of homes and families, communities and countries. Prostitution is big business in many places. And the public argument, which I have

---

[124]   Isaiah 29:13.
[125]   Hosea 8:7, Galatians 6:8, Proverbs 22:8; Romans 1:21-24, 28-29.

seen and heard on radio and TV, goes like this in some quarters, *"I am doing it to earn a living and feed and educate my family."* True, there are real socio-economic challenges, but how intricate and complex the problem of sin in our world! Not love, but *"lip"* service and situational ethics by many regarding this commandment, and sad to say, some professed Christians are involved.

Stealing is not exempt; neither are lying or falsehood, misrepresentation, and covetousness, which were at the heart of Lucifer's sin in heaven. The commandments (numbers 8, 9, and 10) to which these relate are meant to help us to protect the property rights of our fellow human beings and to save us from ourselves and to help us to highly establish and preserve integrity and prevent corruption. If we respect and love others, we will not want to take from them what is not ours and what they have not given to us. Neither will we choose to deceive by lying or misrepresentation. Rather, we will want to cherish the relationship God wants us to have with them as beings who are also made and loved by God.

In many places you still have to watch your back. If you have been deceived and robbed you will understand this. Just recently I was in a store in Florida with someone who told me that her purse was stolen in the store, with no trace of the villain. Because some of these lawbreakers are not caught and punished speedily, it is set in the hearts of men to do evil.[126] That's why many continue to lie and cheat to "get ahead" they claim, risking the embarrassment and the punishment that goes along with being caught for a crime or felony. Yet God loves them too, and there is hope for them if they choose to accept Jesus as Lord of their lives while they area live!

In fact, in some situations, it is difficult to tell who is male and female. God made Adam and Eve and brought them together as a heterogeneous couple (husband and wife) to multiply and replenish the Earth. But so many today have chosen instead same sex couples and even try to call that family.[127] Yet in all my years,

---

[126] Ecclesiastes 8:11.
[127] Romans 1:20-32.

I know that if I want to use an electric iron to get heat to press or iron some clothes, I must insert the male plug leading from the iron into a female electrical outlet or socket.

This satisfies the law of physics made by man. I have never seen it work any other way, or know of any other connection that can get it to work. But, when the time is right, when the cup of the iniquity of sinners is full reaching up to heaven, God will again act, just like He did at the time of Lot in Sodom and Gomorrah. However, if sinners chose to hear His voice and repent, there is hope for their salvation. Let us never forget that God loves them too and died for them. They too can choose to embrace God's Love Language; so never write them off.

The commandments of God are indeed important as they are God's love letter to us which spells out in plain and simple language what we need to know and do (or abstain from doing) as an expression of our love and appreciation for God. Provided herein below are ten (10) of the main reasons why the commandments of God are important.

i) They are from a loving God for His creatures whom He wants to save; and they are universally binding.[128]

ii) They are a transcript of the character of God. Many people will remember a transcript when they want a copy of their academic performance from an educational institution. It reveals a record of their performance. For God, it reveals what God is like. It's a record of His nature, which is perfect, holy, just, good, and spiritual, and therefore, a mirror image of the His character. They reflect the character that God wants us to have. That is why Jesus challenged us to be perfect even as our Father which is in heaven is perfect. See Matthew 5:48. When we possess such a God-like character, we will have joy

---

[128] Ecclesiastes 12:13.

communicating with God through His love language and not via a substitute language of our own devising.

iii) In addition to reflecting God's nature and character, the Ten Commandments are both immutable (unchallengeable and indisputable) and irrevocable or non-cancellable (unchangeable or irrepealably) just like God. Not even God can change His law. After sin emerged, the Son of God died to pay the penalty for the broken law (the greatest act and evidence of grace), because the Law of God is unchangeable.

iv) They contain the seal of God. God's people in the last days, will be identified as those who possess His stamp of approval or seal because they keep His commandments and have the faith of Jesus. This fourth commandment is additionally significant for at least three (3) reasons because it begins with the word:

"REMEMBER".

a) It's important because it is a memorial of creation, hence the need for the weekly celebration of the Sabbath and constant reminder that God is the Creator of heaven and earth. Similarly, many countries will value and observe their day of independence as constant reminder of their beginning of a nation. The principle is no different with God.

b) Remember signifies that you were informed before; therefore, remember suggests a reminder of something that is important.

c) Humans have the tendency to forget, just like ancient Israel forgot many of God's goodness to them. So God's didn't want us to forget Him as Creator, or His seal, which is also a sign of our redemption.

v) They are God's moral standard (divine principles) of righteous living.

vi)   They summarize our relationships, viz; love to God (God/man vertical relationship) and love to fellow human beings (human/human horizontal relationship) and define acceptable behaviour and conduct. In this regard, they are the best expression and definition of the content and quality of God's Love Language. There can, therefore, be no doubt as to what language God requires us to use in communicating with Him. That is, His language of love and not our counterfeit language of selfishness and self-centeredness.

vii)   They define the basis or standard by which all human beings are judged in the judgment, enter heaven, given eternal life and right to the tree of life or receive eternal damnation in hell.[129]

viii)   The Ten Commandments law of God is a moral law, a spiritual law, a positive law, a simple law, a unique law, a delightful law, a comprehensive law, and yet a law containing universal principles.

ix)   They are the equitable basis by which God will provide rewards to all human kind at the appropriate time of His choosing.

x)   They are central and critical to an understanding of God's Love Language. They are a requirement that vouch for our love for Jesus. In John 14:15, Jesus said: *"If ye love me keep my commandments."*

In addition to being important, the Ten Commandments of God have many purposes. Outlined herein below are (6) of their main purposes.[130]

i)   **To reveal God's will and purpose for humanity**, while **demanding perfect obedience** (possible only through the power that the indwelling Holy Spirit provides)

---

[129] Revelation 14:12; Isaiah 26:2.
[130] SDA Beliefs, Chapter 18 - The Law of God

107

which is vital to salvation. *"For whoever shall keep the whole law, and yet stumble in one point, he is guilty of all"* (James 2:10).

Jesus Himself said: *"If you want to enter into life, keep the commandments"* (Matthew 19:17).

ii)   **To point out sin in the lives of humanity** and function like a mirror or looking glass. The Ten Commandments are necessary for persons to conspicuously see God's holiness in contrast to their own guilt and, therefore, their need to repent. If human beings do not recognize that they are in violation of God's law, they will not sense the magnitude of their sin, sinfulness or lostness, and hence their need of the atoning blood of Jesus, the Son of God. Because the law of God functions as a mirror, it will help people to see their true condition, and hence their need to turn to the Saviour whose blood is able to wash away their sin, which is the transgression of God's law.[131] The law of God cannot save, it has never saved anyone, and never will. The law simply points out our sin, and this recognition of sin, is what drives or directs us by the prompting of the Holy Spirit, to Jesus. When we repent (at the Holy Spirit enabling), confess, and forsake our sins, and ask God to forgive us, He will forgive and cleanse us of all unrighteousness,[132] and give us the power to live a holy life.[133]

iii) **To act as an agent in our conversion.** Conversion is a change from wrong doing to right doing, a change from sinful living to rectitude or righteous living, a change of

---

[131]   James 1:23-25; 1 John 3:4; Romans 3:20, 7:7.
[132]   1 John 1:9; 1 Peter 1:16.
[133]   John 1:12.

allegiance from Satan to God, which obviously involves a noticeable change in the thought, feelings, beliefs, philosophy, and behaviour. The Psalmist, David, helps us to understand that God's law is the instrument that the Holy Spirit uses to bring us to conversion. In the Book of Psalm he cites this principle as follows: "*The law of the Lord is perfect, converting the soul*" (Psalm 19:7).

iv) **To restrain evil and bring blessings.** It can be restated unequivocally here that where there is narrow to widespread disregard for God's moral law or Decalogue, this has resulted in a domino effect or multiplier increase in crime, violence, immorality, and wickedness affecting the guilty: whether individual, nation and or the world. Contrastingly, where God's moral law or Decalogue is accepted and adopted, it restrains sin, promotes right actions, and becomes a means of establishing righteousness. Nations that have incorporated the divine and universal principles of God's moral law into their laws have experienced great blessing. On the other hand, those nations that have abandoned these said principles, have experienced a steady decline, and even extinction, as in the cases of Babylon, Sodom and Gomorrah.

The reality is that, as the Old Testament times bear record, God often blessed nations and individuals in proportion to their obedience to His law. It's a principle of the law of cause and effect out lined in subsection 6.1 in Chapter 6. Here are a few references that vouch for this conclusion. "*Righteousness exalts a nation,*" and a "*throne is established by righteousness.*" (Proverbs 14:34; 16:12). Those who refused to obey God's commandments encountered calamities (Psalm 89:31, 32). "*The curse of the Lord is on the house of the wicked, but He blesses the habitation of the just"* (Proverbs 3:33; Leviticus 26; Deuteronomy 28). The same general principle is true today.

v) **To function as a standard for God's judgment**. The law of God sets the standard of righteousness. Accordingly, each one of us will be judged by these righteous principles, and not by our consciences. The wise man Solomon explicitly outlines for our understanding the following: *"Fear God and keep His commandments,"......"for God will bring every work into judgment, including every secret thing, whether it is good or whether it is evil"* (Ecclesiastes 12:13, 14). James also contributes the following: *"So speak ye, and so do, as they that shall be judged by the law of liberty."* (James 2:12). Because human consciences vary from "weak," "defiled," "evil," to being "seared with a hot iron" (1 Corinthians 8:7, 12; Titus 1:15; Hebrews 10:22; 1 Timothy 4:2), telling us that we must do right, but not telling us what is right; they must be "set" by some accurate standard to be of value. Therefore, only consciences set by God's great standard—His law— can keep us from straying into sin. However, those who lead a lifestyle of loving obedience to God and His commandments, will not be afraid of the judgment.

vi) **To provide true freedom.** Jesus declares in His word: *"he shall know the truth (the law of God is truth) and the truth shall make you free."*[134] He also said that *"whoever commits sin is a slave of sin"* (John 8:34). Therefore, when we disobey, transgress, or break God's law, we have no liberty; for we then come under the condemnation of the law. It is obedience to the Ten Commandments that assures us of true freedom; and it is this obedience that underscores our appreciation and love for God's Love

---

[134] John 8:32; Psalm 119:142.

Language. When we live within the confines of God's law (under the jurisdiction of the law), we have liberty from sin. This liberty means freedom from that which accompanies sin—the continual worry, wounding of the conscience, and increasing guilt and remorse that wear out life's vital forces. The psalmist puts it this way: *"I will walk about in freedom, for I have sought out Your precepts"* (Psalm 119:45, NIV). James referred to the Decalogue as "the royal law," "the perfect law of liberty" (James 2:8;1:25).

A motorist who commits a traffic offense and is charged for exceeding the speed limit may understand that he/she is under the condemnation of the Road Traffic Act, as it is called in some countries. He/she is under the condemnation of the Act and is required to pay the traffic fine. If the motorist commits no traffic offense that motorist will experience the freedom that comes with compliance with the Road traffic Act. So is it with the law of God.

We can know for sure that the Ten Commandments of God are binding upon all people of all nations around the world. Can you imagine for a moment our world, which is so reliant on computers, having computers without any source codes, operating software and the set of guidelines for their effective operation? Can you imagine the manufacturer of the Benz or BMW motor vehicles completing and shipping off their vehicles with no instruction manuals? Or can you imagine a large multinational, multibillion dollar company operating successfully without policies and guidelines?

Why then would God, Omnipotent, Omniscient, and Creator of heaven and earth, make people on earth, and give them dominion over earth without

providing them with a set of rules and guidelines?
He wouldn't; He couldn't and He didn't. He is too wise.
Heaven, God's throne has laws; and so too does earth.
This we can know for sure. Provided below are four
(4) reasons for **establishing that God's moral law is
universally binding**.

i) **The law of God was in existence before sin and the
creation of human beings**, just as how the Garden of
Eden was in existence before Adam and Eve were placed
in it. Similarly, it was in existence before it was written
by God upon tables of stone and given to Moses on
Mount Sinai. Friend, God believes in order and proper
sequencing, and much more so than we have learnt by
experience the importance of the proverbial expression
of "putting the horse before the cart." So it was necessary
to have the guidelines or the moral blue print in place
long before the creation of the first human being as the
law that was, and still is intended to, be the guiding
principles for righteous living for all people of all ages
and in all generations.

Lucifer was the first sinner, not Adam (the first human
sinner). What was his sin? Rebellion (against God), murder, and
false witness! How do we know? By the Word of God and law of
God, and the evidence of his own actions over time! The fact that
Lucifer sinned from the beginning, meant that the law of God
must have been from before the beginning, when he sinned. This
is what the reliable and unerring record tells us.[135]

> *"Ye are of your father **the devil**, and the lusts of
> your father ye will do. He was a **murderer** from the
> beginning, and **abode not in the truth**, because
> there is **no truth in him**. When he speaketh a lie, he*

[135]   John 8:44; Revelation 12:7-9.

*speaketh of his own: for **he is a liar**, and the father of it."*

*And there was **war in heaven**: Michael and his angels fought against the dragon; and the **dragon fought** and his angels, And **prevailed not**; neither was their place found anymore in heaven. And the great dragon was cast out, **that old serpent, called the Devil, and Satan**, which deceiveth the whole world: he **was cast out into earth**, and his angels were cast out with him.*

How would we know and how could we know about Lucifer's sin without the law? Likewise, how would we know whether someone in any of the continents of the world sinned without the law of God? This is how the apostle Paul relate to this matter in the New Testament record.[136]

*Wherefore, **as by one man sin entered** into the world, and death **by sin**; and so death passed upon all men, **for** that all have **sinned**:"*

*"Therefore **by the** deeds **of the law the**re shall no flesh be justified in his sight: for **by the law is the knowledge of sin**."*

You know many sinners; so do I! But how do we know? By virtue of the law, which came before sin. Sin is only revealed because there is a law and indeed the law of God, which had to be in existence before mankind for all mankind.

I know someone very well, who some years ago was recruited to head a sub-business unit of an important multimillion dollar company and to introduce a new product. One of his very first tasks upon assuming the responsibilities was to prepare the policies and

---

[136] Romans 5:12; 3:20.

procedures, a business plan, then acquire the resources and prepare applications forms. The last task was to advertise and hire staff. The necessary board approvals were obtained; then the resources were acquired and last of all personnel were recruited. This was a case of putting the horse before the cart, order and sequencing. This is what God did, but perfectly, unlike man who is imperfect, in preparing man for existence on planet earth. He ensured that His law was in place early.

ii) **The law of God is a transcript of the character of God, which existed before** Lucifer and man were created. It divine contains principles which are universally applicable. God in His wisdom knows the value of relationships and the variableness of man's sinful nature, and therefore made a law to guide man's relationship with God, His Maker, and his fellowman.[137] The wise man Solomon reinforces this principle of the universal applicability of God's law to all humanity at all times as follows: *Fear God and keep His commandments, for this is the whole duty of man (Ecclesiastes 12:13).* So where ever man is found, his duty stands.

iii) **Nations around the world have adopted some aspects of God's moral law** in their system of law. Can you think of any nation or country where there is not a law respecting and protecting right to life, property, and home and family?

iv) **All the world will be judged by God's Law, the perfect law** of liberty, and the standard of righteousness.[138] If this law was not meant to be universally applicable, then God would have revealed what other standard He would be using to judge the world.

---

[137] Jeremiah 10:22-24
[138] Ecclesiastes 12:13-14; James 2:12.

d) Summary of God's Love Language

Before moving on to discuss Endorsement of God's Love Language, let us quickly summarize what has been stated so far in this subsection 3.2 and conclude with a few important pointers. **God's Love Language is a lifestyle of loving obedience to God and His moral law or Ten Commandments.** Like human love languages, God's Love Language is a unique vehicle that God's people use to communicate their love for God. This vehicle has the components of a lifestyle of pleasing God, volitional loving obedience to God (who is singular, yet plural) for their awesomeness, unimaginable and demonstrated, incomparable goodness, love, forgiveness, and capacity to save repentant sinners like you and me, and their perfect law of liberty which serves as a lamp to our feet and light to our path in this world permeated by sin. So, in using God's Love Language (the lifestyle acceptable to Him) and not your own, you are demonstrating love and respect for God and opening up yourself and providing opportunities for God to bless you.

Unlike human love languages, God's Love Language transcends all human love languages. Whereas with human love languages one hundred percent (100%) is used by people to express, give or receive, or simply communicate love to another, and thereby make a person in the relationship feel loved, with God's Love Language only six out of the Ten Commandments relate to sharing love with one another. The remaining four (which are the first four as cited to in Table A) relate to people sharing their love with God. But by fulfilling this dual role of loving God and fellowmen, the individual child of God is satisfying the requirement of the said law of God, which is not a law of man, but a divine law.

Furthermore, **the lifestyle required in God's Love Language is one that results from an experiential knowledge of** God the Father, God the Son, and God the Holy Spirit or for short, the triune God, or Trinity. **This lifestyle comes through ongoing and aggregate decision making that involves** diligent study of God's word and by practical living for Him and sharing Him with others. **This lifestyle is chosen volitionally and willingly, yet intentionally and deliberately, and knowingly by the individual for the long-term** and is anchored by nurturing and maintaining consistency in behaviour despite and in spite of testing and difficult challenges. **It also involves non-separable love and (willing) obedience for God in this sequential order. This love for God will always result in obedience to God's revealed will and His commandments, which are a transcript of His Character which He wants to be reproduced in our character.** This love for God and obedience to His (Ten) Commandments also mean living by His set of divine principles (and not ours), which will cause us to love our fellowmen who were also made by God, in His image. This also means that God wants us to be true ambassadors for Him wherever we are and go, and whenever we get an opportunity to speak for Him. This is what God loves and what brings joy to Him.

iii) Endorsement of God's Love Language

A thorough review of the Bible reveals that God's Love Language has been endorsed by many different persons. These persons include kings, patriarchs, prophets, outstanding leaders, persecutors and the persecuted, as well as persons and beings, some of whom lived on earth and some of whom are now immortal and living in heaven. The endorsements of seven of these persons are presented herein below. These seven persons are: Jesus, the spotless, sinless Son of God and second member of the Godhead; His disciple, John, the revelator; the apostle Paul, the persecutor, who became Christian, joining the rank of the persecuted; the wisest man and son of a king, Solomon, who also became king; the patriarch and prophet, Moses, who died, was resurrected, and seen by Elias (Elijah) and Peter on the mount of transfiguration and who is living in heaven; the Psalmist and man after God's own heart, David, who was the second anointed king of Ancient Israel; and the Holy Spirit, the third member of the Godhead.

The endorsement of each of these persons is presented in the order listed. I encourage and beseech you to join this illustrious list of eminent persons. If you do, it will transform your life here and now. Plus you will one day meet them in heaven.

1. **Jesus endorses 'God's Love Language'** even though He did not use those verbatim words. But notice **His own words** on the subject of love and obedience to God and His commandments as follows in the gospels of John and Matthew cited below.[139]

   "If ye love me keep my commandments." "He that hath my commandments, and keepeth them, he it is that loveth me: and he that loveth me shall be loved of my Father, and I will love him, and will manifest myself to him."
   "Ye are my friends, if ye do whatsoever I command you." "Jesus said unto him, Thou shalt love the Lord thy God with all thy heart, and with all thy soul, and with all thy mind. This is the first and great commandment. And the second is like unto it, Thou shalt love thy neighbour as thyself. On these two commandments hang all the law and the prophets."

It is crystal clear from Jesus' statements in these texts above in St. John and St. Matthew that there are some very important conclusions Jesus wants us to draw and messages He wants us to grasp in a very explicit manner regarding God's Love Language.

i) According to Jesus, God's Love Language is based on divine principles and order- sequence of **love** first, followed by **obedience**, just a show Joe A. Webb living many years after, described it.

---

[139] John 14:15, 21 and John 15:14, Matthew 22:37- 40 respectively.

ii)   God's Love Language is about our expression and communication of our love in two spheres or at two levels: first and foremost to God, and secondly to our neighbour. Also, God's Love Language reflects the depth and magnitude of our love (See Chapter 7 for more details) for God and our neighbour.

iii)   God's Love Language reflects the relational nature of our communication of love; rightly understood, we cannot keep it to ourselves. It's a reciprocal and symbiotic type of relationship that also requires a right attitude towards God and His Word, and all His children.

iv)   His summary of the Ten Commandments into two is as follows: The first Commandment is love, and the second Commandment is love. Therefore, love and commandment are synonymous and symbiotic; and genuine and true love will always precede obedience, and they are inseparable, as on these two commandments ('love' and 'love' or 'double love') hang all the law and the prophets. The honest and genuine "keeping of God's Ten commandments or moral law" is, therefore, a dependent variable in contrast to "loving Jesus",which is the independent variable (to use the mathematical terminology). You cannot have a dependent variable,if there is no independent variable, and the independent variable always comes first.

v)   This love relationship is volitional but carries responsibility. Jesus says: "**If** ye **love** me **keep** my commandments...." and **not** "*you must love me.*" He is not seeking to legislate or force any one to love God. We must of our own freewill choose to fall in love with Jesus and accept the attendant responsibility of expressing and communicating love.

vi)   Jesus states that the keeping of the commandments is a requirement or commandment from Him (our Creator, Redeemer, Sustainer, and soon coming King). Because

He is superior in rank and position, He has the right and moral authority to state the commandments to be kept or satisfied.

vii) Loving Jesus involves not just a mental note ('hath my commandments') but, also and more importantly, the practice (actually doing or 'keeping') His commandments (love and love), which flows from a revived and reformed life. Such obedience to God's will is the evidence of all true revival. When we reach this point in our love relationship with Jesus, He declares that we will be loved by His Father and He will love us and **manifest** Himself to us. Oh what an assurance that loving Him brings reward! This provides a guaranteed basis to be secured in His love. Sadly, this security is lacking in so many marriages.

The Contemporary English Version (CEV) instead of using the words *"manifest himself to us"* uses the statement: *"show you what I am like."* Again, according to Jesus in St. John 15:14 cited above, it is when we reach this stage in our loving obedience relationship with Him and are willing to do whatever He commands us, that He calls us His friends.

What a testimonial and transcript from Jesus! This seems to me to be synonymous with the complete surrender of ourselves to, and the merging of our wills with that of Jesus.

2. The apostle **John**, the beloved disciple of Jesus, also **reaffirms and endorses Jesus' position on the matter of obedience and commandment keeping in relation to God's Love Language.** This is evidenced by his quotation shown below.

*By this **we know** that **we love the children of God, when we love God, and keep his commandments**. For **this is the love of God, that we keep his commandments**: and his commandments are*

not grievous."[140] *"Now by this we know that we
know Him, if we keep His commandments. He
who* **says, 'I know Him,'** *and does* **not** *keep* **His
commandments, is a liar, and the truth is not** *in
him. 1 John 2: 3-4*

Let us pause for a moment to reflect, meditate, and analyse
this text so as to gain the powerful message on both *agape* and
phileo love that John wants to communicate to us on the subject
of God's Love Language. Also, a few pertinent questions will help
us to grasp the substance of the matter.

   i)   How do we know that we love the children of God?
   ii)   What is the love of God?
   iii)   How are these commandments described?

The quotation above from John contains the answer to these
three questions, so let's examine it carefully so as to ensure that we
comprehend the love principle they contain, including the **two
critical points** which **emerge** as follows.

   i)   **We know** that we **love the children of God**,when

          a) we love God (Father, Son and Holy Ghost) and
          b) keep His commandments or moral law;

   ii)   **We have the love of God** when we keep
          His commandments.

          This is in truth what we have said that God's
          Love Language is all about: a lifestyle of loving
          obedience to God and His commandments. So,
          John is confirming it in a very straight forward
          manner.

---

[140]   1 John 5:2-3.

iii)   For question iii), the answer is that God's commandments are not grievous. That is, contrary to what many think, do, debate, these commandments of God are described as "not grievous", meaning that they do not cause grief, pain, anguish, sorrow, and are not burdensome or oppressive. On the contrary, they are according to the apostle Paul, just and good.

According to John, we can do all the talking and bragging we want. We can receive all the praise of men. **But, God knows who His people are; and they are neither liars nor imposters.** His Word declares that **the proof** is not in the talking or wishing, but in the **exercise of love, which is riveted and engrossed in obedience to His commandments (God's Love Language).** It is only then that there is demonstrated evidence that we **have** the love of God and love our fellow men, who are the children of God, fearfully and wonderfully made in God's own image.

It is crystal clear that John is talking about **God's Ten Commandments**, the same moral law or the Decalogue, **written with the very finger of God**, first upon the **two tables of stone**, which were broken by Moses and rewritten again with the finger of God. The first writing is recorded in the Genesis Account and the second writing or replacement for the first one broken by Moses is recorded in the Account given in Deuteronomy.[141] **Later on, God wrote the commandments on the fleshy tables of our hearts**, so that God's law could be known and read of all men.[142]

But you ask: how do I know for sure that John is talking about the Ten Commandments? Where is the evidence? Answer: It is by the Ten Commandments that we know who are liars. The ninth commandment states that we should not bear false witness. For indeed, by the law is the knowledge of sin.

---

[141]   Genesis 31:18; Deuteronomy 9:10.s
[142]   See 2 Corinthians 3:2-3.

In theology, divine providence is God's intervention in the world. It is by **divine providence, and not by chance or coincidence, that** love to God is engraved on the first table, because unless we truly practice loving God (*Agape* love) we will not be able to truly love our fellowmen (*Phileo* love) who are children of God. John, the beloved disciple, in reaffirming and enhancing his endorsement of God's Love Language, puts it in crystal clear perspective the icing on this spiritual cake as follows:

> *"We **love** him, because **He first loved us**. If a man say, I love God, and hateth his brother, he is a liar: for he that loveth not his brother whom he hath seen, how can he love God whom he hath not seen? And this commandment have we from him, That **he who loveth God love his brother also**."*[143]

So according to John, we respond to God's love based on God's pro active action. Our response to God's love is reciprocal: *"We love Him because He first love us."* So, only when we love God, as our response to His proactive action, will we be able to also love our brother. The last thing that many guilty persons want, is to be caught and to face possible retribution for their wrong. That's why we as sinners, left on our own, would not approach God who dwelleth in the light and knows all that we did even before we did them. So while we were yet sinners, Jesus took proactive action for our benefit; Christ died for us to give us the power to resist sin and to become sons and daughters of God.

3. The **third endorsement** comes from the apostle Paul who was a zealous, former persecutor of those who lovingly obeyed God and the law of God. He was converted while in the very act of persecuting God's people (of the way) on the road to Damascus. After his conversion, he truly knew and practiced what loving obedience and surrender of self

---

[143]   *1 John 4:19-21.*

to God meant. Look at and meditate on his testimony in the book of Galatians.[144]

*"**I am crucified with Christ**: nevertheless **I live; yet not I**, but **Christ** liveth in me: and the life which **I** now live in the flesh **I** live by the faith of the Son of God, who loved me, and gave himself for me."*

So, he not only had a loving obedient relationship with God which he lived, but he was also a prolific writer and he wrote much about God's law, love, faith and obedience. Cited below is one of his own testimonies and comments on the law of God from the book of Romans where he acknowledges God's law as a transcript of God's character it terms of its qualities.[145]

*"Wherefore **the law is** holy, and **the** commandment holy, and just, and **good**."*

Paul also adds the following: *"For it is not the hearers of the law who are righteous before God, but the **doers of the law who will be justified**." Romans 2:13(ESV).*

4. Here is the **fourth endorsement**. The wise man Solomon and also former anointed king of Ancient Israel, who understood very well what pomp, power, possession, and position meant, fully endorsed God's Love Language in the beautiful backdrop of the duty of mankind and the coming judgment. He was coming to the close of his life, having had time to review his life and fluctuating relationship with God, when he recorded his profound endorsement. Come with me to the Book of Ecclesiastes[146] (KJV, CEB), for his endorsement which is cited herein below.

---

144 Galatians 2:20.
145 Romans 7:12.
146 Ecclesiastes 12:13-14.

*"Let us hear the conclusion **of** the **whole** matter: **Fear God, and keep his commandments:** for this is the **whole duty of man**. For God shall bring every work into judgment, with every secret thing, whether it be good, or whether it be evil"(KJV).*

*"So this is the end of the matter; all has been heard. **Worship God and keep God's commandments** because **this is what everyone must do**. God will definitely bring every deed to judgment, including every hidden thing, whether good or bad."(CEB)*

Solomon, having tried various options with their attendant pain and disappointments, concluded in his wisdom that everyone must **love** (implied from the words "fear God"), **worship God, and keep His commandments,** which is not part of, but **the whole duty of man.** Then he concludes by bringing into his analysis the matter of mankind's accountability to God, who will bring every work or deed, good or bad, right or wrong, done in the light of day or the dark of midnight, into judgment. Clearly, when he penned his comments, he was moving through the time continuum from his past, to his present, and to the future judgment, when all must stand before the judgment seat of God and give account for their life's deeds or misdeeds. The good news is that those who endorse God's Love Language will be very happy in that day. And guess what, you can choose to be among them!

5. The **fifth endorsement** by Moses is very unique. This is because Moses is very special and in a class all by himself. He was the meekest of all the men that walked upon planet earth. But this was after he was a murderer, who was forgiven by God, and experienced both God's love and grace, which are available to all. He paid a dear price (not making it to the earthly Promised Land)for disobeying God's commandment when he struck the rock instead of speaking to it as God had commanded.

Moses is a classic example of what a divine-human love and obedient relationship is all about. He spoke to God face to face. He was God's representative to King Pharaoh in Egypt. He was the one to whom God gave His Ten Commandments on two separate occasions. He encouraged the children of Israel to love God and keep all His commandments. He writes profusely on this and other matters in the first five books of the Bible, called the Pentateuch. Presently he lives in heaven with God as a result of embracing God's Love Language. Here are some of his comments endorsing God's Love Language.[147]

> *"And he declared unto you his covenant, which he commanded you to perform, even Ten Commandments; and he wrote them upon two tables of stone."*

> *"Know therefore that the **Lord thy God, he is God, the faithful God,** which **keepeth** covenant and **mercy with them that love him and keep his commandments** to a thousand generations;"*

> *"Therefore thou shalt **keep the commandments of the Lord thy God**, to walk in his ways, and to fear him."*

> *"Ye shall walk after the Lord your God, and fear him, and **keep his commandments, and obey his voice,** and ye shall serve him, and cleave unto him."*

6. The **penultimate endorsement** is from the Psalmist David, a former murderer, and king, who suffered immensely for his disobedience, but repented in remorse, and embraced God's love and grace and led a

---

[147]   Deuteronomy 4:13, 7:9, 8:6, 13:4.

transformed life. He has much to say on this subject. Here are a few of his comments.[148]

*"O how **love I thy law**! it is my meditation all the day." "I hate and abhor lying but **thy law** do **I love**". "The **law of the Lord is perfect**, converting the soul: the testimony of the Lord is sure, making wise the simple." "Thy righteousness is an everlasting righteousness, and **thy law is the truth**."*

7. **Finally**, the Holy Spirit of God, the third member of the Godhead, adds His weight of endorsement to what I have called God's Love Language. John tells us that He reproves the world of sin (*transgression of Gods' law*) and of righteousness (*rectitude, compliance or obedience to God's law*) and of judgment to come; and that **He will guide us into all truth (*includes the Jesus and the Law of God*).** He also glories Jesus. (John 16:8,12, 14). Because the Holy Spirit is God's representative on earth in the absence of Jesus, and who is very interested in our salvation, the apostle Paul warns us against grieving the Holy Spirit. The Holy Spirit does this reproving because He knows that the law of God is to be kept and that it is the divine standard that will be used in the judgment.

iv) Attitude towards God and His love language.

Attitude refers to our mind-set or state of mind, approach, way of thinking, posture and disposition. Our attitude, which is influenced by a myriad of factors including your belief system, will definitely affect how we relate to God's Love Language, which **is designed** to help us improve our love and obedience to God and His commandments. It is also designed to help us improve the quality of our relationship with our triune God. Revival and reformation are integral to that relationship with our triune God.

So, if persons have wrong attitude in this matter, they will pile up scorn on revival and reformation, and are therefore,not likely to be in an attitude of gratitude towards God and anything that is godly. Accordingly, if you believe with all your heart that God is a toy, then your behaviour will reflect that perception, and treat Him as a play thing. If you believe that God is your peer, then you will respond accordingly. If you believe that He is a bully or a tyrant based on your past experience with some church members, employers, or even a spouse, or one of your parents, etc, you may choose not to have a relationship with Him. If you are an infidel, an agnostic, or an atheist, then your philosophy will likewise influence your preferences, tastes, choices, beliefs, and behaviour concerning God.

Where our attitude and perceptions do not match with the reality of who God is, and where our knowledge of Him is partial and or inadequate, our response to God's love will likewise fall short of the mark that God expects. Hence, it is important for each one of us to have a correct perception and attitude of, and an adequate knowledge of Him in order to please Him, because **life at its best is about pleasing God.** And of course, faith, belief, obedience, and right judgment are critical to having a right grasp of who is God.

The Apostle Paul, in Hebrews and Acts, contributes the following to help with our understanding of this matter:

> "But **without faith it is impossible to please him**: for he that cometh to God must **believe** that he is, and that he is a rewarder of them that diligently seek him."[149]
>
> [22] Then Paul stood in the midst of Mars' hill, and said, Ye men of Athens, I perceive that in all things ye are too superstitious. [23] For as I passed by, and beheld your devotions, I found an altar with this inscription, To The Unknown God. Whom therefore ye ignorantly worship,him declare I unto you. [24] **God that made**

---

[149] *Hebrews 11:6.*

127

the world and all things therein, seeing that he is Lord of heaven and earth, dwelleth not in temples made with hands; [25]*Neither is worshipped with men's hands, as though he needed anything, seeing he giveth to all life, and breath, and all things;* [26]*And hath made of one blood all nations of men for to dwell on all the face of the earth, and hath determined the times before appointed, and the bounds of their habitation;* [27]*That they should seek the Lord, if haply they might feel after him, and find him, though he be not far from every one of us:*

[28]*For in him we live, and move, and have our being; as certain also of your own poets have said, For we are also his offspring.*

[29]*Forasmuch then as we are the offspring of God, we ought not to think that the Godhead is like unto gold, or silver, or stone, graven by art and man's device.* [30]*And the times of this ignorance God winked at; but now commandeth all men everywhere to repent:"*[150]

In the context of the above**, practicing God's Love Language will require changes in our mindset** as is outlined by both revival and reformation. This "**revival** signifies a **renewal** of spiritual life, a **quickening** of the powers of mind and **heart**, a **resurrection** from spiritual death, whereas **reformation** signifies **a re-organization**, a **change** in ideas and theories, habits and practices."

E. G. White adds further as follows on the subject of Revival and Reformation**:**

"Obedience to God's will is the evidence of all true revival. Our Lord longs for a revived people whose lives reflect the loveliness of His character. There is nothing that Jesus desires more than a people who are passionate about personally knowing His love and sharing that love with others."

---

[150] Acts 17: 22-30.

It is the **condition** of our heart and spirit that determines whether or not we will have the right attitude that is required to embrace God's Love Language and whether we will, by extension, show forth God's praises in our lives, home and family, work, school, and play, as well as in our choices of occupation, career, partner for life; what we see, read, speak, eat, play, listen to; and our deportment. If we do not have the right attitude, and where our heart is not right, we may call ourselves Christians or God-fearing, and yet be greedy, impulsive, impetuous, impertinent, abrasive, antagonistic, and even abusive to those in our own household. We may even be very pious in worship; we may be eloquent and dynamic preachers, and yet be bigots.

It is only when **Jesus reigns in the heart and mind, when His rules and His values become ours and operate at the deep level, that we will have the right attitude and conscience towards God and display consistency between what we belief, teach or preach and practice.** It is the **absence** of surrender (**love and obedience**) to Jesus why there is such a dichotomy; as was evident in the life and attitude of the Pharisees. They read the Bible and prayed frequently (which was good) and openly (but sadly) it was for others to see their piety. Their value system was all wrong as they **placed greater value** on the Word of God, **than on its Author**. But to what avail? If prizes were being given out for piousness they would be faster to the finish line than Carl Lewis in his time or Usain Bolt in this twenty-first century, post-modern era. Yet they planned, plotted and implemented their involvement in the crucifixion of Jesus, the sinless one, who came also to save them. That's why Jesus said:

*"He came unto **his own**, and **his own** received him not."*

It is difficult to orchestrate to kill someone you love. But their actions proved what was inside, drought and absence of love for Jesus. What was the problem? Their attitude! They had misplaced values, emphasis and priorities. Their value, emphasis and priority was on themselves, the external, and ostentation. Their love for themselves, their desires, preferences and tastes, power and position, and a following, was greater than their love for God. They saw themselves in constant competition with Jesus for attention, and for a greater following, and were among His most vehement enemies that played a key role in the crucifixion and death of Jesus. This was because their love language was love for themselves, power and position. Hence they saw and had no need to embrace God's Love Language. It is no wonder that history is replete with the suffering and punishment, including the holocaust, meted out to the Jews.

Jesus accurately assessed their hearts and characters and summed it up concisely as follows:

> *"Woe to you, teachers of the law and Pharisees, you hypocrites! You are like whitewashed tombs, which look beautiful on the **outside** but on the **inside** are full of the bones of the dead and everything unclean. In the same way, on the **outside** you appear to people as righteous but on the **inside** you are full of hypocrisy and wickedness."*[151]

This is a very scathing rebuke from Jesus. You see, Jesus read their hearts and lives like an open book. Sadly, with all of this revelation from Jesus as to how we ought not to be, and how deceptive our hearts can be, many who profess to be followers of the law of God are sometimes among the most vehement and caustic critics, accusers and even persecutors of the humble, truly obedient followers of Jesus, who in their eyes have more and sometimes less accolades, including those who sometimes make genuine mistakes.

How can we ensure that we are not like those Pharisees, and that we do not borrow or copy their attitude of self- centeredness? It is by **choosing to love Jesus enough** that we will obey (surrender self to) Him. We must internalize and embrace His teachings and philosophy of love, forgiveness and grace. Because, it is only when our values, which operate at the deep level, are right that our

---

[151]   *Matthew 23:27-28(NIV).*

behaviour (what is seen on the external) will be right, according to Dr. Erica Puni.[152]

On the same matter of obedience, Carsten Johnsen, concludes:

"Obedience is the highest praise man can offer to God."[153]

This is the attitude of gratitude that God wants us all to have. And this is what God's Love Language wants to accomplish in your life and mine.

v) Challenges

A challenge is a request, claim or demand, that is made on a Christian or non-Christian, the non-fulfillment of which threatens continuity of the religious liberty rights of either person, and the fulfillment of which requires the individual to break God's law and or compromise on his/her relationship with God, ethics, and or religious rights. The challenge may originate from varied sources whether explicitly or implicitly, directly or indirectly, using coercion or non-coercive means, in return for reward or refusal/denial of reward, financial or non-financial.

A decision to caress a lifestyle of loving obedience to God can be quite challenging. And the Bible speaks profusely on this particular matter. It makes it clear that there are two beings that seek our obedience and allegiance. They are God and the devil. God means us good as the Old Testament prophet, Jeremiah, tells us. By contrast, the devil does everything possible, including force and even the use of false prophets such as Hananiah[154] during the time of the true prophet of God, Jeremiah, to distract and detour us from God in order to deceive, control, defeat, and destroy us.[155]

---

[155]   See 1 Peter 5:8.

Although man (in the generic sense: man and woman, boy and girl) has free moral choice, he is often caught in the midst of this great controversy between God and the devil, the two contrasting forces of good and evil. And because the devil is deceptive and cunning in his attempt to control mankind, he does everything possible to make the path and life of all those who serve, and would like to serve, Jesus, and embrace God's Love Language as difficult and as challenging as possible.

But we are not to be surprised by it. Rather we are to expect challenges and persecution. Notice that the apostle Paul informs us about it in his second book of Timothy:

> *"Yea, and all that **will live godly in Christ Jesus** shall **suffer** persecution."*[156]

The apostles Peter and John, the revelator, also corroborate on this matter in 1 Peter 4:12, 16 and Revelation 2:10 respectively as follows:

*"Beloved, **do not think it strange concerning the fiery trial** which is to try you, as though some strange thing happened to you; Yet if anyone suffers as a Christian, let him not be ashamed, but let him glorify God in this matter."*

*"Fear none of those things which thou shalt **suffer**: behold, the devil shall cast some of you into prison, that ye may be tried;"*

I like how the Apostle Peter, the prophet Jeremiah, and the Psalmist sum up the matter and put things in contrasting perspective, in the three following texts respectively:[157]

*"**Be sober**, be vigilant; because **your adversary the devil**, as a **roaring lion**, walketh about, **seeking whom he may devour**." "For I know the thoughts that I think toward you, saith the Lord, thoughts of peace, and not of evil, to give you an expected end."* KJV.

---

[156] 2 Timothy 3:12.
[157] *1 Peter 5:8(KJV and NIV 1984); Jeremiah 29:11(NIV 1984).*

"For I know the **plans I have for you,** *"* declares the Lord, **"plans to prosper you** *and* **not to harm you, plans to give you hope and a future.** *"* **NIV 1984**

The challenges of a lifestyle of loving obedience to God and His commandments are quite real. Given this reality, the apostle Peter challenges us to be both sober and vigilant. We need to be likewise fully clothed in the armor of God. This is because he also knows that the devil uses all the tricks available to discourage those who would embrace God's Love Language. The devil allies include the use of human beings and organizations. He even moves the world to hate God's people. *"**Marvel not, my brethren, if the world hate you.** If the world hate you, ye know that it hated me before it hated you." "If ye were of the world, the world would love his own: but because ye are not of the world, but I have chosen you out of the world, therefore the world hateth you."*[158]

I know of cases where persons who, after becoming Christians and keeping the fourth commandment, have been asked to resign their jobs, sit examinations on the Sabbath, denied promotion, demoted, denied employment, and in some instances fired. In some countries, some have been tortured, imprisoned and even killed.

Ellen G. White puts it this way in her book, The Great Controversy:

*"**Those who endeavor to obey all the commandments of God will be opposed and derided.** They can stand only in God. In order to endure the trial before them, they must understand the will of God as revealed in His word; they can honor Him only as they have a right conception of His character, government, and purposes, and act in accordance with them"*[159]

This is because the devil will continue to throw his darts at you, as he has done at so many before, for he is a roaring lion.

---

[158] 1 John 3:13, John 15:18-19.
[159] E.G. White, The Great Controversy, Chapter 37: The Scriptures a Safeguard, page 594; accessed at http://www.whiteestate.org; used by permission.

Although the devil seeks to *devour and* destroy, Jesus promises to give us (His people) power to gain the victory over him, as is recorded by the beloved disciple, John, and cited below:

*"But as many as **received him***, *to them **gave he power to become the sons of God***, *even to them that believe on his name:"*[160]

Despite all the challenges that the devil places in the path of God's people, in the end they will overcome. John, the revelator, gives us the secret of their victory (as quoted below) for us to be courageous when faced with diabolical challenges. Notice also that obedience to God is more important to them than their own lives.

*"And **they overcame him** (the devil) by the **blood of the Lamb** and by the **word of their testimony***, *and **they did not love their lives** to the death." Revelation 12:11.*

vi) Divine solution and the question of trustworthiness

Friends, God has a remedy to this intricate, yet perplexing human problem that causes people not to want a lifestyle of loving obedience to God and His commandments. Because the problem involves sin, and the sin of humans in the world, it is a spiritual problem and requires a spiritual solution. Let us make no mistake about this! It is a problem that involves the human heart and, therefore, the solution must begin with God fixing the human heart. And that is why other solutions (monetary and economic, technological, legal, educational, etc.,) though being useful for certain situations, have not worked, and will not work; that's like applying band aid rather than suture, to a major surgery. God's solution also involves human response to God's prescription in a divine human relationship. **It involves human beings leading a lifestyle of loving obedience to God and His moral law, the Ten Commandments**. It involves surrender of the heart and self to

---

[160]   John 1:12.

God. In summing up the Ten Commandments, the Bible states the following in **Matthew 22: 34-41 shown below:**

> *But when the Pharisees had heard that he had put the Sadducees to silence, they were gathered together. Then one of them, which was a **lawyer**, asked him a question, tempting him, and saying, Master, which is the great commandment in the law?*

> *Jesus said unto him, **Thou shalt love the Lord thy God with all thy heart, and with all thy soul, and with all thy mind.** This is the first and great commandment.*

> *And the second is like unto it, **Thou shalt love thy neighbour as thyself.***

> *On these two commandments hang all the law and the prophets.*

In essence, **the solution is love to God and love to our fellowmen.** Sadly, many persons are mere actors and performers when it comes to the real test of complying with God's commandments. Their words and actions go in opposite directions. Some call this practice "lip" service to God and His commandments.

How many lawyers are asking questions today, not to know and walk in the truth about God and His love, but just to tempt Jesus and His faithful followers? As the person reading this book right now, are you doing or are you planning to do the same thing; or are you going to persuade others to join you? How many from other professions or no professions at all, are doing the same thing: asking, but not to know, believe, love, obey, and surrender to Jesus and walk in the path of truth in order to have real joy, wonderful joy, and peace that passeth all understanding?

How many persons are still going back to setting-up false gods which cannot save, or quack doctors who cannot heal? How many are going back to image worship and to mocking God by taking His name in vain? How many will read this book and go back to set-up a parallel and counterfeit Sabbath that is not a memorial of God's creation?

The Lord is right! Indeed, the prophet, Isaiah is right; the apostle Mark is also right, when under inspiration they wrote as follows herein below, that the people honour the Lord with their lips (indeed lip service) but their hearts are far from Him. Doesn't this sound like acting? But isn't the right word for this kind of behaviour: hypocrisy?

*"Wherefore **the Lord said**, Forasmuch as this people draw near me **with their** mouth, and **with their lips** do honour me, but have **removed their** heart far from me, and **their** fear toward me is taught by the precept of men:"*[161]

*"He answered and said unto them, Well hath **Esaias prophesied** of you **hypocrites**, as it is written, This **people honoureth** me with **their lips**, but **their** heart is far from me."*[162] It is important to reinforce the fact that collectively the Ten (10) Commandments are a transcript of the character of God and reflect the divine standard of rectitude and righteous living that God has set for mankind. Speaking of the Ten (10) Commandments, the apostle Paul states:

*"Wherefore the law is **holy**, and the commandment **holy**, and **just**, and **good**."*[163]

So by obeying God's Ten (10) Commandments, or better yet, by embracing God's Love Language or leading a lifestyle of obedience to God and His commandments, God is calling and positively challenging each human being and each human family on planet earth to a higher, nobler, and exalted plateau of existence. This calling is also to a lifestyle that is holy, just and good; yes, one that involves purity and **trustworthiness** or faithfulness.

---

[161]   *Isaiah 29:13.*
[162]   *Mark 7:6.*
[163]   Romans 7:12.

By rejecting God's commandments, we are caressing sin, a fatal attraction for a love language of our own selfish devising, and a lifestyle that is unholy, unjust, and bad. Sin is rejecting God and His law, which is also equated with missing the mark, also referred to as rebellion against God.

So, the problem is not with God, who is holy, just, and good. Neither is the problem with God's law, which is also holy, just, and good. Prudence and the harsh realities and experiences of life stare us clearly in the face that the problem is with human beings, including you and me, as shown above by the texts in Mark and Isaiah.

However, we have a difficulty making the needed change. Why? This is because the human heart is both deceitful and desperately wicked. That's why the wife beater (or any abuser) keeps on beating his wife (or victim) and continues the cycle of abuse, despite repeated reconciliation (apologizing, giving of excuses, etc). Like the Dead Sea that receives but does not release any of its salty water, like hell which is never full, and like greed that does not know moderation, sin is never satisfied. It wants more and more of the same. This is how the prophet Jeremiah puts it in his prophetic book:

"The heart is deceitful above all things, and desperately wicked: who can know it?"[164]

That's why we cannot change ourselves. Then Jeremiah further asks the pertinent question to sink home the reality of the inability of man on his own to change his perverted ways.

*"Can the Ethiopian **change his** skin, or the leopard **his spots?** then may ye also do good, that are accustomed to do evil?"*[165] (Read the whole Chapter of Jeremiah 13.)

However, because God, our Creator, knows our heart and condition, He tries the heart and can fix the problem **when we surrender ourselves to Him**. But, since God is not a dictator, nor

---

[164] *Jeremiah 17:9.*
[165] *Jeremiah 13:23*

a thief that breaks down our doors to take what he/she wants, nor a gunman pointing a gun to our face to coerce us to yield to his/her illegal demands, ***we must surrender ourselves to Him*** for Him to work on us and in us to effect the desired spiritual change. Carefully note that God is also the greatest (spiritual and multi-skilled professional) surgeon of all times, and He knows that He will have to perform a spiritual heart transplant on all those who are lovingly, willingly obedient, and who warm to, and want to lead a lifestyle and lifelong loving and obedient commitment to Him.

Notice from the quotations below from the Old Testament books of Jeremiah and Ezekiel, how God operates in fixing the problem of humanity.

"*I **the** LORD search **the heart**, I **try the** reins, even to give every man according to his ways, and **according to the** fruit of his doings.*"[166]

> *"Cast away from you all your transgressions, whereby ye have transgressed; and make you a **new heart and a new spirit: for why will ye** die, O house of Israel?" And they shall come thither, and they shall take away all the detestable things thereof and all the abominations thereof from thence. And **I will give them one heart**, and **I will put a new spirit within you**; and I will take the stony heart out of their flesh, and will give them an heart of flesh: That they may walk in my statutes, and keep mine ordinances, and do them: and **they shall be my people, and I will be their God**.*[167]

> *Then will I sprinkle clean water upon you, and ye shall be clean: from all your filthiness, and from all your idols, will I cleanse you. A **new heart also will***

---

166   *Jeremiah 17:10*
167   Ezekiel 18:31, 11:18-20.

*I give you, and a **new spirit will I put within you***:
and ***I will take away the stony heart out of your
flesh***, *and I will give you an heart of flesh. And I will
put my spirit within you, and cause you to walk in
my statutes, and ye shall keep my judgments, and do
them.*[168]

This must be a miracle of all miracles. A heart transplant
without the spillage of a single milliliter of blood, and each patient
lives! **Can God pull it off? Yes He can**; and yes He has done it
before! Moses in his Genesis account asked: *"**Is anything too hard
for the Lord?**"* Jeremiah after stating that the Lord God had made
the heaven and the earth by His great power and stretched out
arm concluded confidently in his book with the answer: *"there is
nothing too hard for thee"*[169]

But then you stoutly retort, "That is dealing with nature,
but dealing with the complex human heart is really dealing with a
horse of a different colour". "Yes, that may be so for you, but the
Bible is filled with answers also." It tells us that He caused barren
Sarah to get pregnant and give birth way beyond childbearing age
range. He healed the sick as in Jairus' daughter and resurrected the
dead as in Lazarus and Moses. And of course, you know well the
story in the Genesis account, how God created man from the dust
of the ground.

So a heart transplant, without the shedding of blood, is really
simple stuff for God! God is not daunted by position or rank,
neither is He fearful of faces. He gave King Saul this transplant, but
Saul's system rejected the spiritual heart transplant after the surgery
because of his non-compliance with the after surgery spiritual diet
regimen. His chosen lifestyle of non-compliance with God's Love
Language eventually led to his own peril. Read the details in Case
Story 2 in Chapter 6.0.

---

[168] Ezekiel *36:25-27.*
[169] Genesis 18:14; Jeremiah 32:17.

King David, by contrast, asked for it and got this heart transplant after committing adultery and murder. So, there is hope for you, if you request and embrace it. But, you exclaim in wonder and astonishment: "adultery and murder in corridors of a kingdom!" "Yes! you are correct." "But King David surrendered to God and repented of his sins." Reader, he caressed God's Love Language and was among those faithful giants who gave their endorsement to it. "He also followed to the letter and spirit, the required after surgery spiritual diet regimen and *lifestyle with a very positive outcome.*" **Listen to David's own testimony!**

> ¹*Have mercy upon me, O God*, *according to thy loving kindness: according unto the multitude of thy tender mercies **blot out my transgressions**.* ²***Wash me throughly from mine iniquity, and cleanse me from my sin.*** ³*For **I acknowledge my transgressions: and my sin is ever before me.*** ⁴***Against thee, thee only, have I sinned,*** *and done this evil in thy sight: that thou mightest be justified when thou speakest, and be clear when thou judgest.*

> ⁵*Behold, I was shapen in iniquity; and in sin did my mother conceive me.* ⁶*Behold, **thou desirest truth in the inward parts***: *and in the hidden part thou shalt make me to know wisdom.*

> ⁷***Purge me with hyssop and I shall be clean: wash me, and I shall be whiter than snow.*** ⁸*Make me to hear joy and gladness; that the bones which thou hast broken may rejoice.* ⁹***Hide thy face from my sins, and blot out all mine iniquities.***

> ¹⁰***Create in me a clean heart***, *O God; and **renew a right spirit*** *within me.* ¹¹*Cast me not away from thy presence; and **take not** thy **holy spirit** from me.*

¹²Restore unto me the joy of thy salvation; and uphold me with thy free spirit.

*¹³Then will I teach transgressors thy ways; and sinners shall be converted unto thee. ¹⁴**Deliver me from blood guiltiness, O God, thou God of my salvation:** and my tongue shall sing aloud of thy righteousness. ¹⁵O Lord, open thou my lips; and my mouth shall shew forth thy praise. ¹⁶For thou desirest not sacrifice; else would I give it: thou delightest not in burnt offering. ¹⁷The sacrifices of God are a broken spirit: a broken and a contrite heart, O God, thou wilt not despise.*[170]

What a terrific surgical success story and testimony to the great spiritual surgeon, who is our (yours and mine) God? What a testimony! What confession of sin! What repentance! What humility! **What an amazing transformation!** What a godly sorrow for sin and desire for spiritual change! What a shift in paradigm! **What a changed man David became?** No wonder he was called a man after God's own heart. **So it can be for all of us.** It does not matter your position or station in life, whether king or civilian, professional or unprofessional, slave master or servant. God loves us all with an everlasting love, regardless of class or position or religious standing: sinner or saint. The critically relevant and timely question is: "Do we/I love God enough to trust Him enough to perform this most needed and urgent surgery on our / my heart - "which is above all things desperately, wicked?"

If you don't trust God, if you reject His divine remedy, should God trust you, knowing that you cannot change yourself for the better? If God cannot trust you to respect your neighbour's goods and spouse down here, why should He run the risk of trusting you with heaven and eternal life? If He cannot trust you to spend

---

[170]   *Psalm 51:1-17.*

quality time (secondary love language) with Him by keeping His Sabbath day (the seventh-day of the week or Saturday) holy or to use His Holy time to His honour and glory, why should He trust you with eternity? If you will not stop stealing, lying, and homicide down here on planet Earth or refuse to accept that stealing, lying, murder are all sins; why should God trust you with heaven, the holy city, or the New Earth, where there are streets of gold? You would want to dig up the street of gold, go in search of a goldsmith or jeweler to sell it for cash, and then lie and kill anyone who you see and perceive would hinder your diabolic ambitions.

If you were deceived by one or more of those very clever, unrepentant Ponzi schemers as well as operators of the failed unregulated financial organizations (UFO)/institutions, you would have come to realize that they cannot be trusted. Even though you may not have lost money (own funds/personal or borrowed) in those schemes or UFOs, you may know of persons or even organizations that have. These persons may include your own family members, relative(s), friend(s), as well as others that you may have heard about in the news media (whether electronic or print). Very likely, they will never ever trust those fraudulent persons (fraudsters) again. If you, as well as other victims, have reasonable, justifiable, and legal reasons not to trust them again, why would God trust them either? God cannot take that chance!

On the other hand, would any unrepentant sinners, including these crafty schemers, be happy in God's visible presence? I doubt it. They would be most unhappy and feel imprisoned there as they wouldn't be able to live there by deception. Neither would the womanizers be able to have girls by the dozen. Likewise, unrepentant homosexual and lesbians, liars, kleptomaniacs, drug pushers, and others of that ilk, would be most unhappy there too. In fact, they will not make it there. If you can honestly and truthfully conclude that they should not be there, why then should God take unrepentant sinful people there? Grace will get you to the pearly gates of the City of God. But it is justice (love and obedience to God's moral law) that will take you pass the entrance into the

City, God's paradise. They would be out of place there, as after all their years on planet earth, they have not learnt obedience or self-surrender to God or have no desire to.

So **in the final analysis, if God cannot trust persons to be obedient to Him on earth, the battle ground of the devil, and testing ground** for development of the fitness of our characters for God's paradise, **then He should not want to trust such persons in Heaven**. Why? Because we may yield to lead a rebellion there also, if He was to make the mistake and take the risk of giving us right of access there.

So we need not be in any doubt; no need to "guess and spell" as they say in common parlance on this matter. God specifically tells us what He requires of us and wants us to do. So if we want, we can know where we stand with Him on this all-important matter. *He tells us His love language.*

One thing is certain, and that is, after the matter of the great controversy here on earth is finally resolved and settled, *"affliction shall not rise up the second time."*[171] A husband who truly loves his wife will seek to find out and communicate with her using her love language and likewise the wife. So too, will a loving parent use the love language of the son or daughter to demonstrate parental love and bring out the best in the child. So too must a church brother or sister do, or a person who neither attends church nor has any interest in church. **Why should it be any different in principle regarding our relationship and communication with God?**

A spouse, a parent, a child, a sibling, a church member, and employee or employer, or a friend or neighbour, may or may not know his or her love language, and even when it is known, may choose to refuse to communicate it. *But God is not like that.* He knows what is the love language that He expects us to use in communicating our love to Him. He also tells us, repeatedly, in His word what His love language is. He is **not about withholding** on this all important matter, which **carries eternal implication.**

---

[171]   Nahum 1:9.

He tells us because He loves us and He wants to save us that we may have an eternal relationship with Him. **That's why He died on Calvary's cross**. It was that important.

That act of loving us to the point where He actually died for our sins was **Jesus' way of providing evidence of His great unlimited and unconditional (agape) love for us**. This is the **platform or foundation for His divine solution**. But it also **speaks to the immutability of God's law, which is a transcript of God's character**. Notice that the wages of sin is death. See Romans 6:23. And sin is missing the mark, breaking of God's law, and rebellion against God, our supreme Lover. So, as a result of the sins of humanity, God's law was broken, and the penalty had to be paid for the broken law of God. **Because the law is unchangeable, it required the life of the sinless, spotless, Jesus to pay the wages or penalty for our sins.** Can you, therefore, appreciate why God's Love Language and a lifestyle of obedience to God's commandments are such an important, urgent, decision to make and an irrevocable and timely step to take? **Now it's our turn to show that we love Him**, and that He can trust us; yes, to let Him know that we truly love Him. And we do this by using His love language of obedience, requesting, and accepting His divine solution.

3.3 Prerequisites (preparation) for using God's Love Language

i) Present prerequisites:

There are at least four (4) prerequisites that a sincere seeker of righteousness who wants to lead a lifestyle of loving obedience to God and His commandments needs to satisfy. These include the following:

a) Believe that God exists.[172]

---

[172] Heb 11:6.

b) Know God.[173]
c) Exercise faith in God.[174]
d) Wisdom from God[175]

The word **"believe"** mentioned herein above means to "accept as true especially without proof" and "to have religious faith" is one that must lead to action. If I believe that God exists then my action must show it. John 3:16 carries the same principle and sentiment. The apostle Paul puts it this way: *".... for he who comes to God must believe that He is..."*[176] If I say in words that I believe that Jesus died to save me but don't take action to give credence to my belief, then it's all in vain, and I will die in my sins.

Years ago, I was told a story of a man who at a circus pushed a wheelbarrow across a tight rope that was hoisted at some distance above the floor of the circus. The crowd, with bated breath, cheered in amazement as the man successfully accomplished the feat. The man repeated the feat to a thunderous applaud from the crowd. After pushing the wheelbarrow across the distance and before making the returned leg, he asked the crowd if they believed he could repeat the feat. The response was an astounding yes. And rightly so, for they witnessed the amazing feat accomplished with their own eyes, in their very presence! Then for the acid test, to establish proof of the genuineness of their verbalized belief, he asked to stand those who would allow him to push them in the wheelbarrow across the rope. Only one little boy stood to his feet, as his expression of belief and trust in the pusher of the wheelbarrow. So many of us are just like that. We talk, we say the right words with our mouths that we believe, but when the time of action and test comes to prove to God that we love him, by keeping his commandments, we choose to remain where we were in our comfort zones imprisoned by disbelief and fear.

---

[173] John 17: 3.
[174] Heb. 11:6.
[175] Proverbs 4:7, Psalm 111:10; James 1:5.
[176] Hebrews 11:6.

The required preparation is progressive. We must move from the point of belief to the place where we come to **know God**. The disciple, John, quoted Jesus in John 17:3 as follows:

> *"And this is eternal life, that they may **know** You, the only true God, and Jesus Christ whom You have sent."*

The Adult Sabbath School Lesson Guide, in Lesson 8, carried the following definition and explanation of "to know God:"[177]

> *To **know God** is a major goal of religious experience. To **know God** means the **development of a sensitivity to the guidance of God, a trust in the wisdom and love of God**, and an **eagerness for a relationship with God**. This experience comes to the sincere person who prays, who meditates, who reads God's words, and who commits himself to God.*

Until we make knowing God a major religious goal, we will only be marking time spiritually and beating the air. Clearly, knowing God is more than a head knowledge of God; it includes an experiential knowledge of Him as well. The little boy at the circus also demonstrated implicit trust in the pusher of the wheelbarrow. When we come to know God, our trust in God's wisdom and love and an eagerness for a relationship with Him will be even greater than that exhibited by that little boy. You will be able to share or tell how He has lead you, and identify things that He has done for you in your journey of experience with Him. Reread the (to know God) definition and until you know it verbatim.

Our belief in God will also be a function of our knowledge of Him. With some exceptions for what is practiced in certain cultures and caste, it is very unlikely that a person in his/her right

---

[177] Adult Sabbath School Lesson Guide, Third quarter: July to September 1980, Lesson 8, Page 71

mind will marry someone he/she does not know. So we need to know Him more than we know subjects (such as Mathematics, Physics, Biology, Accounts), our sport, jobs, and careers. This is vitally important because Jesus wants us to be in a spiritual marriage relationship with us, His people, His Church. Notice how the prophet, Jeremiah states this in Jeremiah 3:14, as follows:

*"Return, O backsliding children," says the LORD; "for **I am married to you**."*

The apostle, Paul, states a similar spiritual relationship that God wants to have with us in 2 Corinthians 11:2, as follows:

> *"For I am jealous for **you** with godly jealousy. For I **have betrothed you to one husband**, that I may present **you** as a chaste virgin **to** Christ."*

The marriage relationship has been described as the most intimate relationship among human beings. No wonder Christ uses the imagery of the marriage relationship to describe the relationship between Himself and His People, the Church. Such a relationship is to be nourished, cherished, protected, defended, and lasting. In this context, we can understand why Jesus equates knowing Him/God with eternal life.

As a result of His love for us and our eagerness to have a relationship with Him, we will seek out opportunities to know as much as possible about Him. So we will want to know that He is the resurrection and the life; that He gave His life for all and rose again to tell us that He is alive. As part of that knowledge, we will know for sure that death lost its sting with Him and that the grave could not hold Him down; and that when it was time for Him to fulfill prophecy of staying three days in the tomb, He arose, is alive, and is now in Heaven. We will also seek to know that the angel told the story of His resurrection; that the apostles and many others saw Him after His resurrection, and many witnessed His ascension. We will become familiar with the record that Stephen said he saw Him in heaven; the apostle Paul says that He will return at the sound of the trumpet and will come with angels. Likewise, **we will believe** that Matthew says He will come again, as did other Bible writers, such as John, the revelator, who said that He will come with clouds of angels and every (living)eye will see Him. So, the more we know about Him, the more will belief Him. Seek to know as much as you can about Him.

Given the above, God is not someone you or any reasonable person would want to disbelieve and distrust based on all the available and indisputable body of evidence. Jesus said that He will be going to Heaven and if He goes, He will come again. Well, guess what! He did go, and there is ample reason to believe that He will come again:

a) For His people;
b) To reward the wicked;
c) To put an end to sin and wrong forever;
d) To be with His people;
e) As a fulfillment of His Words and prophecy.

To be truthful, I believe Him. For me, the evidence is overwhelming. I have more than enough reasons to *know* Him and believe Him, and to relate to Him using His love language of living a lifestyle of obedience to His commandments. I know of no better option. Do you?

When we know God, it makes it easier to **exercise faith** in Him. Faith is a confiding trust in someone. E. G. White, in her book, *Education, page 223,* states that "Faith is trusting God – believing that He loves us and knows best what is for our good." The Apostle Paul states that without faith it is impossible to please Him/God. One of my friends who was the best man at my wedding shared with me the following acronym for faith. It's quite profound.

F = Forsaking
A = All
I = I
T = Take
H = Him.

Mary, who did just that, was healed and she and her sister even saw their brother, Lazarus, raised to life. But for faith to be real faith, it must be exercised. Indeed, it is our faith in Him that will help us to overcome this sinful, slipping, sliding earth. Read 1 John 5:4. And this faith comes by hearing the Word of God. Read Romans 10:17.

The fourth, final, and perhaps the most important of all the prerequisites is **wisdom** that comes only from God. The fact that this word 'wisdom' is used over two hundred times in the Bible is indeed very significant. Divine providence is signaling to us that it is critically important to life on planet earth and to our eternal salvation. Similarly, we must have it in order to believe in God, know God, and exercise faith in God, as well as to appreciate God's Love Language and have a demonstrable lifestyle of loving obedience to God and His commandments.

Wisdom is, therefore, much more than knowledge. It is the ability to use knowledge aright. But, it is also more than the ability to use knowledge aright. This is because, even though many people have knowledge they don't seem to be any better off; many knowledgeable people make unbelievable mistakes, do some very crazy things, and even take their own lives or the lives of others.

There is, therefore, something that is very special and unique about wisdom. It has a divine component that enables people to use knowledge to have abundant and fulfilled lives. Dr. Benjamin Carson defines wisdom as *"knowing what is to be done, how it is to be done; when to do something, when not to do something; knowing what you can do and what you can't."* Understandably, Solomon, in Proverbs 10:19, adds that: *"the wise knows when to speak and when not to speak."* The Adult Sabbath School Lesson carried what I consider to be a most thought provoking definition of wisdom as follows: *"Wisdom is to **think and to act as God would** in any situation in life."*[178] When we reach that place in our spiritual relationship and journey with God, we are well on our heaven-bound way. This is

---

[178] Adult Sabbath School Guide, Fourth Quarter 1991, page 6, 7.

because God cannot lie; neither does He make a mistake.

The apostle Paul gives a mirror image of the above definition as well as characteristics of wisdom as follows:

> *Let this **mind be in you which was also in Christ Jesus" and for it is God who works in you both to will and to do for His good pleasure**. Do all things without complaining and disputing, that you may become **blameless and harmless, children of God without fault** in the midst of a crooked and perverse generation, among whom **you shine as lights** in the world, **holding fast the word of life**, so that I may rejoice in the day of Christ that I have not run in vain or labored in vain. Philippians 2:5,13-16.*

Notice how James corroborates some of the characteristics of wisdom as follows:

> *"But the **wisdom** that is from above **is first pure**, then **peaceable**, **gentle**, and **easy to be in treated**, full of **mercy and good fruits**, without partiality, and **without hypocrisy**. And the fruit of righteousness is sown in peace of them that make peace."*[179]

These quotations help us to understand that the desired behaviour is made possible only through the working of God in our lives.

Furthermore, this **wisdom** is not obtained from any earthly university; neither can it be purchased with money from any earthly manufacturer, distributor or retailer. It is obtained only from God. James, Jesus' brother, affirms that **wisdom is from God**. Benjamin Carson assures us also that wisdom is from God. He states that "technical skills or knowledge is something you acquire, but wisdom is from God." And the apostle Paul informs us that it

---

[179] James 3:17-18.

is a **gift** of the Spirit of God.[180] Knowledge says "Jesus is Saviour;" wisdom says "make Him Lord of your life." So, whereas knowledge is factual, **wisdom is functional**. That is why we cannot think and act like God without being like Him in character and behaviour. Therefore, wisdom in action is life at its best. Thus, we can write the formula for wisdom as follows:

WISDOM = LOVE + OBEDIENCE
(Proverbs 4:7) (Psalm 111:10) (John 14:15)

In conclusion, wisdom is a summary of love for God and obedience to His commandments. And since wisdom has God at its centre, all who possess this wisdom of God will embrace His love language.

3.4 Other things to know about God's Love Language

John, the Revelator, summed up the picture explicitly and beautifully for us, regarding four (4) other things we need to know and never forget about God's Love Language.

a) It's the key identifying mark and patience of the saints.

> "Here is the patience of the **saints**: here are they that keep the commandments of God, and the faith of Jesus."[181]

Some of these saints are in their graves, while some are living on earth. They are the ones who will be saved and go to heaven at Jesus' second coming. But, here is a thriller; there is a third category of saints. These lived on earth, but are now in heaven. Why? Because they loved God so much and kept His commandments that God thought it fit to take them to heaven as first fruits. They

---

[180] 1 Corinthians 12:8.
[181] Rev. 14:12.

include Enoch (who walked with God), Moses (a man of great humility who spoke to God face to face while he was on earth), and Elijah, the prophet who ascended to heaven in a chariot of fire. See Chapter 4 on Blessings and Benefits.

The truth is that God will not, and cannot, change His Word, which He has magnified above His name.[182] His Word has established these three-fold characteristics (patience, commandment-keeping, and faithful or trustworthy) of the saints and, therefore, He will not accept those who knowingly choose an opposite path. He is too loving, having created the human family with the power of choice, not to respect and accept their choices so that they can reap the consequences.

b) God's Love Language is practiced by His true Church here on earth. God is also seeking for other honest people (also called the 'other sheep')[183] to become true worshippers and members of His Church here on earth. Matthew and John tell us that all who labour and are heavy laden are to come unto Him and He will give them rest and he who cometh to Him, He will in no wise cast out.[184] The Bible also refers to God's Church as the (pure) woman. According to John, the revelator, she satisfies the following.

i) She is the remnant (meaning God's true Church in the last days before His Second Coming, that has the same characteristics of the early Church);

ii) She keeps the commandments of God as a result of her being in love with God;

iii) She has the testimony of Jesus, which is the Spirit of prophecy.

She obeys and honours the (fourth) commandment that contains the seal of God. The chances are you know persons who

---

[182] See Psalm 138:2.
[183] John 10:16.
[184] Matthew 11:28; John 6:37.

are members of this Church, as you may have seen them going to Church on the same day that God blessed, rested on, and sanctified or set aside for holy use. This is the same day that Jesus kept as Sabbath while He was here on earth. Or you may have read about them or heard about them.

c) The devil is wroth with this Church (see 'b' above) that has a lifestyle of loving obedience to God and His commandments.[185] This is because he is unable to break their love relationship with God. Jesus calls them sheep. He then gives them eternal life and an irrevocable guarantee which states in part: *"neither shall any man pluck them out of his hand."*[186]

d) God's Love Language provides the fairest, most equitable, universal basis, metric, and standard for providing rewards to those whom Jesus will save and those that will be lost.

> *"Blessed are* **they that do his commandments, that they may have right to the tree of life**, *and may enter in through the gates into the city." For without are dogs, and sorcerers, and whoremongers, and murderers, and idolaters, and whosoever loveth and maketh a lie."*[187]

The lifestyle of loving obedience to God and His commandments provides our guarantee to heaven and access to the tree of life, the leaves of which will be for the healing of the nation. This guarantee is better than any country's passport and visa, which lasts only for a time. In fact, this love language provides a right that no one can take away, and it lasts throughout eternity.

Because the commandments are also a transcript of God's character, and because God wanted to ensure that those who would

---

[185] Revelation 12:14, 17.
[186] John 10:27-29.
[187] Rev. 22:14,15.

be saved reflect His character in their lives,[188] the Word of God stated repeatedly the requirements for gaining access to heaven and the tree of life. References to do, obey, keep, the commandments of God are so numerous in the Bible and Word of God, that it would be easy for any genuine seeker of truth and righteousness to find them and choose to keep them. This is one of the distinctive qualifying marks of the persons who choose to satisfy the requirements of God. They are the **one who get the victory over self** (as they are meek and humble), the beast, and over his image, and over his mark and over the number of his name, and John sees them (who also sing the Song of Moses, the servant of God, and the song of the Lamb) **stand on the sea of glass in heaven.**[189] What made this possible? The love of God and their love for God - the perfect symbiotic and win-win relationship!

THE LOVE OF GOD[190]

The love of God is greater far
than tongue or pen can ever tell;
It goes beyond the highest star,
and reaches to the lowest hell;
The guilty pair, bowed down with care,
God gave His Son to win;
His erring child He reconciled,
and pardoned from his sin.

By: Frederick M. Lehman

---

[188] Philippians 2:5-6.
[189] Rev. 15:2, 3.
[190] *Frederick M. Lehman @ http://library.timelesstruths.*
org/music/The_Love_of_God/

CHAPTER 4

BLESSINGS AND BENEFITS OF USING GOD'S LOVE LANGUAGE

THE BLESSINGS AND benefits outlined in this Chapter and consequences as outlined in Chapter 6 are the results of our decision making. Let's just pause to review your definition of decision making and compare it with the one that follows. *Decision making* may be defined as a thought process that involves identifying, developing and analysing options or alternatives followed by the making of a choice in pursuit of an objective or goal. Life as we know it is full of decision making and choices (the last part of decision making). Without them life would be robotic, programmed like a machine. Decision making and choices are inescapable to human existence and have two crucial outcomes: i) favourable such as blessings, rewards or benefits; and ii) unfavourable consequences.

According to the Bible, God made mankind with the capacity for making decisions and the power of choice. See Genesis 2-3 and Deuteronomy 30. Here are two (2) classical examples in Genesis 2:15-17 (of our fore parents Adam and Eve), and in Deuteronomy 30:15-20 (of ancient Israel), of the opportunity to exercise their God given power of choice in the context of decision making.

And the Lord God took the man, and put him into the garden of Eden to dress it and to keep it. 16 And the Lord God commanded the man, saying, Of every tree of the garden thou mayest freely eat: [7]*But of the tree of the knowledge of good and evil, thou shalt not eat of it: for in the day that thou eatest thereof thou shalt surely die. Genesis 2:15-17.*

[15]*See, I have **set before** thee this day **life and good**, and **death and evil;** *[16]*In that I command thee this day **to love the Lord thy God, to walk in his ways, and to keep his commandments and his**

statutes and his judgments, that thou mayest live and multiply: and the Lord thy God shall bless thee in the land whither thou goest to possess it. [17]*But if thine heart turn away, so that thou wilt not hear, but shalt be drawn away, and worship other gods, and serve them;* [18]*I denounce unto you this day, that ye shall surely perish, and that ye shall not prolong your days upon the land, whither thou passest over Jordan to go to possess it.*

[19]*I call heaven and earth to record this day against you, that I have* **set before you life and death, blessing and cursing**: *therefore* **choose life**, *that both thou and thy seed may live:* [20]*That thou mayest love the Lord thy God, and that thou mayest obey his voice, and that thou mayest cleave unto him: for he is thy life, and the length of thy days: that thou mayest dwell in the land which the Lord sware unto thy fathers, to Abraham, to Isaac, and to Jacob, to give them. Deuteronomy 30:15-20.*

You may know or recall that the results of our fore parents' choice to disobey God and to eat of the forbidden tree were unfavourable outcomes: sin, suffering, sorrow and death. This is recorded in Genesis 3. Notice carefully that they were free to eat of all the trees in the garden, except one. Only one tree was reserved and forbidden by God; and to the reasonable and prudent minded person, this must be seen as an easy, or the mildest, test for them. Yes, it was a test and trial to determine whether Adam would be obedient as the loyal angels of heaven or disobedient. If he passed the test, "*his instruction to his children would have been only loyalty. His mind and thoughts would have been asthe mind and thoughts of God. He would have been taught by God as His husbandry and building. His character would have been moulded in accordance with the character of God.*"[191]

If Adam and Eve had obeyed God by abstaining from eating of the fruit from the forbidden tree, they would have passed the test and be trusted with immortality. But if they disobeyed and thereby failed the test, they would have proven to be disloyal and distrustful,

---

[191]   Source: Ellen G. White, Letter 91, 1900, Used by permission.

and would be subject to facing the negative consequences of their disobedience, which included being barred from the Garden of Eden and their ultimate death. Needless to say, they failed the test. Not only did they die, but all their descendants were now subject to sin and death. What a price to pay for their sin of disobedience to God's command? This is how the apostle Paul sums up the outcome of Adam's choice in Romans 5:19 as well as the outcome of Jesus' (the second Adam) successful choice to redeem mankind (including Adam and Eve) from sin.

*"For **as by one** man's disobedience many were made sinners, so **by** the obedience of **one** shall many be made righteous." Romans 5:19.*

This text is a reaffirmation of the reality of decision making and choice, mentioned herein above. Adam's choice of disobedience brought the consequences of sin and death in the human family. By contrast, the decision and choice of obedience ("by the obedience of one") Jesus, "shall many be made righteous."

In the second example in Deuteronomy 30:15-20 cited herein above, Moses recounts for the information of ancient Israel the two and only glaring outcomes of choice: life and good or death and evil; life or death; blessings or curse. If we are wise, we will make a choice only after defining the objective or goal, identifying and evaluating the options or alternatives and their related costs and benefits (disadvantages and advantages), and then selecting the best possible option, which is the option or alternative with the least cost or negatives and the best possible positive results. We should recognize the value of wisdom in making the right decision and ask God for help in this regard.

This book provides an opportunity for each reader to make a decision and a choice regarding God's Love Language. This chapter relates specifically to the benefits of choosing to accept and obediently speak God's Love Language. The consequences of not accepting God's Love Language are dealt within Chapter 6. Chapter 5 speaks to excuses that individuals make. Please don't make excuses for not choosing life and good. Life is too precious and too short here on planet earth to make that kind of choice. Like Moses who asked ancient Israel to choose life and good, I ask you to choose too speak God's Love Language (by loving God and keeping His Ten Commandments) which is synonymous to choosing God's blessings and eternal life.

4.1 The concept of return and benefits

In our world of business and entrepreneurship, many entrepreneurs and investors will not invest one dollar ($1.00) unless they are sure and satisfied from the very outset that they will be getting real return on their dollar (i.e. a rate of return that is equal to or greater than the rate of inflation). In the realm of social entrepreneurship, social investors will be hesitant to make social investment in social entrepreneurship ventures and organizations unless they are satisfied that there will be adequate social return on their investment (SROI). Social entrepreneurs also want to make sure that they will bring about positive social change. Prudent depositors and savers with extra amount of funds will not normally put away their funds on investment in a bank or in other financial and investment institutions unless they are satisfied that they are safe and secure and that they will make a reasonable return on their funds, and be able to retrieve their funds when they need them.

Likewise and more so, the God who created human beings understands this yearning of the human heart for benefits and returns, because He made humans as stewards who are accountable to Him for the resources at their disposal. In the parable of the talents, Jesus praised the two servants who each made 100% return on their two (2) talents (units of money) and five (5) talents respectively. But He called the servant who received the one talent, unprofitable and a bad example of a steward. This is because, rather than investing his lord's money, he went and hid it in the earth, then turned around and railed at his lord.

It is no wonder or surprise then to find that the Word of God outlines the many advantages, blessings, and benefits, for those who choose to invest in a lifestyle of loving obedience to God and God's commandments (God's Love Language). The returns from such an amazing investment are factually real and incomparable. These returns we may call spiritual return(s) and spiritual dividends. Some have already been mentioned throughout the text so far, though not using those verbatim words. However, some of the main ones are brought together under this heading and are shared herein below under two categories, viz: i) benefits on earth, and ii) benefits in heaven and the Earth made New.

4.2 Benefits on Earth.

There are many benefits, blessings and rewards that those who embrace God's Love Language will enjoy while living on earth before Jesus returns at His second coming. Some will result in great financial savings. Others will result in the creation, stimulation, building, growing, and maintaining of quality relationships that are priceless, the returns of which cannot be computed using common, perishable earthly measurements of sinful human beings. Rather, by embracing God's Love Language, the obedient will be making and sending deposits to the bank of heaven to swell their accounts. It is their deposits to these accounts that the heavenly intelligences recognize, which will also qualify them for benefits in heaven and the New Earth.

i) Assurance of the presence of the Spirit of Truth.

Loving Jesus and keeping His commandments will create a readiness in our lives for the fulfillment of the prayer that Jesus prayed to His Father. This prayer states in part that *"**He shall give you another Comforter** (the Spirit of truth), that **he may abide with you forever.**"* It's a wonderful experience and assurance to know that God singles out each one of us for special mention in such a way that we can know that His presence will be with each one of us as long as we shall live. This comes about after building and maintaining this precious relationship with Him.[192] So you are **not alone, I am not alone; we need not be alone** in the struggles and challenges of life on this planet called earth. What greater confidence can we have? This means less stress, good vital health signs and less money to pay to the doctor, and therefore, great financial savings.

ii) Assurance of being led into all truth.

Practicing God's Love Language provides assurance that we will be led into all truth (not just some that we like and are comfortable with) by the Spirit of Truth, the Holy Ghost, who will show us things to come. See John's record of this spiritual truth below:

*"Howbeit when he, **the Spirit of truth**, is come, he **will guide you into all truth**: for shall not speak of himself; but whatsoever he shall hear, that shall he speak: and he will shew you things to come."*[193]

This will definitely help to keep us away from errors, sin, and out of the path of the roaring lion, the devil. The truth includes the law of God, the 10 commandments, including the keeping of the Sabbath, the day between Friday (the preparation day) and Sunday (the first day of the week), and the day between Easter Friday and Easter Sunday, as the following quotations from Dr. Luke make very clear for us. The first is from the King James Version (KJV) and the second, which is repeated for emphasis and clarity, is from the Good News Translation (GNT).

*It was **Preparation Day**, and the Sabbath was about to begin. The women who had come with Jesus from Galilee followed Joseph and saw the tomb and how his body was laid in it. Then they went home and prepared spices and perfumes. But **they rested on the Sabbath in obedience to the commandment**. On the **first day of the week**, very early in the morning, the women took the spices they had prepared*

---

[192] Read Proverb 3:5-6.
[193] John 16:13.

and went to the tomb."[194]

"*It was* **Friday***, and the* **Sabbath** *was about to begin. The women who had followed Jesus from Galilee went with Joseph and saw the tomb and how Jesus' body was placed. Then they went back home and prepared the spices and perfumes for the body.* **On the Sabbath they rested, as the Law commanded.** *Very early on* **Sunday** *morning the women went to the tomb, carrying the spices they had prepared."*[195]

Read and even reread these passages also from the New English Bible (NEB), the Today's Living Word (TLV), and the Good News Bible (GNB). The weekly cycle, which includes the Sabbath (or Saturday), was instituted by Jesus (as "all things were made by Him;…") during the creation week. He made it for man, just like how He made the woman for the man.[196] What would mankind be like without the woman? Similarly, He made the Sabbath for man, for his happiness and joy, so that he could rest, be refreshed, and glorify His Maker (as a result of spending a whole day weekly of quality time with God, as specified by God, - God' secondary love language).

Even though He, Jesus, is Lord of the Sabbath,[197] He kept it while He was here on Earth. He kept it with His disciples on numerous occasions. This is one of the Ten Commandments that He has commanded us to keep. It is the same commandment that we will meet again in heaven and in the Earth made New. Oh friend, what a joy it will be on that day when the redeemed families of earth and all ages, join with the family of heaven to worship God. Can you visualize the scene?

Imagine meeting Daniel there, who was thrown in a den of ravenous lions for refusing false worship! Imagine meeting the woman at the well who had five husbands and the one she had when she met Jesus was not hers! Why will she be there? Because

---

194   Luke 23:54 -56; 24:1 KJV
195   Luke 23:54 -56; 24:1 GNT
196   See 1 Corinthians 11:9.
197   Mark 2:27-28.

she fell in love with Jesus, who forgave her of all her sins. She said, *"Come see a man who tells me everything I did. This must be the Christ."* She discovered Jesus, the way the truth and the life. And there are many others who we will meet there, if we are likewise loving, obedient, and trustworthy. The Spirit of Truth led them too into all truth, and to know, Jesus, who also is truth. This same Spirit of Truth is ready and willing to lead me, you (us) today, right now, into the same truth if you choose to let Him.

The Bible specifically identifies the following as truth: Jesus; the Law of God (which includes the Sabbath); the Word of God (which records the 10 commandments); the Holy Spirit of God; and God, the Father. The Psalmist highlights the significance of the Law as follows:

*"Thy righteousness is an everlasting righteousness, and **thy law is the truth**."*[198]

The Spirit of God also helps the believer to understand prophecies.[199] So, there will be no need or desire to walk in darkness or in error, once you honestly love Jesus. Here is the reason why many walk in error.

"Jesus answered and said unto them, Ye do err, not knowing the scriptures, nor the power of God."[200]

iii) Longevity and quality of life

Length of days, longevity, and quality of living fortified with great peace flow to those who do not forget God's law, but allow their hearts to keep God's commandments. The psalmist speaks to the magnitude of the peace as follows:

"Great peace have they which love the law and nothing shall offend them."[201]

These commandment lovers and keepers have a calmness and tranquility of soul that Jesus gives them because they are reflecting His character. They will neither be cynical, shifty, nor offensive; quarrelsome nor rude; loud nor hostile and destructive; abusive nor violent. Why? Because they have *a peace that passeth all understanding*. So, though storm winds blow, they will not be offended. Plus the length and quality of life that they enjoy on earth is but a tip of the ice berg experience that they will have in heaven and the Earth made New. Moses records God's promise of freedom from certain diseases for His obedient children while on earth as follows.

*"And said, If thou wilt diligently hearken to the voice of the LORD thy God, and wilt **do that** which is right in **his** sight, and wilt give ear to **his commandments**, and keep all **his** statutes, I will put none of these diseases upon thee, which I have brought upon the Egyptians: for I am the LORD **that** healeth thee."*[202]

iv) A barricade against sin and evil

Because lovers and speakers of God's Love Language have hid the Word of God in their hearts, just like the Psalmist[203] did, it becomes a lamp and a light of truth to them, pointing out the way they ought to tread, and guiding them and keeping them away from sin, in this dark, gloomy, and violent world of evil.[204] As a barricade against sin, they will in this life be spared many of sin's consequences here on this piece of dirt called earth. They will also be spared from the second death as they will be translated or be in the first resurrection. This is also due to the fact that the Lord who is faithful will keep them from evil. This is shown below as follows:

*And that we may be delivered from unreasonable and wicked men: for all men have not faith. **But the Lord is faithful, who shall stablish you, and keep you from evil**. And we have confidence in the Lord touching you, that ye both do and will do the things which we command you. And the Lord direct your hearts into the love of God, and into the patient waiting for Christ.*[205]

---

[202]   *Exodus 15:26.*
[203]   Psalm 119:11, 105.
[204]   Read John 16:13, Psalm 119:105, 11, and Proverbs 6:23.
[205]   *2 Thessalonians 3:2-5.*

v) Peace with your enemies

Your enemies will be at peace with you, because your way pleases the Lord.[206] This defies sinful earthly human logic. It baffles human wisdom and reason. The wicked do not understand it, but the wise does.[207] This is how the prophet Isaiah describes the security picture of the saints of God, who love and keep God's commandments.

"....*When the enemy shall come in like a flood, the Spirit of the Lord shall lift up a standard against him.*"

vi) Natural love for God's law

We will love God's law so much that it becomes our daily meditation.[208] This provides the basis for our purity. We are what we think, do, and eat. For out of the abundance of the heart, the mouth speaketh. If we want pure thoughts, pure words, pure action, behaviour and mannerism, we must feed out minds with what is perfect, just, good, which is the law of God. When we do this, it will become so natural like the fresh air that we breathe. The prophet, Jeremiah, shares his own experience regarding the Word of God as follows:

> ***Thy words were found,*** *and* ***I did eat them; and thy word was unto me the joy and rejoicing of mine heart:*** *for I am called by* ***thy name, O LORD God of hosts.***[209]

The Psalmist has said some fascinating things about the law and some specific benefits that we can obtain. A few are cited below.

"*The* ***law of the Lord*** *is* perfect, ***converting the soul****: the testimony of the Lord is sure, making wise the simple. The statutes of*

---

[206] Read Proverbs 16:7.
[207] See Daniel 12; 10.
[208] Read Psalm 119:97, 127, 142.
[209] Jeremiah 15:15-17.

*the Lord are right, rejoicing the heart: the commandment of the Lord is pure, **enlightening the eyes….**" More to be desired are they than gold, yea, than much fine gold: **sweeter also than honey and the honeycomb.** "*[210]

If you want to be perfect, if you want your soul to be converted, if you want purity, if you want your eyes to be enlightened, and if you want good taste, make the law of the Lord your daily meditation. With all these benefits of the law of love: perfect, converting the soul, pure, enlightening the eyes, more to be desired, sweet, sweeter than honey and the honeycomb, is it any wonder that David made it his daily meditation? If we have taste for what is good, we will want to replicate in our lives David's example of best practice.

vii) The joy of being loved by God

Isn't it wonderful to experience the joy that comes from being greatly loved by someone significant in your life? It sure is! Then what about the more wonderful experience of being in love with God? This is the joy that comes from the experience of a lifestyle of loving obedience to God's commandments or moral law, which is the truth. The prophet, Isaiah, posts on his Facebook wall (to use postmodern computer age phraseology) a masterpiece statement about this matter.

*"I will greatly **rejoice in the Lord**, my soul shall be **joyful** in my God; for he hath clothed me with the garments of salvation, he hath covered me with the robe of **righteousness**, as a bridegroom decketh himself with ornaments, and as a bride adorneth herself with her jewels."*[211]

What a comforting assurance to know that it isn't just you alone, but all of God's people, who keep His commandments that are greatly loved and called beloved. This knowledge provides peace, joy, and a feeling of spiritual security. The prophet, Daniel,

---

[210] *Psalm 19:7-8, 10.*
[211] *Isaiah 61:10.*

who refused to pray to the sinful king Darius, was one of them that enjoyed that level of recognition and reassurance given by God. This is recorded by the prophet, Daniel, and cited below as follows, as a source of encouragement for us:

> *"And he said unto me, O Daniel, a man **greatly beloved**, understand the words that I speak unto thee, and stand upright: for unto thee am I now sent. And when he had spoken this word unto me, I stood trembling."*

> *«Then there came again and touched me one like the appearance of a man, and he strengthened me, And said, O man **greatly beloved**, fear not: peace be unto thee, be strong, yea, be strong. And when he had spoken unto me, I was strengthened, and said, Let my lord speak; for thou hast strengthened me."*[212]

viii) You walk in integrity and your children are blessed after you.

What wonderful example will we set for those around us in our family, and what greater legacy can we leave for our children![213]

ix) The people rejoice

"When the righteous are in authority, the people rejoice".[214] The righteous lead a life of rectitude. They are upholders of the law of God and righteous principles. When they are in authority,people do take notice, and are happy, because of their governance that

---

[212] Daniel 10:11, 18-19.
[213] See Proverbs 20:7.
[214] Proverbs 29:2.

is characterized by fair play, justice and equity. This is in sharp contrast to what happens when the wicked rule. *"... When the wicked beareth rule, the people mourn."*

x) We receive what we ask.

This is perhaps one of the greatest benefits. Think about it seriously and objectively. To receive whatever you ask! Only persons with great resources can make and honour that kind of promise: to grant an asker, whatever he or she asks. But man's resources are finite and sometimes tainted. However, if mankind can promise and deliver on a promise, what says God, whose resources are infinite, immeasurable, and abundant? That is why He can "bestow more abundant honour" (1 Corinthians 12:23), and wants us to *"know the love which I have more abundantly unto you" (2 Corinthians 2:4).* This is because according to the apostle Paul, **God *"is able to do exceeding abundantly above all that we are able to ask or think,*** *according to the power that worketh in us." Ephesians 3:20.*

Our God is not a play, play, or toy God. He is the Creator of the entire universe who hangs the world on nothing. Astronauts who went to the moon brought back pictures that shows our world in open space, hanging on nothing. What a mighty, amazing God we serve! He truly has power and resources to supply what we ask.

John, the beloved disciple, as well as Matthew, another disciple, summed it up beautifully, and they state the reason why we will receive what we ask as follows. Then the apostle Paul, under inspiration, gives us information on the supply side, also cited below respectively.[215]

"And whatsoever we ask, we receive of him, because we keep his commandments, `and do those things that are pleasing in his sight."

"And all things, whatsoever ye shall ask in prayer, believing, ye shall receive."

"But my God shall supply all your need according to his riches in

---

[215]   *1 John 3:22; Matthew 21:22; Philippians 4:19.*

glory by Christ Jesus."

If you ask God for a loving husband or wife, for the conversion of a friend, etc., God will grant your request. This is because we ask, keep His commandments, and do those things that are pleasing in His sight. But, we must ask for the best gifts, which include "wisdom" and the Holy Spirit, who guides us into all truth.

xi) Deliverance in the time of trouble.

Before Jesus returns to earth the second time, we are told in prophecy that there will be a time of trouble such as never was, since there was a nation. It will be a time of trouble for God's people who love Him and keep His commandments. It will be a time of great social, economic unrest, emotional and spiritual distress resulting from the withdrawing of God's spirit from the earth. Merchandising will not be as before as challenges will face many. Consequently, many won't be able to buy or sell. But Michael, the Son of God, will come to the defense of His people and will stand up for and deliver them. The prophet Daniel captures the scene succinctly as follows.

> *"And at that time shall Michael stand up, the great prince which standeth for the children of thy people: and there shall be a time of trouble, such as never was since there was a nation even to that same time: and* **at that time thy people shall be delivered**, *every one that shall be found written in the book."*[216]

xii) Spirit of power, love, and of a sound mind and the absence of a spirit of fear.

This particular benefit promotes radiant health, cost effectiveness, quality of life, wholesome and loving relationships, and a capacity to accomplish great things. Many are unable to sleep

---

[216]   *Daniel 12:1.*

without tranquilizers such as valium, because they are possessed or controlled by fear, which in turn affects their mental health, quality of life and wallet or purse. Here is where those who practice God's Love Language have special advantages and endowments.

> *"Hearken unto me, ye that know righteousness, the people in whose heart is my law; fear ye not the reproach of men, neither be ye afraid of their revilings."*

> *"For God hath **not** given us the spirit of fear; **but of power, and of love, and of a sound mind.**"*[217]

Based on the content of these two quotations, we must thank both the prophet, Isaiah, and the apostle Paul for sharing their spiritual inspiration with us.

4.3 Benefits and rewards in a sinless world to come: Heaven and the New Earth

Despite all the existing challenges, life on earth is still verily important. The reason for this is that it is how you live here, and not so much how you die, that really matters. Make no mistake about it. Allow no one to "turn you round" or "spin you round" on this critical matter. **It is the decisions that you make in this life that will determine one of the two places of your final destination**: Heaven and the New Earth or (ii) hell; or to put it another way: (i) the first resurrection or (ii) the second death.

So, as you read this section of this book, stop and think carefully. Reflect on your life to this very moment and ask yourself: "where do I want to spend eternity"? The choice is yours (insert your name here).

Whatever your decision, make sure you choose to embrace

---

[217]   *Isaiah 51:7; 2 Timothy 1:7.*

God and His love language. That is what accepting God's grace through faith will lead you to do. That is what will entitle you to the benefits cited is this section of this chapter of this book. These benefits are incomparable; they "put the icing on the cake", to use the familiar phrase. But as you will agree, the benefits on earth (listed herein) are really just a tip of the iceberg compared to what God has prepared for all those who will enter heaven at the second coming of Jesus. Additionally, the word of God is crystal clear on this matter of rewards. Rewards are coming! And there will be rewards (good or evil) for everyone. John, the Revelator, gives us this assurance in the apocalyptic book of Revelation in Chapter 22:12 stated herein below that when Jesus comes again He comes with rewards.

"And, behold, I come quickly; and my reward is with me, to give every man according as his work shall be."

i) Passport and visa rights

Have you seriously considered the need for a passport and visa rights for entry into Heaven, access to the tree of life, and the resulting happiness? If you have, then it would be prudent to take a look at what two tried and proven prophets: Isaiah and John, the revelator, have said on this vitally important matter.[218] The reason for this is that if you fail to get the passport and visa for heaven and eternity, you would have missed it all. This is because the other benefits that you will be entitled to in heaven and the New earth are dependent on this one.

Consider this! The heavenly reward far supersedes access and entrance to Disney Land, Paradise Island, the Atlantis, the Holy Land, and the countries of the first, second and largest economies of the world. It is better than the best holiday you have enjoyed, or will ever enjoy anywhere on this sinful earth, even if with all expenses paid or prepaid. The heavenly passport and visa rights will

---

[218]   Read Isaiah 26:2; Revelations 22:14.

entitle you to spend one thousand (1,000) years (the millennium) vacation style in heaven, where there will be peace and tranquility and the absence of poverty, crime and violence. It will be 1000 years of bliss. Then it will be accompanied by eternal life, in a country where the presence of God will be throughout the ceaseless years of eternity. This is how the apostle Paul, writing under inspiration, sums up the bright future for all those who embrace God's Love Language.

> *"But as it is written, Eye hath not seen, nor ear heard, neither have entered into the heart of man, the things which **God hath prepared for them that love him**.*
>
> *But **God hath revealed them unto us by his Spirit**: for the Spirit searcheth all things, yea, the deep things of God."*[219]

What an invaluable dividend that is promised to those who embrace God's Love Language?

ii) Immortality plus

What great rewards: immortality, incorruption, and eternal life free from any and all illness! Take a reading trip with the apostle Paul to two historical countries: Corinth and Rome, and discover what he had to say on the subject matter.[220] See the footnotes.

Now, this one will "blow us away". It is living forever, yes, life without end! And not just any kind of life, but quality life which is not subject to morbidity, death or dying (i.e. mortality), free from physical decay and from the quality of being corrupt or corruptible, unending longevity, and freedom from all forms or kinds of maladies and illnesses. This is life at its best. There is no other life that is even remotely comparable to this gift of life and

---

[219] 1 Corinthians 2:9-10.
[220] Read 1 Corinthians 15:42,53; Romans 2:7.

existence; it is called the abundant or everlasting life. It is a life that involves enjoyment of perfect health and perfect quality of life and living.

Imagine the scene if you can! Stretch your imagination to the limit! Here is an excerpt of a song I learnt in Church many years ago that gives a glimpse or 'bird's eye view' of what life then will be like. The song is entitled: "O What a Day That Will Be."[221]

> *"They'll be no sorrow there no more burdens to bear, No more sickness, no more pain, no more parting over there; And forever I will be with the One who died for me, What a day, glorious day that will be!"*

This means that there will be no more hospitals; no more doctors; no doctor and hospital bills; no more health insurance companies, cards and costs; no more morgues, autopsies, funeral homes and parlors; no more funeral processions, mourners or hired mourners; and no more places of internment and cremation. Why? Because these former things and sorrows will be forever passed away. Read below how John, the revelator, describes the scene in heaven and the earth made new in wonderment.

> And **I saw a new heaven and a new earth:** *for the first heaven and the first earth were passed away; and* **there was no more sea.** *And I John saw the holy city, New Jerusalem, coming down from God out of heaven, prepared as a bride adorned for her husband. And I heard a great voice out of heaven saying, Behold, the tabernacle of God is with men, and he will dwell with them, and they shall be his people, and God himself shall be with them, and be their God.*

---

[221] O What a Day That Will Be by the covenant Four Quartet, posted online at http://www.angelfire.com

*And **God shall wipe away all tears** from their eyes; and there shall be **no more death, neither sorrow, nor crying, neither shall there be any more pain: for the former things are passed away.** And he that sat upon the throne said, **Behold, I make all things new.** And he said unto me, **Write: for these words are true and faithful.***

*And he said unto me, It is done. I am Alpha and Omega, the beginning and the end. I will give unto him that is athirst of the fountain of the water of life freely. **He that overcometh shall inherit all things; and I will be his God,** and he shall be my son.*[222]

iii) Many mansions

Before Jesus returned to heaven, He left a promise for all mankind and especially those who would embrace it. That promise involved undeniable access to mansions in heaven prepared for those who love Him and keep His commandments (God's Love Language). Read the quotation cited below.

*"Let not your heart be troubled: ye believe in God, believe also in me. **In my Father's house are many mansions:** if it were not so, I would have told you. I go to prepare a place for you. And if I go and prepare a place for you, I will come again, and receive you unto myself; that where I am, there ye may be also."*[223]

Friends of mine, this is a golden and invaluable opportunity I would not want to miss, and cannot afford to miss by the help of God. "Do you, and should you?"

---

[222] *Revelation 21:1-7.*
[223] *John 14:1-3.*

iv) Privilege in Judgment

Privilege to participate in the judgment of the wicked is for real!

The Bible records that God's people, while in heaven during the millennium, which is before the executive phase of the judgment upon the wicked, will judge the wicked. This will provide a golden opportunity for the saved commandment- keeping people of God to review the records of the lives of the wicked and see and understand the reason(s) why they were lost and not taken to heaven with the saved at the second coming of Jesus. This review will also involve the judgment that is to be meted out to Satan and his host of evil angels before their final elimination from the universe that will be forever free from sin and wrong. The apostle Paul in relating to the matter of judging angels, provides the reason why God's people on earth, before the second coming of Jesus should settle disagreements among themselves and not have to go to earthly courts and judges who are unjust.

> *Do ye not know that the saints shall judge the world? and if the world shall be judged by you, are ye unworthy to judge the smallest matters?*
>
> *Know ye not that we shall judge angels? how much more things that pertain to this life? If then ye have judgments of things pertaining to this life, set them to judge who are least esteemed in the church.*[224]

v) Construction and inhabitation of perfect residential dwellings and an agrarian economy.

In the earth made new, the saved will have well-deserved opportunities to build and inhabit magnificent residential dwellings. We will also have agrarian farms, for we shall plant

---

[224]   *1 Corinthians 6:2-4.*

vineyards and eat the fruits of them. This is so much unlike what exists in some places in this sinful world where many cannot afford to purchase a plot of land, let alone build a tiny dwelling place and where many are unable to get and or pay their mortgages. Many here on earth experience foreclosures, tears, disappointment, grief and sorrow. But in God's new world, there will be nothing like this. We will both build and inhabit, and long enjoy the work of our hands. The prophet Isaiah gives us a glimpse of what the new and beautiful building and living arrangement will be like.

> *"And they shall build houses, and inhabit them; and they shall plant vineyards, and eat the fruit of them. They shall not build, and another inhabit; they shall not plant, and another eat: for as the days of a tree are the days of my people, and mine elect shall long enjoy the work of their hands."*[225]

When I reached this point in writing this book, I surfed the Internet to get a picture of what some of the most beautiful and the most expensive houses in the world looked like. From the images that I found, two memorable ones stood out in my mind. One was the most beautiful[226] and the other was the most expensive[227] house in the world. The second was entirely of glass. Both, especially the most expensive house would wow you! Why? They were extremely beautiful. Imagine a residential dwelling with over twenty floors, over five hundred feet tall, made entirely of glass and costing a billion dollars! Many can only dream of houses like these! They may never behold, enter, own or live in one like that. But, believe it or not, know it or not, like it or not, none of these can come even near to what homes will be like in the

---

[225]   *Isaiah 65:21-22.*

[226]   Source: http://decorationchannel.com/randomdesigns/ most-beautiful-house-world/

[227]   Source:http://blog.yaaree.com/ top-10-most-expensive-houses-in-the-world.

Earth Made New that the saints, who are redeemed from Earth will have and enjoy.

vi) Perfect nutrition

In the new world to come, we will have all the food and healthy nutrition we want and will ever need. And there will be nothing to taint our diet. There will be perfect nutrition. There will be the tree of life, which bears twelve manner of fruits, the leaves of which shall be for the healing of the nation. Nothing presently on earth, even in the best of times, can remotely compare to what God will make available for the saved in terms of dietetics, nutrition, and radiant health. In the Bible (Revelation 15:2, 21:18, 21) reference is made to sea of glass, clear glass and transparent glass in the new heaven and the new earth. It is a breath-taking sight to behold. Let us plan to be there. See below how John, the revelator, in vision captures an imagery of the beautiful, new Edenic scene.

> *And he shewed me a pure river of water of life, clear as crystal, proceeding out of the throne of God and of the Lamb. In the midst of the street of it, and on either side of the river, was there the tree of life, which bare twelve manner of fruits, and yielded her fruit every month: and the leaves of the tree were for the healing of the nations.*
> *And there shall be no more curse: but the throne of God and of the Lamb shall be in it; and his servants shall serve him.*[228]

vii) Earth filled with the knowledge of the Lord

The knowledge of the Lord in the new earth, hitherto not experienced, will cause many in this wonderland to be filled with amazement and joy. Eyes will 'pop open'; mouths will 'drop down'

---

[228] Revelation 22:1-3.

as if they want to run with water. All forms of ungodly lyrics and musical genre that have no place for God will not be there. Unrepentant revelers and orgy planners and goers will not be there. Unrepenters, non-believers, and unrepented midnighters, party lovers and goers, will be conspicuously absent. Heaven and the new earth would be a furnace of hell for them who are steep in their own ways, fatal and self- centered love language. Unlike our present individualistic, slipping, sliding world of sinful paraphernalia and pluralism, there will be one accord and unity in the new world to come. The prophet, Habakkuk tells us exactly how spiritually potent the place there will be.

> *"For the earth shall be filled with the knowledge of the glory of the Lord, as the waters cover the sea."*[229]

There will be one way of worship and one day of worship. Isaiah also comments on this beautiful celestial scene in the quotation below as follows.

> *"For as the new heavens and the new earth, which I will make, shall remain before me, saith the Lord, so shall your seed and your name remain. And it shall come to pass, that from one new moon to another, and from one Sabbath to another, shall all flesh come to worship before me, saith the Lord."*[230]

viii) Innocent, harmless playing in the streets of the city.

Read Zechariah 8:5-8. This one "puts the icing on the cake", as some would say. This is because of the love that, generally speaking, people have for children who can be so innocent, and harmless. Parents who love, appreciate, and understand the bundle of joy that children are, can perhaps at least, dimly picture a scene

---

[229]   *Habakkuk 2:14.*
[230]   *Isaiah 66:22-23.*

characterized by safety and security. And even such a picturing is a far cry for what the prophet Zechariah writes about the children in the city of the New Jerusalem in Chapter 8 of his book, and as cited below.

> *"And the streets of the city shall be full of boys and girls playing in the streets thereof."*[231]

So, parents in the new earth and in the capital, the New Jerusalem, will be happy and jubilant as they know about the safety and the security of the City and their children at play there. This is a mouthful; no, that is too small; rather, it is trailer load of joy throughout all eternity!

Ladies and gentlemen, brothers and sisters, friends of God, readers alike, it wouldn't be surprising if your mouth watered as you read these magnificent benefits. And the list is just a sample of what God has in store for all those that love Him and keep his commandments (caress His love language). **I know of no other love language that can compare, even remotely, and that provides such great returns and guarantees eternal benefits**. Make sure you know, understand and practice this love language in your daily lives. It is exciting to know that we can speak God's Love Language both with our lips and with our lives. With our lips we can praise Him in songs of praise and words of affirmation. With our lives we can obey him and teach and encourage others to do so. When we do this repeatedly, it becomes an incomparable way of life.

4.4 Key requirements for benefits in a sinless world to come

What is the price that we will have to pay for all the above mentioned benefits available for the saved who will gain entry to heaven and the earth made new? How much would you be prepared to pay or give in order to have these benefits? Your bank account! Your automobile! Your real estate! Wouldn't the price be

---

[231]   *Zechariah 8:5.*

peppercorn compared to the invaluable, immeasurable benefits, blessings and rewards? But guess what! The price doesn't involve current nor noncurrent assets! It is that inexpensive and therefore really peppercorn; that is why the rich and the poor alike can satisfy the key requirements! It is simply satisfying two (2) main requirements, all non-monetary,[232] which are stated herein below as follows.

i) God's Love Language

Friends of mine, the first and most important requirement is to knowingly, intelligently, intentionally and willingly choose a lifestyle and lifetime of loving obedience to God and His commandments. John, the beloved disciple of Jesus, recorded Jesus' statement of this requirement as follows:

"If ye love me, keep my commandments." Below are some additional related quotations.[233]

> *"Blessed are they **that do his commandments that they may have right to the tree of** life, and may enter in through the gates into the city."*
> *"And whatsoever we ask, we receive of him, because we keep **his commandments**, and **do** those things that **are pleasing in his sight.**"*
>
> *"And hereby we **do know that we know (love) him, if we keep his commandments.**"*

The principles of love and obedience embodied in God's Love Language are not new; neither are they just applicable only for people of our time, day and age. They were verily applicable for ancient Israel; and they are likewise applicable to modern Israel and to all those who want to become a part of modern Israel.

---

[232] Isaiah 55:1-3.
[233] Revelation 22:14; 1 John 3:22, 3:2.

There is no escaping or getting around it; compliance with God's Love Language was a vitally important condition that ancient Israel had to satisfy in order to enter the earthly promised-land, called Canaan - a land flowing with milk and honey. Similarly, it is a vitally important condition that modern Israel and prospects of modern Israel must likewise satisfy in order to make it to the heavenly promised- land, where God dwells, and then for subsequent habitation of the earth made new.

Review the quotations below from the Book of Deuteronomy. These are provided by Moses (who embraced God's love and obedience), now living in the heavenly Canaan where God is. Notice how he describes the condition that God stipulated for ancient Israel to satisfy in order to gain access to the earthly Canaan.[234]

"Hear, O Israel: The Lord our God is one Lord: And thou shalt love the Lord thy God with all thine heart, and with all thy soul, and with all thy might."

All the commandments which I command thee this day shall ye observe to do, that ye may live, and multiply, and go in and possess the land which the Lord sware unto your fathers. *And thou shalt remember all the way which the Lord thy God led thee these forty years in the wilderness, to humble thee, and to prove thee, to know what was in thine heart,* ***whether thou wouldest keep his commandments, or no.*** *And he humbled thee, and suffered thee to hunger, and fed thee with manna, which thou knewest not, neither did thy fathers know; that he might make thee know that man doth not live by bread only, but by every word that proceedeth out of the mouth of the Lord doth man live.*

---

[234]   Deuteronomy 6:4-5, 8:1-3.

But dear reader and friend, we cannot do it on our own. That is why God woos or draws us. As we experience this act of God, we must choose to accept God's grace, which is saving, abundant and free, but not cheap, through faith in God. It is the exercise of this faith that gives us the victory that we need to embrace God's Love Language.

ii) Faithfulness (trustworthiness) unto death

This second key requirement is a faithfulness that puts love and obedience to God above life itself. Yes, it involves a special kind of **commitment** which knows no leave nor break (of any kind - no vacation leave, no departmental or circumstantial leave, etc.) in continuing the practice of faithfulness (loyalty, devotion, fidelity, constancy, dependability, trustworthiness) to God and His commandments. It also embraces commitment to purity, integrity and principles of rectitude. This kind of commitment reveals the length, breadth, and height of our love for God. Both John, the revelator, and the disciple of Jesus, Matthew, affirm this quality below in the following consecutive quotations.[235]

> *"Fear none of those things which thou shalt suffer: behold, the devil shall cast some of you into prison, that ye may be tried; and ye shall have tribulation ten days: be thou **faithful unto death**, and I will give thee a crown of life."*

> *"His lord said unto him, Well done, good and faithful servant; thou has been **faithful** over a few things, I will make thee ruler over many things: **enter thou into** the joy of thy lord."*

The above quotations from the Books of Revelation and Matthew reaffirm that individuals who embrace this kind of

---

[235] *Revelation 2:10; Matthew 25:23.*

faithfulness or trustworthiness need not possess a spirit of fearfulness for their lives, because they know that, they that loseth their lives for Christ's sake shall find it again or live again eternally.[236]

Writing in the book: Counsels on Health, E. G. White, provides the following comments which are applicable here, not just to believers primarily, but also to all those who will choose to embrace God's Love Language.

"You should not for one moment give place to an impure, covert suggestion; for even this will stain the soul, as impure water defiles the channel through which it passes." Page 616.

Choose poverty, reproach, separation from friends, or any suffering, rather than to defile the soul with sin. Death before dishonor or the transgression of God's law, *should be the motto of every Christian. As a people professing to be reformers, treasuring the most solemn, purifying truths of God's word, we must **elevate the standard far higher than it is at the present time**. Sin and sinners in the church must be **promptly dealt with**, that **others may not be contaminated. Truth and purity require** that we make more thorough work to **cleanse the camp** from Achans. Let **those in responsible positions not** suffer sin in a brother. Show him that he must either put away his sins or be separated from the church.* Ibid, page 626

*The **consciousness of right doing is the best medicine for diseased bodies and minds**. The special blessing of God resting upon the receiver is health and strength. One whose mind is quiet and satisfied in God is on the highway to health. To have the consciousness that **the eye of the Lord is upon us**, and that His ear is open to our prayers, is a satisfaction indeed. To know that we have a never-failing Friend to whom we can confide all the secrets of the soul, is a happiness*

---

[236] John 12:25.

which words can never express.[237]

According to the prophet, Amos, such persons will:

"Seek good, and not evil".

The Psalmist notes that such persons will:

"Depart from evil, and do good; and dwell for evermore"[238] They will sing the wondrous love of Jesus, who died for them and made heaven a reality for them, throughout the ceaseless ages of eternity.

---

[237] Ellen G. White, Counsels on Health, pages 616, 626, 628.
[238] *Amos 5:14; Psalm 37:27.*

WALDON B. WRIGHT

WHEN WE ALL GET TO HEAVEN[239]

Refrain:
When we all get to heaven,
What a day of rejoicing that will be!
When we all see Jesus,
We'll sing and shout the victory!

184

CHAPTER 5

COMMON EXCUSES FOR NOT COMPLYING WITH GOD'S LOVE LANGUAGE

5.1 Excuses and their impact on people

EXCUSES ARE REASONS that people give, overtly or covertly, usually for not doing something that they don't want, or like, to do. Excuses are also reasons people give "forgetting other people off their backs," people who are pushing, pressuring, and sometimes cunningly coercing them to do things they are not yet prepared to do. Excuses are also scapegoats that some people provide when they do not want to carry out reasonable requests from others that they do not like, and or whose personalities conflict with theirs. Excuses also serve to keep people in their comfort zones and prevent them from:

i)   trying something new;
ii) making innovation or improvement of their existing situation;
iii) embracing revival and reformation;
iv) caressing opportunities that could transform their lives into better, best, and propel them to make great accomplishments.

Many persons are where they are in life right now, in the valley of disappointment and doubt, dependency and despondency, fear and or failure, dwelling on past bad and negative experiences, and missed opportunities simply because they refused to try, to advance. They see the cup as "half- empty" rather than "half-full." Don't forget that this is exactly where the devil wants many persons to be. However, if you know what your excuses are, you can do something about them with God's help, as in making a paradigm shift, and go forward into a new life filled with blessings and happiness, and peace of mind.

For persons who have made excuses a way of life, using it to play the blame game, charging that life can be quite challenging and even very difficult, I recommend that they learn this lesson: "it is one of Satan's most successful tools to deceive, defeat and to destroy them." The devil wants people to manufacture and maintain a storeroom full of excuses and scapegoats. This is, because, he knows that it will be more difficult for them to appreciate God's Love Language. God, on the contrary,does not want us to make, save and repair excuses. He wants us to destroy the storeroom of excuses, remembering that He has given us power (*dunamis*), not only of love, but also of a sound mind. So make a paradigm shift today to revisit your storeroom and annihilate all the excuses, skeletons and scapegoats that you may have which are holding you hostage and back from doing what God wants you to do to advance.

5.2 A menu of common excuses

As you review this menu of common excuses shown below, do a honest introspective checkup on yourself and ascertain if any apply to you. If some do, determine in your mind that with God's help, you are going to do something about them and stop holding back yourself from the best that God wants to offer you, not just for time but for eternity.

1. Cultural practices: I have always done it like that, so I refuse to change. I am going to let down my culture if I do.
2. Socialization: That's how I was brought up. I can't deal with a make-over.

3. Confidence in persons who are significant in my life but who are averse to embracing God's Love Language: They will kill me if I change; it will be killing the confidence they have in me.

4. Procrastination and un-readiness for change: I will do it, but not now.

5. I don't believe in God or the Bible: I consider myself to be foolish.

6. Ego: I have a great sense of self-importance; an ego larger than life, and bigger than my relationship with God.

7. Envy: I have a feeling of discontent or resentful longing, aroused by someone else's possession.

8. Avarice: I have an extreme greed for wealth or material gain.

9. Ambition: I have a desire and determination to achieve success.

10. Arrogance and bigotry: I sense that I am better than those around me (even in the church) that I have come in contact with.

11. Stubbornness: I am like a mule; I don't like anybody telling me what to do.

12. Power, position and pride: I have a great and well-paying job that comes with many perks. To take on God's Love Language would be like separating my heart from my chest. I can't do that any time soon.

13. Lack of conversion: I am happy how I am, and doing what I am doing and I do not want to change.

14. "Born come see:" I have been born into a family where I see all my family members either going to Church on Sunday (Friday in some cases) and some not going to Church at all. It's a free and easy life and they want me to maintain the family tradition. Plus, I am not working. I am totally dependent on my parents for everything and am still attending school.

15. Love of the praise of men:[240] I am an entertainer. I love what I do and the praise that I get when I do a performance. This church thing is a very humiliating thing; I don't think that I am ready for that as yet.

16. Love of the things of the world more than love of the things of God.[241] The world is my life. It feeds me and has given me everything that I have.

17. Lack of knowledge of the Scripture and of the power of God.[242] I don't know enough about the Bible or the Word of God to make a decision.

18. Refusal to change and surrender to God: I simply refuse to surrender to God, I am my own big man and big woman.

19. Too many bad examples in the Church: I can't go and join all those 'ginals' (tricksters) that are in the church professing to be followers of God, when in reality they are sheep in wolves clothing.

20. No time, too busy! Some persons claim that they are too busy and just don't have enough time to get involved in this God business.

21. Too wise to evil! Some persons are foolish, without knowledge of God; they have no understanding. They are wise to do evil; but to do good, they have no knowledge.[243]

22. Some have a revolting and a rebellious heart, and thereby refuse to fear the Lord that giveth rain: both the former and the latter rain.[244]

---

240   John 13:43.
241   1 John 2:15-17.
242   Matt 21:22.
243   Jeremiah 4:22.
244   Jeremiah 5:23-24.

23. Many prefer to accept prophets that prophesy falsely and pastors that bear rule by their means, so they have no delight in the Word of God.[245]

24. Some reject advice or to order their steps or to walk in the good way, the old paths of truth, where there is peace. They also refuse to obey God's voice and keep His commandments. They instead substitute their own self-centered, fatal love language, and have chosen defiantly and stubbornly to walk in their own counsels and in the imaginations of their evil hearts, which lead them backward and not forward. Thus, their iniquitous way separates them from God.

5.3 Choosing the path of reason

If your life was threatened with the prospect of death or if you lost everything you had in life, what would you do? Could you live without them and start all over again? If you were sick and had one week (7 days) to live, what would you do differently? What people do is most often a reflection of the situation (including unmet, unsatisfied needs, and broken/ unrealized dreams) that they find themselves in. But, is this how it should be? Shouldn't our ideas, beliefs, decisions and actions be based on principles rather than situations and situational ethics?

Herein below are three (3) amazing but contrasting stories. The first is about someone I know very well, who was in a burning bus. The second is a about a ship which sank at sea, while the third is about a farmer. Each story is different; yet they have some things in common and reveal how the path of reason was chosen or ignored in testing moments with the different outcomes. The first two are true stories, while the third is biblical based and leaves or offers you an opportunity to make a decision and to draw a conclusion.

Many years ago, someone I know very well was a passenger, comfortably seated, on a commuter public passenger bus along the Mountain View Avenue in Kingston, Jamaica, moving in a south to northerly direction. It was a normal, bright and sunny day, with azul skies and not many clouds in sight. It was before noontime and there was neither sight nor scent of rain. Everything was serene, no raucous passengers or laughter. The driver was at the controls and the bus was moving normally; at least so it appeared to an unsuspecting commuter, who was happy to be getting closer to his destination. On approaching the vicinity of the Excelsior High School, everything changed in a moment.

What happened? "The bus was on fire." What was he to do? "Caress reason, good sense and judgment in a moment of crisis." Suppose he said to himself: "I love my seat and I am enjoying this bus ride, I will not get up." Well, you know the answer to that! Fire is not like humans, it does not think nor reason; it has no conscience nor compassion; it simply acts and does what it has to do, and does best, and that is to burn whatever combustible material lies in its path. Because he was clothed in his right mind and having sound reasoning capacity, he quickly arose from hiss eat, and with speed like that of a deer, he headed for the door of the bus, and within a flash, he and the other passengers, exited the bus to safety.

A Jamaica Observer photo appearing online in the September 17, 2013 edition. Used by permission.

Source: http://www.jamaicaobserver.com/assets/9840689/BusFire.jpghttp://
www.jamaicaobserver.com/news/Another-JUTC-bus-catches-fire

Our world is like this bus and the fire represents sin. Sin is what burns and destroys human lives, human relationships, and the divine-human relationships. Sin does not love God nor His love language. Like my friend on the burning bus, we must reason and choose to get out of the path of sin in our burning world of sin, if we want to have a chance of entering a new world free of sin.

I recently learnt about this second story in Church one weekend from a layman preacher. It is a story of a ship that was in trouble at sea one night. The ship was leaking and water was entering the vessel in rapid perfusion. It was a moment of fear and danger as the ship was in grave distress. The captain of another ship which was within distance of the ship in distress recognized that something was wrong, so he moored closer to it in an effort to offer assistance. The captain called out to the captain of the ship in distress: *"Let me take your passengers to safety."* The captain of the distressed vessel replied: *"It is alright, our vessel is leaking, but it will be too risky for our passengers to disembark our vessel and embark another vessel in the dark of night."* The captain replied to the captain of the vessel in distress: *"Since your ship is leaking, let us take your passengers and save their lives."*

The captain of the distressed vessel, now recognizing the increasing rapidity of water coming into his vessel and the increasing risk of loss of life, retorted: *"It is just four (4) hours from daylight and we are within close proximity to the shore."* The captain, who fully understood the implications of a ship in distress from leaking in the night, repeated his offer to rescue the passengers of the distressed, leaking vessel. But, it was to no avail! The captain of the leaking, sinking vessel, had another mindset, and repeatedly refused the offer of help. The good Samaritan neighbouring captain watched in dismay and disbelief as the distressed vessel went under and all on board that ship perished.

Distressed vessel   **(ii) Samaritan Vessel**

Source:

https://www.google.com.jm/search?sxsrf=ALeKk00fStWgKPeTZTPhfgLOBD
1P0p3uRg:1611861204784&source=univ&tbm=isch& q=non-copyrighted+
pictures+of+ships&sa=X&ved=2ahUKEwii26b 0qr_uAhWGtlkKHSGyDbcQ
7Al6BAgOEAo&biw=818&bih=746 (ii)https://www.google.com.jm/search?s
xsrf=ALeKk00fStWgKPeTZTPhfgLOBD1P0p3uRg:1611861204784&source
=univ&tbm=isch& q=non-copyrighted+pictures+of+ships&sa=X&ved=2ahU
KEwii26b 0qr_uAhWGtlkKHSGyDbcQ7Al6BAgOEAo&biw=818&bih=74
6#im grc=ANloJ7pCSKGbHM

What kind of reasoning is that by the Captain of the distressed vessel, who decided to wait four hours, at the risk of the lives of his passengers, to reach the shore before accepting an offer of help, which was right in sight and within his grasp? What kind of excuse is that, when the pace of the water intake is faster than the speed required to reach the shore? What kind of thinking,reasoning, and decision-making is that, to make decisions for others when that decision will guarantee the needless, untimely death of people? What kind of captain is that who trades the sure (safety of his passengers)for the unsure (making it to the harbour with a rapidly leaking, sinking vessel in the dead of night)? Shouldn't a captain, if he is to be true to form, be concerned first with the safety of his passengers?

Who is the captain of your life? Is your captain encouraging you to embrace God's Love Language? What kind of excuses is he/she making for you and what are the consequences? Will the captain of your life guarantee you eternal life or eternal death? Make sure that you have the right answer before your earthly probation is closed and while you are still alive.

Here is the third and final story. It is based on a Biblical principle. A man had a farm. In it he planted some trees. He did very little for them to grow. As they grew into big trees, he decided one day to cut one down. He used a portion to cut into lumber. Another portion he used to build a boat. And still another portion, he used as wood for the fire to keep himself warm. Then from the remnant, he cut out a log. Using a planar, he planed it. Using a chisel he chiseled it, then cut, carved and shaped it into an image, which he called his god. Then he set it up in his house, fell down and worshipped it. What would you think of, and do with, such a man?

Honestly and truthfully, consider your own excuses and blame game. Would you call any of them idols? Consider God, the Creator of heaven and earth, who knows all things as well as our hearts and intentions. He is looking at and watching each reader who has a list of excuses, or who is making one right now, or who will make one in the future. Does your list carry any excuse(s) for not choosing or serving Him, embracing His love language, or for not being faithful or trustworthy with Him?

What conclusion do you draw for yourself? What conclusion of you, do you think God will draw? How different would it be from the one you would draw in the story above? Our God is a reasonable God. He wants us to think and reason. He wants us to **use** reason in our choices, tastes and preferences, and our position on matters and issues in life.

Don't allow your choice of excuses to allow God to choose to hate[246] you and cause your prayers to be an abomination,[247] when there is so much more to your life. By God's powerful and enabling grace, you can choose to be lifted by His love from the sinking doldrums of sin.

LOVE LIFTED ME[248]

I was sinking deep in sin, far from the peaceful shore,
Very deeply stained within, sinking to rise no more,
But the Master of the sea, heard my despairing cry,
From the waters lifted me, now safe am I.

CHAPTER 6

CONSEQUENCES OF KNOWINGLY IGNORING GOD'S LOVE LANGUAGE

6.1 Law of cause and effect

THERE IS A general principle in life regarding the relationship between cause (or event) and effect (a second event). If, for example, I put my finger in the fire (first event), it will be burned (second event or effect), unless a miracle takes place. The fire won't say: *"Finger, I love you, so I will not harm or burn you."* The fire is not gifted with that kind of reasoning and interactiveness. So, it does not know, nor need to know, the difference between a finger and a combustible material (such as a piece of wood) in the fire. It only knows how to burn whatever comes into its path.

This principle is also referred to as causality or causation, (either of which is somewhat different from the concept of reciprocity). So effects (the pain from the burning finger, i.e. the second event, in the example) are the results of causes (first event - putting my finger in the fire). We may, therefore, say that cause is the independent variable and the effect is the dependent variable. It is also a principle observed in the sciences. For example, when you throw (cause) a ball into the air, it falls (effect); it does not remain in the air. This principle is captured in the Universal Law of Gravitation developed by Sir Isaac Newton. When as a young teenager, I fell off my neighbour's mango tree, the Universal Law of Gravitation was very much alive and well as it is today.

For cricketers to do well (effect) in their game, they must practice (cause) in a consistent and disciplined way. World champion and Olympian athletic champion Usain Bolt will tell you that in order to have accomplished his record breaking performance on the tracks, he had to train real hard and consistently. If business persons do not consistently follow prudent business principles, including ethical principles of honesty and integrity, their businesses will not in the long run achieve the best performance results possible. So, to put it another way, if you are committed and sure that the goal is worthwhile (effect), then you must be willing to pay the price (cause).

This is not only true in the world of business, sport and science, as mentioned above; but it is also true in the religious world,especially when it comes to relating to God, and spiritual truths. It is true that God is a God of love, mercy, forgiveness and grace; but He is also a God of justice, judgment and equity. Unlike the fire, human beings are creatures of reason, choice, and interactiveness. So, if we knowingly do what is wrong (lead a life of disobedience to God's commands, that is, the cause),or refuse to do that which is right, just and good (omitting God's Love Language), the results (the effect or second event) will not be the same as when we knowing do what is right, just, and good (lead a life of obedience to His commands). The effect of knowingly going contrary to the expressed commands and will of God can be quite costly and even tragic. Let us quickly look at a few texts (highlighted and bold with a few insertions in brackets for emphasis) from the Bible on this specific point.

> *Behold, the Lord's hand is not shortened, that it cannot save; neither his ear heavy, that it cannot hear:* [2]*But* **your iniquities (cause) have separated (effect) between you and your God, and your sins (cause) have hid his face from you, that he will not hear (effect).**

> [3]*For your hands are defiled with blood, and your fingers with* **iniquity;** *your lips have spoken lies, your tongue hath muttered perverseness.* [4]*None calleth for*

justice, nor any pleadeth for truth: they trust in vanity, and speak lies; they conceive mischief, and bring forth iniquity.[249] *(Both verses 3 and 4 are causes.)*

The two case stories that follow in this chapter are classical examples of the principle of cause and effect in the realm of religion and in the divine-human relationship. They demonstrate that in God's eyes the principle of cause and effect (which truly started with God) is real and that there are consequences (effect) for disobedience and sin (cause). They also demonstrate that God does not, has not and will not, force the will of anyone. Both man and maiden are always free to choose, just like pastors (priests or prelates) and laypersons, kings and subjects, leaders and followers, believers and non-believers, members and non-members, faithful and faithless. But once the choice is made, they must be prepared for the consequences (effects), good or bad.

6.2 Case story 1: The man of God, the lying prophet,and consequences

This true story of the lying prophet[250] is one that underscores the importance and urgency of practicing (cause) God's Love Language (and not your own) on a timely and on-going basis under all circumstances. It also reminds me of the following statement made by Pastor Glen Samuels[251] in a crusade held at the National Heroes Circle Park in Kingston, Jamaica, in 2010, in which he was the preacher. He said that: *"it is a dangerous thing to know what God tells you to do, and refuse to do it, or to know what God's word says is right, and not to do it or do what is wrong."* Moses, in the Book of Chronicles, puts it this way:

---

[249] *Isaiah 59: 1-4.*
[250] 1 Kings11-13.
[251] At the time of writing, Pastor Glen Samuels was Ministerial Secretary of the Jamaica Union Conference.

*"O children of Israel, fight ye **not against the Lord God of your fathers**; for ye shall not prosper."*[252]

The following quotations from Galatians and 2 Chronicles are quite instructive as a prelude to the story. Sectional quotations from the story are also highlighted (in bold) or in *italics* for emphasis.

*I marvel that ye are so soon removed from him that called you into the grace of Christ unto another gospel: Which is not another; but there be some that trouble you, and would pervert the gospel of Christ. But though we, or **an angel from heaven, preach any other gospel** unto you than that which we have preached unto you, **let him be accursed**.*[253]

*"And the LORD said, **who shall entice Ahab king of Israel, that he may go up and fall at Ramothgilead? And one spake saying after this manner,** and another saying after that manner. Then there came out a spirit, and stood before the LORD, and said, I will entice him. And the LORD said unto him, wherewith?*

*And **he said, I will go out, and be a lying spirit in the mouth of all his prophets**. And the Lord said, Thou shalt entice him, and thou shalt also prevail: go out, and do even so. Now therefore, behold, the LORD hath put a lying spirit in the mouth of these thy prophets, and the LORD hath spoken evil against thee."*[254]

i) Background

Here is a **summary** of the background to the story that is recorded in 1 Kings 11.[255]

a) Solomon had been blessed by God and endowed with special wisdom.

b) The 12 kingdoms of Israel had much peace during his reign when he served God and obeyed His commandments.

c) But a sad and dramatic change with far reaching consequences for himself and the kingdom took place in his life.

d) He loved many strange women (cause). He had seven hundred (700) wives, princes, and three hundred (300) concubines,and his wives turned away his heart (effect) from serving God.[256]

e) When he was old, his wives turned away his heart after other gods; and his heart was not perfect (cause) with the Lord, his God, as was the heart of David, his father. He did evil in the sight of Lord. He built high places to the heathen gods as well as for his wives.[257]

f) The Lord was angry (effect) with Solomon because of this as he turned away his heart from God who had appeared unto him twice.

g) *The Lord told Solomon that He will surely rend the kingdom from* him and give it to his servant, Jeroboam, and leave just one tribe to his son, for David's sake.[258]

h) The **prophet of God, Abijah,** using the symbolism of the a new garment which he rend into twelve pieces, **informed Jeroboam**, Solomon's servant, at God's direction, of the rending of the kingdom and gave him ten (10) pieces. He also told him the **reason,** i.e. because "they have forsaken me, and have worshipped Ashtoreth the goddess of the

---

[255] 1 Kings 11:1-14, 26, 30-38.

Zodians, Chemosh the god of the Moabites, and Milcom the god of the children of Ammon, and have not walked in my ways, to do that which is right in mine eyes, and to keep my statutes and my judgments, as did David his father. V. 30-40. *He also informed Jeroboam that if he walked in the ways of God and keep his commandments, God will be with him.* But Solomon, who didn't like the messenger of God nor his message, even tried to kill him (Jeroboam), but was unsuccessful.

ii) Jeroboam's wayward path

a) After the death of Solomon, *Jeroboam* was invited to, and returned from Egypt, where he had fled earlier when he escaped from Solomon, and was made king overall Israel, but *quickly started on a wrong path that included pagan worship*.[259]

b) **A man of God appeared unto Jeroboam** as he was standing by the altar to make an offering and informed him of the birth of Josiah as well as of God's punishment for his waywardness. Jeroboam was also informed by the man of God who cried out against the altar, that

-   Josiah will sacrifice the priests of the high places who at the time made offerings there,
-   human bones will be burned on the altar;
-   a sign of these things happening is that the alter shall be split the same day, and the ashes on it shall be poured out;

King Jeroboam didn't like the word of the Lord about what would happen on the altar, as coming from the man of God. So, he stretched out his hand to seize the man of God (cause) and

---

[259] 1 Kings 12:20, 28-33.

his hand dried up (effect) as a result of his ***departing from God's commandment***. See 1 Kings 13:1-6.

c) Jeroboam in treated the Man of God to pray to God for him that his hand be restored. The man of God did so and his hand was restored.

d) ***Jeroboam invited the man of God home for a meal and for a reward.*** *But the* ***man of God refused*** *outlining that he had explicit instructions from God not to go home with him and not to eat bread, nor drink water and not to return the same way he came.*

e) ***The man of God refused there ward and meal and returned another way.***

iii) The lying prophet and its consequences[260]

a) *Another prophet,* an old man, enters the scene, and who having been briefed by his sons of the developments, journeyed by ass to find the man of God, and *invited the man of God home to eat bread.* **Initially, the man of God refused** *to go, but yielded after the lying prophet told him that he too was a prophet and that an angel spake by him by the word of the Lord that he should bring the man of God back with him into his house that he may eat bread and drink water.* Sadly, the man of God fell for it (deception and hoax) and went home with the lying prophet and ate with him.[261]

b) It is ironical that while they sat at the meal table, the Word of the Lord came unto the *lying prophet,* who then told the ***man of God:***

> *Thus saith the LORD,* ***Forasmuch as thou hast disobeyed (cause) the mouth of the LORD, and hast not kept the commandment which the***

---

[260] 1 Kings 13:11-30.
[261] Review 1 Kings 14-19; Galatians 1:7; and 2 Chronicles 18:19-22.

LORD thy God commanded thee, [22] *But camest back, and hast eaten bread and drunk water in the place, of the which the Lord did say to thee, Eat no bread, and drink no water;* **thy carcass shall not come unto these pulchre of thy father (effect or consequence).** [262]

c) The **man of God**, after departing for home, **suffered for his disobedience**, by being slain by a lion.
d) The ass that the man of God rode on is unhurt.
e) Persons who passed by saw the carcass of the man of God, his unhurt ass standing by, and reported the tragedy to the lying prophet.
f) When the old lying prophet who brought the man of God to his house heard the tragic news, he said:

"It is the **man of God,** *who was* **disobedient unto the word of the LORD (cause):** *therefore the* **LORD hath delivered him unto the lion, which hath torn him, and slain him (effect),** *according to the word of the LORD, which he spake unto him."*

Notice that from the description received, and before physically going to the location of the tragedy, the lying prophet was able to confirm that it was the man of God. He even ventured to state the reason why the man of God was slain, and thereby leaves no room for doubt or speculation. After his sons saddled his ass, the old lying prophet went to the scene of the death of the man of God.

Three important bits of information are recorded in 1 Kings 13:28 for our learning:

i) The old lying prophet found the carcass of the man of God in the way;
ii) The ass that the man of God rode on, as well as the lion that slew the man of God standing by; and

---

[262]   *2 Kings 13:21-23.*

iii)   The lion had not eaten the carcass, nor torn the ass.

It is interesting that the old lying prophet took up the carcass of the man of God, brought it back to mourn and to bury him. The old lying prophet laid the carcass of the man of God in his own grave, mourned over him and exclaimed: "Alas, my brother!"

g) It's unclear as to **why God chose to use a lying prophet to play such an important role** in the story, but the **message is clear: the disobedient man of God** received the **penalty** from God *for his disobedience to the clear and specific commandment of God.*

iv) Comments on the disobedient prophet

There are some important observations, comments, and conclusions that can be made/drawn, in addition to those mentioned above.

a) God means what He says; therefore, it is always dangerous to know what God says is true, right, just and good, and choose to decline and depart from obeying God's commands.

b) **When God gives a command** (including keeping the 10 commandments), **always obey,** unless He Himself instructs you to do otherwise. This is **a timely reminder** that we should not ignore God's Love Language.

c) When you/we disobey God, /we play into the hand of the devil and leave yourself/ourselves exposed to his attacks.

d) Because **God is God, He can use any vessel to point out our sin or wrong**: whether member, right or wrong doer, friend or foe (also as in the case of the witch of Endor in Case story 2 that follows). Make sure that you understand this: **God does not lead any one into sin, neither can He be tempted to lead any into sin.** Satan can and does orchestrate with his evil angels to lead people, including professed people of God, into sin, and to reject God's Love Language. **We must stand our ground in the strength of**

WALDON B. WRIGHT

the Lord, for he who is weak in a crisis is weak indeed.
It is the tests that prove who, and how strong, we are. God
saw and knew what happened, but did not force the freewill
of the man of God, neither will He force ours: to choose to
obey or disobey.

e) It is quite interesting and instructive to know, note, and
never forget that the devil is deceptive. He uses any available
person and means to cause us to sin against God.

> *".... He was a murderer from the beginning, and
> abode not in the truth, because there is no truth in
> him. When he speaketh a lie, he speaketh of his own:
> for he is a liar, and the father of it."*[263]

Therefore, we must **always take God at His word**. Had
the man of God done so, the old lying prophet would not have
deceived, lied to, and misled him into disobedience against God.

f) *We must be very careful about those who would lead us*,
and whom we allow to lead us, into sin and away from God.

Like the old lying prophet, those whole lead us into sin may be
the first to pronounce our verdict and punishment for disobeying
God often when it is too late for us to repent. They may be a
witness at our graveside; they may even bury us, but that won't
change the punishment for our disobedience and guilt. *They may
brag* about what they did to cause our "untimely" calamity and
death, and yet *live after us to rejoice or gloat over our sin* and
may even repent of their error and wrong doing (knowingly or
unknowingly, deliberate or otherwise) in leading us astray. They
may even be saved, when on the other hand, our probation is
already closed, and we would have been dead, gone, lost, as there
is no repentance in the grave.

---

[263] *John 8:44.*

g)   Ellen G. White comments on this story as follows:

i)   "All the sins and excesses of Solomon can be traced to his great mistake in ceasing to rely upon God for wisdom and to walk in humility before Him … *Our safety, our wisdom, is in recognizing and heeding God's instructions.*"[264]

ii) The man of God had been fearless in delivering the message of rebuke. He had not hesitated to denounce the king's false system of worship. And he had refused Jeroboam's invitation, even though he promised him a reward. But he allowed to be over-persuaded by the one who **claimed** to have a message from heaven. **When the Lord gives a man a command**, such as He gave this messenger, He (God) himself must **countermand** the order. Upon **those who turn from the voice of God to listen to counter orders, the threatened evil will come.** Because **the messenger obeyed false orders, God permitted him to be destroyed.**[265]

6.3 Case story 2: Saul's transgression against God and the consequences

Inspired council provides the following advice which is worthy of note, especially for those who are aspiring to leadership. *Never should one be exalted to a responsible position merely because he desires it. Those only should be chosen who are qualified for the position.* Those who are to bear responsibilities should first be proved and given evidence that they are free from jealousy, that they will not take a dislike to this or that one, while they have a few favored friends and take no notice of others. God

---

[264]   Health Reformer, May, 1878.
[265]   Ellen G. White Manuscript 1, 1912.

grant that all may move just right in that institution.[266]

Do you know of anyone who audibly expressed the desire to be exalted to a responsible position, and who turned out to be disappointing, if not a dismal failure, because the mask was removed in the on-going presence of the test and rigor of quality leadership? Well, Saul's case is very interesting and informative because he was not one of those who aspired, wanted nor desired a position of leadership. So we can conclude that whether leadership is desired by, or entrusted upon the incumbent, a position of leadership can be fraught with special challenges and difficulties. And this situation may be improved or worsened depending on the decisions and choices that are made upon assuming, and during, leadership especially on the matter of who is our master.

i) Overview and Background

The story of Saul is most unfortunate, but contains object lessons of eternal importance. In many ways it speaks of a life of wasted opportunities, privileges, and of what can happen to anyone who refuses to follow the clearest leading, advice, counsel, instructions and commandment of God. Notwithstanding, king Saul's almost endless possibilities and potential for great and excellent accomplishments for God and the kingdom that he led, **he allowed ego**, envy, ambition, jealousy, lack of self-control, **stubbornness, lack of faith and trust in God,** and ultimately rebellion (all causes) against God to lead him astray.

All of these unfortunate characteristics were apparently imperceptible at the beginning. And this is the nature of sin and how it operates. If you allow yourself to be led by sin (use whatever nomenclature of your choosing to label and call it), it will fool you. Also, it will decoy you as to where it is taking you; but the devil, the leader and master of deception and sin, knows. When sin and

---

[266]   Ellen G. White, Testimonies for the Church, Vol. 1,
p. 567 (1867); Councils on Health, page 372.

its sinful characteristics, in the life of anyone, remain unchecked, ignored or underestimated, for what they really are, then such as inner is on a dangerous,downward, fatal path. This can happen to anyone who knowingly rejects God's Love Language.

It happened to Saul. Why? Because, he, Saul, could not, or refused to, see beyond his nose in terms of where sin would eventually lead his aspiration of self-centeredness and the embracing of his own love language. His egoistic thinking of himself more highly than one ought to think, permitted a diabolical garden for sin to be nourished, germinated, and flourished within him. **His repeated acts of ignoring God** (which became easier over time), who permitted him to rise from humble beginnings to the exalted position of first King of the nation of Israel played a major role in **guaranteeing his** unrepentant, uncontrollable, downward journey to self- destruction, demise and eternal loss.

This happened to him because he resisted and rejected all prudent advice and counsel from: his family (including from his own son, Jonathan), his advisers in the palace, his friends, the priests and prophets of God (including Samuel). He crossed the line of no return and committed the unpardonable sin. Therefore, there was nothing more that God could do to reach, restrain, restore, and save him; for indeed, God had done everything possible, but to no avail. Reader and friend, remember that God doesn't force our will.

Notice very carefully, as you review his story, that it was not an overnight fall for Saul. This was a lengthy and progressive downward spiraling to his own demise. **He ignored all the red flags and warning signs,** including all the advice from those close to him and wanted the very best for him. The critical multimillion dollar question is: Could something like this happen to you? Answer: Yes, it can if you make the same or similar mistake of setting up yourself as a demigod, and diabolically so! Also, if it happening to you, would you know in time what to do to curtail its far reaching lethal effects? You may deny it, but the truth is: "Time, will tell!"

Saul enters the scene against a particular background of

transition. Samuel, who was invested by the God of Israel with the three-fold office of judge, prophet, and priest, had become old, and his sons whom he had made judges over Israel, walked not in his ways. They had turned aside after lucre; took bribe, and perverted judgment. Consequently, all the elders of Israel gathered themselves together and came unto Samuel. They requested that he make them a king to judge them like all the nations, because he, Samuel, was old and his sons walked not in his ways. Samuel took this request of the people for a king as a personal indictment and as a rejection of his leadership.

Have you ever noticed that the unconsecrated and world-loving are ever ready to criticize and condemn those who have stood fearlessly for God and right? If in fact a defect is seen in one whom the Lord has entrusted with great responsibilities, then all his former devotion is forgotten, when an effort is made to silence his voice and influence.

However, as he normally does, **Samuel presented the matter to the Lord**. The Lord comforted and reassured him, that it was not a rejection of his leadership, but a rejection of the Lord as their leader because they no longer wanted the Lord to reign over them. (Could it likewise be true of you that you no longer want God to be your leader? If so, you, like Saul are in the danger zone.) The Lord told Samuel to go ahead with their request and to select a king.

When we want something very badly, including that which is not good for us, God in His wisdom may permit us to get it. This is because He respects our choice: good or bad. He also knows that the unfolding of the consequences (effects) sometimes serves to awaken in us how sinful the human heart can be, to lead us to accept His will for us, even though we would have suffered immensely in the process.

The Lord communicated to Samuel guidelines and instructions for selecting the new king. He also informed him of the manner of the king that would rule over them and the desire and nature of the kingly office, the demands it would make on the people (their sons and their daughters) and the consequences of having a king rule over them. The consequences would be so grave that the people would cry out because of the oppression from their chosen king and that the Lord would not hear them in that day.

As God requested, Samuel related all these things to the people, but **they refused to obey** his voice as they wanted to **be like all the nations** around them that had kings. They wanted their king to judge them and to go before them to fight their battles. Having listened to the words of the people, Samuel rehearsed them before the Lord. And the Lord told him to make them a king.

The selection and anointing of Saul as king is most unique. The asses (donkeys) of his father were lost, and his father, Kish, sent him along with one of the servants to go with him in search of the asses.[267] Unable to find the asses after much journeying and searching, Saul tells the servant that it is time to return less his father stop caring for the asses and become concerned about them. He decides to return to the city wherein he remembers that there is a prophet of God, also referred to as a seer, who could guide them in finding the asses. They decided to go to see the prophet and take a gift with them.

They enquired as they went along and were given directions to find the prophet of God, who was on his way to the place of worship to eat with invited guests. When they reached the city, Samuel had come out also to go up to the place of worship (also called high place). This is because God had told Samuel the previous day, that about this time He will send him a man of the land of Benjamin, whom he, Samuel, is to anoint as captain over the His people, Israel, that he (Saul) may save His people out of the hand of the Philistines. The Lord had also told him that He had looked upon the people as their cry had come up to Him.

As Saul approached, God told Samuel that this was the man, so Samuel recognized him. Not recognizing Samuel, Saul asked him for directions to the seer's house. Samuel told him that he is

---

[267]   See 1 Samuels 9:8.

the seer, and directed Saul to the place of worship where he would join him for a meal, and also informed him that the asses that he was in search of were found, and that he could depart on the morrow when he would tell him all that was in his heart, as well as that on him was all the desire of Israel. Saul gave a very humbly response. He said: *"Am not I a Benjamite, of the smallest of the tribes of Israel? And my family the least of all the families of the tribe of Benjamin?* Wherefore then speakest thou so to me?"*[268]

Then Samuel brought them into the dining room at the place of worship and guided them to sit in the main place (places of honour) among the thirty (30) persons that were gathered for the dinner. Samuel asked the cook to bring out the best piece of meat which he had previously given her. She brought it and gave it to Saul, and Saul ate with Samuel that day. After the meal, they returned from the place of worship to the city. And Samuel communed with Saul from the top of the house. Saul slept at Samuels' house that night. Early the next morning, Samuel told Saul on the roof that it's time to get up that he may get started on his way. They left together and as they were approaching the end of the city, Samuel requested that the servant to go ahead of them, so that he could relate to Saul the word of God.

Then Samuel took a vial of oil and poured it upon Saul's head, kissed him and said, *"Is it* not because the Lord has anointed you commander over His inheritance?" *1 Samuel 10:1 NKJV.* So Saul was chosen as Israel's first king. This changing of the guards was a simple anointing event: no fanfare, no beating of drums, no parades, no crowd of hundreds or thousands of guests, no noisy gun salute; just Saul and the prophet Samuel in attendance, but watched by the heavenly intelligences.

What was going on in Saul's mind? He knew he was the smallest of the tribes of Israel, and that his family was likewise the least of all the families of the tribes of Benjamin. But did he know then that he was the tallest among the people, from shoulder upwards?

---

[268] 1 Samuel 9:21.

This anointing development was not the reason why he had left his father's house. He left on another assignment, **in obedience to his father's command** to find the asses which were lost. He came in contact, face to face, with the unexpected. What would you have done? How would you have reacted or responded? As to why God chose that quiet anointing service I may never know until I get to heaven. But I have to trust His wisdom and judgment because God knows and does what is best. Job puts in this way:

*"He does great things **past finding out**, Yes, wonders without number."*[269]

Then the Apostle Paul contributes the following:

*"**Oh, the depth of the riches both of the wisdom and knowledge of God!** How unsearchable are His judgments and His ways **past finding out**!"*[270]

ii) Saul's election and confirmation

Despite the quiet unobtrusive, anointing service, and from all appearance, Saul was off to a good start. Then the prophet, Samuel, prophesied of three (3) encounters that Saul would face after departing from him, and told him that he should do as the occasion warrants **for God was with him.**[271] Did you get that point? "God was with him."

The third encounter involved meeting a company of prophets coming down from the place of worship (high place) with a psaltery, a tabret (tambourine), a pipe, and a harp. The company of prophets shall prophesy, and that he, Saul, would prophesy because the **Spirit of the Lord would come upon him, and he shall be turned into another man.**

Commenting on this third encounter, Ellen G. White states:

---

269 Job 9:10.
270 Romans 11:33.
271 1 Samuel 10: 2-7.

The Lord would not leave Saul to be placed in a position of trust without divine enlightenment. He was to have a new calling, and the Spirit of the Lord came upon him. The effect was that he was changed into a new man. **The Lord gave Saul a new spirit,** *other thoughts,* **other aims and desires than he previously had.** *This enlightenment, with the spiritual knowledge of God, placing on him on vantage ground, was to* **bind his will to the will of Jehovah."**[272]

In fact the Bible tells us in 1 Samuel 10:9 that when he turned his back to go from Samuel, *"**God gave him another heart"** and all the things that were prophesied by Samuel came to pass that day.

Now Saul, the new king must be presented to the people. So, Samuel called the people together unto the Lord to Mizpeh. He recounted how the Lord God had led them over the years and delivered them out of Egypt and Egyptian bondage and despite all God's goodness to them, they had chosen to reject God as their leader and to have instead a king to rule over them. He asked the people to present themselves before the Lord by tribes and by thousands. When he had called all the tribes to come near, the tribe of Benjamin was taken, and when by families, the family of Matri was taken, and Saul, the son of Kish was taken.

But, ironically, when they sought for Saul, he could not be found. Could it be that stage fright, the reality dawning on him, and shyness and timidity were all caving in on him? They enquired of the Lord, and the Lord responded that he had hidden himself behind the baggage. They ran and fetched him.

When he stood among the people, he was "more than a head taller than anyone else." Samuel presented Saul to the people and said:

---

[272] Ellen G. White, Letter12a, 1888.

212

> *"See ye him whom the Lord hath chosen, that there is **none like him** among all the people?" "And all the **people shouted**, and said, **God save the king. 25** Then Samuel told the people the manner of the kingdom, and **wrote** it in a book, and laid it up before the Lord. And Samuel sent all the people away, every man to his house."*[273]

So, Saul received all the confirmation that anyone in that position could have hoped for, perhaps even exceeding his best expectation. This was indeed, not only a historic moment, but also a defining moment in the life of the people of Israel. Never before did they have a king. Never before had he served in such a position of trust and honour.

But it was also significant for two (2) other reasons outlined herein below.

a) The weight of responsibility and accountability that would rest upon his shoulders, notwithstanding the fact that he was entering into uncharted paths and untested waters.
a1) His level of responsibility would be proportionate to the level of his knowledge. Like other persons in positions of power, any mistakes that he made would have huge consequences. Stephen Cover, author of The Seven Habits of Highly Effective People, defines "Responsibility" as "your chosen response to what happens to you in life."
a2) His level of accountability would likewise be proportionate to the level of his responsibility.

Accountability is giving account to someone or an authority who entrusted you with responsibility for resources at your disposal for the effective and efficient carrying out of the roles and function you have been entrusted with. To reject, downplay, or

---

[273] 1 Samuel 10:24-25.

underestimate the importance of accountability is to embrace irresponsibility, which is anchored in egocentricity, bigotry, and anarchy. This is applicable for all persons in positions of leadership and authority. Furthermore, the greater the position of a leader, the bigger is the impact of the leaders' decisions. So too, it must be for Saul and for all those who choose a leadership by exception rather than leadership by principle and example. In a similar fashion, we are accountable to God as to what we do with His Love Language.

When Lucifer, the first sinner, (who began his diabolical mission with the angels that were under his command), sinned (cause) in Heaven, and therefore, by his own choice became the great dragon, the serpent, the Devil and Satan (effect), one-third of the angels-hitherto sinless beings in Heaven chose to sympathize with him and conjoined in his sin. This is clearly an evidence of the impact that the decisions of those in exalted positions have had, and can have, on others including peers, lesser mortal and subordinates. And so, Lucifer, who had made himself into a devil, and by so doing embarked on a path of no return, apparently not knowing the devastating downhill path (including making war against God, sinister and diabolical plots to kill Jesus) where it would lead. Having forsaken all council and rebuke from God, Lucifer was unfit to remain in heaven having disqualified himself from further tenancy and residence there. God, who could no longer trust him with honour and supremacy, rightfully cast him out from Heaven and barred him from gaining any re-entry there.[274]

Consequently, Saul too, like other **leaders** (including those of the cloth), **must be held to an extremely high standard of rectitude.** When we reject or fight against accountability and

---

[274] See Revelation 12:7-10, 17, and Review and Herald, January 28, 1909.

or efforts to enthrone accountability, we by our own actions are revealing the intent and will of our hearts, and that we are unfit for leadership. We must, therefore, be held accountable, and be removed from our positions to save us from ourselves, and to safeguard the integrity of the office as well as to send a signal message to those that would choose to follow in our misguided course of spiritual ineptitude in judgment and sin. We may recall that Moses, the prophet and servant of God, was denied entering the earthly Canaan because he struck the rock in the presence of the people, disobeying God's explicit commandment to speak to the rock. This is another example to show that God does mean what He says.[275]

b)   His (Saul) **greatest**, consistent **and on-going test** would be **how he related to God's Commandments** especially as exemplified in his destruction of the Amalekites and ridding Israel of idolatry and witchcraft.

b1) God was disappointed with Israel for wanting a king to be like all nations. He wanted His people to **be above all nations,** and **not like them** as a result of loving and obeying Him and all His commandments (component of God's Love Language). One of the specific commandments of God that was given to the Children of Israel upon entering the Land of Promise was to destroy the Amalekites, who had no respect for God. They were enemies of God's people. They were descendants of Amalek, who was a descendant of Esau, who was born unto Timna and Esau'a son, Eliphaz, who Esau had with Adah, one of his three wives. (Read more about this in Genesis 36:9-14,Numbers 24: 19-21, and Deuteronomy 25:16-19). The Amalekites were constantly attacking, fighting, and trying to destroy God's people. Their major ambition was to rid the world of all Jews and to return the planet to idolatry, paganism

---

[275]   See Numbers 20:7-12.

and barbarism. **Saul was to be tested in how he related to God's commandment which required destroying in battle the entire nation of the Amalekites** down to the last cow. See the subheading below "Saul's sparing of Agag, king of the Amalekites".

b2) The Bible describes rebellion as the sin of witchcraft, and stubbornness (Saul's major problem) as iniquity and idolatry.[276] In fact, in Israel, King Saul, put to death those that were involved in this sinful practice. King Saul was also tested on this subject, as is outlined below under the subheading: Saul seeking counsel of the witch of Endor."

iii) Saul's transition and the consequences

Not withstanding the challenges, Saul had great potential and capabilities. E.G. White commenting on this subject writes:

> *Saul had a mind and influence capable of governing a kingdom,* **if** *his powers had been submitted to the control of God, but the very* **endowments that qualified him for doing good could be used by Satan,** *when* **surrendered** *to his power, and would enable him to exert widespread influence for evil. He could be* **more sternly vindictive,** *more injurious and determined in prosecuting his unholy designs, than could others,* **because** *of the superior powers of mind and heart that had been given him of God.*[277]

Another multimillion dollar question is: What happened to Saul; what caused this great transition or turn around in his life that he, after rising from humble beginnings to kingship, could have descended from head of state of one the greatest kingdoms

---

[276] 1 Samuel 15:23.
[277] Ellen G. White, Signs of the Times (ST) Oct. 19, 1888.

on earth at the time, to the point where he was so depressed that he would later take his own life, and was subsequently beheaded? Read on!

The commentary above gives us some insight into the answer. The Bible and life experiences teach us that we become the servants of whosoever, by our own choice, we yield ourselves servants to obey. And either way we choose (cause), each has its own set of very far reaching rewards or consequences (effects). Here are some things that we can be sure about.

a) Having a mind and influence capable of governing a kingdom is no guarantee of ending up on God's side and getting eternal life.

b) Those God given endowments may be used either way, either for good or for evil, each with a difference outcome (law of cause and effect).

c) There are two contenders only in the battle for our mind and influence, heart, soul, spirit, and strength; and they are God and Satan. The first is God, our Creator, sustainer, redeemer, and friend. He existed before the world began and before man was created. The other, the devil and Satan, is a created being, who is the originator of sin.

As outlined by Moses in the Genesis account, and subsequently by John the Revelator, the devil is a liar and deceiver, who wants us to distrust God and side instead with him, and by so doing to deceive ourselves that we will accomplish more and rise to a higher plane of existence. And for a time he can make it happen (or appear to happen); that's why he is so deceptive. But he showed his true character when he planned and deceived the angels in Heaven that sinned. He also deceived humans and carried out his orchestrated designs to have Jesus crucified on the cross. But Jesus endured the humiliation to save us and is now in Heaven. But Satan and all who side with him will be destroyed at the close of the millennium in the fire that was prepared for him and the angels who sinned and together were cast out of Heaven.

d) The critical decision to take (and step to follow) is to align ourselves on the right side, God's side, and in obedience to His commandments.

Yes, **Saul's** sinful **fall** occurred over a period of time and as a result of his **repeated disobedience to God's explicit commandments** and repeated decisions to allow the devil to use him to exalt himself. In many ways, his life involved highs and lows, sinning and repenting, until the cup of his iniquity was full and the Holy Spirit of God, which leads into all truth, left him. He started off on a good footing, with God changing him into another and better person. However, his desire to please his ego and (perhaps thinking that like Judas, he was so smart and could out-smart the others) his fascination with having his own way and his own love language, as well as his pride, and position of power all led to his eventual downfall as he chose to let the devil use him. This was as a result of having refused to learn from his mistakes and God's guidance.

Look, for example, at how he mistreated David and tried to kill him after he defeated the Philistine giant, Goliath. This was because the people sang that Saul had slain his thousand but that David is ten thousand. After that failed attempt, look at how for a number of years he continually tried to kill David, using his soldiers to hunt him down like a bird, day and night. Why? Because God had rejected him from being king and chosen David to be his successor.

But why did God reject King Saul?

There are many reasons that can be cited from the Scriptures, but three (3) significant ones are stated for our learning, that we don't make the same error. For indeed, we do err if we don't know the Scriptures nor the power of God.

i) Saul's presumption at Gilgal[278]

Saul had been king for some three years. The Philistines, one of the enemies of the nation Israel, gathered themselves together at Michmash to fight with Israel, having a contingent of 30,000 chariots, 6,000 horsemen, and with people as the sands of the sea. The men of Israel recognizing that they were outnumbered and in a strait, hid themselves in caves, in thickets, in rocks, in high places and in pits, and some went over Jordan to the land of Gad and Gilead. Although Saul came to Gilgal, all the people followed him trembling. He tarried there seven days according to the time set by Samuel. But Samuel was delayed and so the people were scattered from him.

Then Saul was impatient and acted rashly, requesting that he be given a burnt offering, and peace offerings. His actions were truly **rash and foolish** because **the offering of sacrifices was a role reserved by God for the priests only.** But Saul proceeded and offered the burnt offering. Soon after he offered the burnt offering, Samuel came. Samuel asked him what he had done. He gave an answer riddled with scapegoats, as he stated that:

a) he saw that the people were scattered from him;
b) Samuel did not arrive within the agreed seven (7) day period;
c) the Philistines had gathered themselves together at Michmash and that they will come down upon him to Gilgal, and
d) because he had not made supplication unto the Lord.

Notice Saul's conclusion: *"I have forced myself therefore, and offered a burnt offering."* (verse 12) Samuel's response in pointing out his error and sin of disobedience was quick, candid, and explicit. Samuel said to Saul:

Thou hast done foolishly: *thou hast* **not kept the commandment of the Lord thy God,** *which he commanded thee: for*

---

[278] 1 Samuel 13:1-14.

now would the Lord have established thy kingdom upon Israel forever. ***But now thy kingdom shall not continue:*** *the Lord hath sought him a man after his own heart, and the Lord hath commanded him to be captain over his people, because* ***thou hast not kept that which the Lord commanded thee.***

Although this is the first indication of Saul's rejection as King, the prophet's message is loud and clear, and the reason is explicitly stated. The prophet's revelation also clearly points out to Saul the heart of the matter.

a) He acted foolishly;

b) He had not kept the commandment of the Lord;

c) To refuse to keep the commandment of the Lord is equivalent to acting foolishly;

d) His foolish action revealed the content of his heart;

e) Saul's heart was not right as God's was not at its centre.

f) Saul's reign was to end prematurely because of his own wrong choosing.

g) When God rejects a leader who refuses to carry out His will of obedience to His commandment, He will replace him with someone whose heart is right with God, even though in the eyes and mind of the deposed leader, it may appear otherwise.

h) Although the pronouncement of the discontinuance of Saul's reign was made the moment of Saul's disobedience, yet his removal from office was not immediate.

Like at the time of the flood, there was a (seven day) period of "probation", but sadly that period did not witness any meaningful transformation, remorse or genuine repentance on the part of the Saul. He should have learnt from this experience, but he chose to go further on the downward path of jealousy, persecution and rebellion.

Saul's sparing of Agag, king of the Amalekites[279]

When we do something that is wrong and someone comes to point out our error, wisdom dictates that we should be remorseful and learn from our mistake so that we may become better persons. Sadly, however, sometimes imprudence seems to be easier and more fashionable, and many don't choose to learn from their mistakes. King Saul was a typical example. Instead of responding favourably to the reproof from Samuel, the prophet and priest of God, he chose to sink deeper into the "I" sickness syndrome. Let's pickup the story in 1 Samuel 15.

Samuel rehearsed for Saul his obedience to God's commandment in anointing Saul as King over His people, Israel. **He instructed Saul to heed the word of the Lord by smiting Amalek and destroying all that they had including man and woman, infant and suckling, and animals: ox, sheep, camel and ass.** The prophet reminded the King how Amalek mistreated the Israelites when they were liberated from Egypt.

Commenting on this battle with the Amalekites E.G. White, writes:

> *God did not wish His people to possess anything which belonged to the Amalekites, for His curse rested upon them and their possessions.* ***He designed that they should have an end,*** *and that His people should not preserve anything for themselves which He had cursed. He also wished the nations to see the end of that people who had defied Him,* ***and to mark that they were destroyed by the very people that they had despised.*** *They were not to destroy them to add to their own possessions, or to get glory to themselves, but to fulfill the Word of the Lord spoken in regard to Amalek.*[280]

---

[279] 1 Samuel 15:1-35.
[280] Ellen G. White, Spirit of Prophecy (1SP), Volume 1, page 364.

*That wicked people [the Amalekites] were dwelling in God's world, the house which He had prepared for His faithful, **obedient** children. Yet they appropriated His gifts to their own use, without one thought of the Giver. The more blessings He poured upon them, the more boldly they transgressed against Him. Thus they continued to pervert His blessings and abuse His mercy.*[281]

In response, King Saul gathered his troops, 200,000 footmen and 10,000 men of Judah and went to battle with the Amalekites. He met with what appears to be initial success, for he destroyed "all the people" with the edge of the sword. He smote the Amalekites **bu**t he and the people spared Agag, the king of the Amalekites, and the best of the sheep, oxen, fatlings, the lambs, and all that was good, and would not utterly destroy them; but everything that was vile and refuse, that they destroyed (verse 9). Strangely, but of course not surprisingly, Saul was satisfied that he had done well.

Meanwhile, the prophet, Samuel, may have been a waiting there turn of Kind Saul to get an up-to-date report of the outcome of the battle. This seems to have been taking some time. And of course, God who is not like man, must have mused to Himself and said, "I better get to Samuel first, because Saul, like some other persons who love praise of men above their love for God, is preparing a report riddled with lies and deception to give to Samuel." So, God spoke unto Samuel, His servant as follows: *"It **repenteth me** that I have set up Saul to be king: for **he is turned back from following me**, and hath **not performed my commandments**."*[282]

These words are familiar to the prophet. But, he can't believe that Saul had gotten worst. He is so disappointed. He is so grieved that he cried unto the Lord all night.

---

[281] Ellen G. White, Signs of the Times (ST) August 24, 1882.
[282] 1 Samuel 15:11,13.

Samuel arose early in the morning and is on his way to meet Saul, when he got word that Saul is also on his way to meet the prophet. Can you imagine Saul's illusory word of greeting to the prophet?

*"Blessed be thou of the Lord: **I have performed the commandment of the Lord.**"*

Can you imagine if you were Samuel for a moment, what you would do, if after hearing that kind of verdict from God regarding the disobedient Saul, that he approaches you with that monstrosity of a greeting about performing the commandment of the Lord? Would you laugh? Would you cry? Would you chase him away or would you feel sorry for him? Would you say: "what an audacity?" Or would you say: "what level of presumption?" Was the king's case hopeless at this point? Would you conclude that God's review, assessment, summary and conclusion is bang on target?

According to E.G. White, stubbornness made Saul's case hopeless. In her comments in Review and Herald, May 7, 1895, she wrote:

*"It was **Saul's stubbornness** that made his case hopeless, and yet how many venture to follow his example. The Lord in mercy sends words of reproof to save the erring, but **they will not submit to be corrected.** They **insist that they have done no wrong,** and thus resist the Spirit of God."*

Listen to the wisdom in the words of the prophet of God, wrapped in tact and humility of a divine nature, as he addressed King Saul. He neither accuses nor condemns him! He uses the question method of Jesus, the Master questioner and Teacher of all times.

"What meaneth then this bleating of the sheep in mine ears, and the lowing of the oxen which I hear?"

By asking a question, the prophet of God, provides an opportunity for the king to explain himself. The king could choose to confess his sin and error of stubbornness or he could seek to cover it up, defend or justify his action, or find someone to blame, in an attempt (futile of course) to shift responsibility for his action and thereby attempt to veil and avoid accountability. What would you have done if you were in Saul's pickle? Would you come clean? Or would you do as some other leaders do, pass the buck or blame to someone(s) lower in rank in a ghastly attempt to veil the truth and to avoid embarrassment and punishment when you are caught, found wanting in the area of accountability as it relates to God's Love language? Honestly speaking, just what would you do? Well, let's see exactly what Saul, the first King of the combined Kingdoms of Israel, did! This is his response to the prophet's question in 1 Samuel 15:15:

> *"And Saul said,* **They** *have brought them from the Amalekites: for* **the people** *spared the best of the sheep and of the oxen, to sacrifice unto the Lord thy God; and the* **rest we have** *utterly destroyed."*

Well, were you correct in your answer? Were you that perceptive? Well, if you did, you read his heart as that of an open book. For the king once again played right into the hand of the devil and Satan. His answer revealed the humanity of man when not connected to God. For, instead of standing up as a true Trojan, admitting his error like a true leader, and choosing the high path of confession, surrender and forgiveness, he fell right into the trap of Satan, who by this time had the king as one of his true allies.

If you are a leader, there are times when you must lead from the front. If you are a church leader, do you lead your congregation into obedience to God's Love Language? If you are a follower, a member, do you encourage your leader(s) to help you obey God Love Language?

Saul was the commander of the armed forces of Israel. He must give the orders. He is not just another soldier. This task to destroy all the Amalekites and their possessions perhaps may have been **his greatest moment of opportunity** to win the visible, **outward, physical, and military battle** against the Amalekites and the unobtrusive, **inward battle with self and stubbornness** and thereby redeem himself in the eyes of God and Samuel. How then can he surrender his responsibility, authority, and accountability to the people, whom he is supposed to be leading, while simultaneously trying to rationalize it? This is indeed another moment of weakness for him. The statement by E. G. White: "*He who is weak in a crisis is weak indeed*" is indeed applicable here. **The king's answer revealed that he cannot continue as leader for he is too weak** when he ought to be strong on the things of God and on side of God. If you are weak in a moment of crisis when you ought to be strong, you are weak indeed, because it is that very moment that tests your mettle and reveals the strength or weakness of your character. But now, is Saul really about to fail the acid test of all time?

What follows next is a very interesting exchange of how God operates, even though in this case through His emissary, Samuel. It brings out the reasonable reasoning nature of God. For as we review the texts, we see how the prophet, judge and priest Samuel, reminds Saul of his divine appointment, and from where God took him and brought him, from humble beginnings, and gave him an opportunity to carry out God's command to destroy the Amalekites. He also told him about God's reason for the command that is, because of their sins, and provided another opportunity for him to explain himself and to give his side of the story by specifically asking him the open-ended question as to why he did not obey the commandment of the Lord.

Signs of the Times carried the following commentary by E.G. White:

> *Here Samuel point out the reason for Saul's appointment to the throne of Israel. He had a humble opinion of his own capabilities, and was willing to be instructed. When the divine choice fell upon him, he was deficient in knowledge and experience, and had, with many good qualities, serious defects of character.*

But the Lord granted him the Holy Spirit as a guide and helper, and placed him in a position where he could develop the qualities requisite for a ruler of Israel.

*Should he trust to his own strength and judgment, Saul would move impulsively, and would commit grave errors. But **if he would remain humble**, seeking constantly to be guided by divine wisdom, and advancing as the providence of God opened up the way, he would be enabled to discharge the duties of his high position with success and honour. Under the influence of **divine grace**, every good quality would be gaining strength, while evil traits would as steadily lose their power. This is the work which the Lord proposes to do for all who consecrate themselves to Him*[283]

As we discover, Saul chose to trust his own strength and judgment, and moved impulsively and defended self repeatedly, when he was knowingly disobedient to God's commandment and obviously in the wrong. In the reasoning with Samuel and Saul introduced above, here is Samuel's question and notice carefully the answer given by Saul, and Samuel's response in the same 1 Samuel 15:19-23, 28-33.

Samuel: *"**Wherefore then didst thou not obey the voice of the Lord**, but didst fly upon the spoil, and didst evil in the sight of the Lord?"*

Saul: *"Yea, **I have obeyed the voice of the Lord**, and have gone the way which the Lord sent me, and have brought Agag, the king of Amalek, and have utterly destroyed the Amalekites. **But the people** took of the spoil, sheep and oxen, the chief of the things which should have been utterly destroyed, to sacrifice unto the Lord thy God in Gilgal."*

---

[283]   Signs of the Times, Issue September 7, 1882.

Amazing! The Lord sends his word of reproof through His prophet, Samuel, to Saul, the King. But the king is still defiant. He refuses to accept the message of reproof and submit to be corrected. He defiantly insists that he has done no wrong. He stands foolishly firm and fatally proud in his stubbornness and sin, as if the frequency by which wrong is repeated makes it right. Then he tries to twist the prophet's arm and attempts to appease God, by what some would call a convincing but monstrous **"thriller."** You have to get it, that is, what the king said!

Saul says it: *"But the **people** took of the spoil, sheep and oxen, the chief of the things which should have been utterly destroyed, **to sacrifice unto the Lord thy God** in Gilgal.*

Get Saul's desperate line of reasoning:

a) The people (foot soldiers, if you may) made the decision, not the King.
b) The people took the spoils, sheep, oxen, and the chief things which should have been utterly destroyed. The king is admitting his disobedience but in a subtle way(as he is one of the people). You will miss it, if you are not a keen observer. How did the king know that these should have been destroyed? The answer is easy and simple. It was part of the commandment that the Lord communicated to him through His prophet, Samuel.
c) So why did (he permit or not prevent) the people take the spoils which should have been utterly destroyed? Here is Saul's answer and hypothesis: **"to sacrifice unto the Lord thy God** in Gilgal."

As we would say in common parlance, this one "takes the pillow and the case." If the things should have been destroyed, how then can they be taken to offer sacrifice unto the Lord? It just does not make any sense. Obviously something went awry with the reasoning and thinking of Saul. Or he thinks that God is a dolly and can't think, reason, or analyse, and make a good judgment.

Paradoxical reasoning if you may! When we depart from God and reject His commandments (i.e. God's Love Language), that is exactly what happens. Like Saul, we are convinced in the logic of our argument to defend our indefensible position and mannequin-like posture. Saul allows himself to be captured and totally deceived by the devil. But the true prophet of God, Samuel, is not deceived. He sees right through Saul and the folly of his ploy to use sacrifice as a bait to catch God, like fishes which are caught by biting on baits. Genuine people of God have the gift of discernment, which they receive from God, and they can quickly reprove those in error and the folly of their ways.

Before turning to Samuel's further response, consider the following:

i) When God's commandment says remember the Sabbath day to keep it holy, and you choose a day of your own making that pleases you, one that requires no sacrifice, are you not behaving like Saul?

ii) When God's commandment says thou shalt not steal, and you chose to work on God's holy time, the Sabbath, thereby robbing God of His time, and the quality time that you should spend with Him, are you not forwarding an argument and hypothesis like Saul to defend your thinking, reasoning, and position?

iii) When God's commandments forbid fornication and adultery, and you participate in premarital and or extramarital sex, concubinage, or trial marriage, overlooking the bewitching power and spell of sin to keep you in error, are you not behaving just like Saul?

iv) How would you like the people of God (who know what is right according to the word of God in such matters) to respond to you? And what would your response be?

The prophet Samuel had a well-reasoned response for Saul that went straight to the heart of the matter and shattered Saul's mask of lip service to God. Look at his response.

Samuel: *"Hath the Lord as great delight in burnt offerings and sacrifices, as in* **obeying the voice of the Lord?** *Behold,* **to obey is better than sacrifice,** *and to hearken than the fat of rams. For rebellion is as the sin of witchcraft, and* **stubbornness** *is as iniquity and idolatry. Because thou hast rejected the word of the Lord, he hath* **also rejected thee from being king.** *"*[284]

This is a very serious indictment on the king and sounds like the last sentence on the last page in the last chapter of his life. His ploy is unmasked and lies bare before his very eyes. Some invaluable and heart searching truths are brought to his attention like the midday sun that he cannot deny.

a) **The Lord delights greater in obedience to His voice** than in burnt offerings and sacrifices.

b) **Obedience is better than sacrifice**, as not all sacrifice is acceptable, clearly not the ones from the Amalekites source, which God had already rejected, and commanded that they be destroyed.

c) God, through his servant, the prophet, Samuel, gets to the core of Saul's sin for what it really is:

Stubbornness! His ego was bigger than his love for, and obedience to, God.

d) Saul thought that his stubbornness (doing as he pleased even with God) was a small or light matter; but God and the prophet, Samuel, thought otherwise and placed it in the category of sin in which it really and rightfully belongs: **iniquity and idolatry.** The first of the Ten Commandments places God as the first and only true God, while the second states that we should not make

---

[284]   *1 Samuel 15:22.*

any images to worship them. Saul had failed the test in regards to these two commandments, because by choosing his own way and love language, and rejecting obedience to God, he placed himself above God. In doing so, he also made himself, his ego and stubbornness, an image and an alternate god, which he obviously revered above and instead of the true God, and which could not help him in his greatest moment of defeat. So, God had to stop him in his tracks, as among other things, a lesson for all who would follow, that you cannot fight against God and win.

e) Saul's action and his words showed that he had rejected the Word/commandment of the Lord. So the Lord also rejected him from being king, as he was no longer representing God, neither as king of Israel, nor Lord of his life.

Commenting on Samuel's response to Saul (in 1 Samuel 15:22-23), the Spirit of Prophecy (1SP) and Ellen G. White Manuscript (MS) carried the following respective statements:

> *"God required of His people obedience rather than sacrifice. All the riches of the earth were His. The cattle upon a thousand hills belonged to Him. He did not require the spoils of a corrupt people, upon whom His curse rested, even to their utter extinction, to be presented to Him to prefigure the holy Saviour, as a lamb without blemish." (ISP 365)*

> *"The first king of Israel proved **a failure**, because **he set his will above the will of God**. Through the prophet, Samuel, the **Lord instructed Saul that as king of Israel his course of action must be one of strictest integrity.** Then God would bless his government with prosperity. But Saul **refused to make obedience to God his first consideration,***

*and the principles of heaven the government of his
conduct. He died in dishonor and despair.*"[285]

Now Saul hears the prophet's pronouncement. It is crystal
clear. There is no mincing of words. It unmasks the king's veil of
ploy, hoax and baits, and gets straight to the heart of the matter:
the king's ego and stubbornness. The king is convinced beyond
any shadow of reasonable doubt of the enormity of his sin and
guilt. Like Judas, who betrayed Jesus, the Pearl of Righteousness,
and who out of his embarrassment rather than remorse cried that
he had betrayed innocent blood, the king said: *"I have sinned:
for I have transgressed the commandment of the Lord, and thy
words: because I feared the people, and obeyed their voice. Now
therefore, I pray thee, pardon my sin, and turn again with me, that I
may worship the Lord."*

Even at this point the king just didn't seem to get it, nor
fully understand the message of rejection from the Lord. He again
blames the people for his action, as if he is in denial. How blinding
can sin get! It is darker than the darkness of midnight. In spite of all
this, the king was still persistent in ego pleasing, and more desirous
to save face than in genuine repentance for his sin and wrong.
Genuine, godly sorrow for sin could possibly be cited like this:

> *"I have sinned against God and in thy sight in that I
> have knowingly disobeyed God's commandment and
> am no more worthy to be king; forgive and pray God
> for me that He may cleanse my heart from its dross
> of self-will and stubbornness, so that I may again be
> obedient and trustworthy."*

But, as is the king's case, like the case of so many unrepentant
sinners, **sin is a tyrant and a bully that is bent on having its own
way.** This is due to the fact that sin is callous, evil, unconscionable,

---

285   The Spirit of Prophecy (1SP) Volume 1, page 36, and
       Ellen G. White Manuscript (MS) page 151, 1899.

persistently demanding to have its own way, and its pound of flesh, that it really does not own. So the king, not only blames the people for his foolish, sinful action, but in the same breath is demanding and dictating to the prophet that the prophet should:

a) *pray for him;*
b) *pardon his sin;and*
c) *turn with him and go and worship the Lord.*

But this is an impossible request that the prophet in his rightful and sanctified mind could not honour, as God had already rejected Saul. When the prophet refused to honour his request, repeating that the Lord had rejected him from being king over Israel, Saul held unto the skirt of the mantle of the prophet as he turns away from him, causing it to rent. This is typical to what a thief would do: demand money from its victim, and when the request is not met, the thief then tries to harm the victim with whatever weapon he/she has with him/ her. But the prophet of God is neither afraid nor daunted. The prophet seized the moment to drive home the nail. For he told Saul, the king,that

> *"the Lord hath rend the kingdom of Israel from thee this day, and hath given it to a neighbour of thine, that is better than thou. And also the Strength of Israel will not lie nor repent: for he is not a man, that he should repent."*

By stating that *"the Strength of Israel will not lie nor repent: for he is not a man, that he should repent,"* the prophet was reaffirming two important points about God and His decision on the matter:

a) God, who is *"the Strength of Israel"* means exactly what He says. And because the judgment pronounced upon Saul was true, fair and final, it could not be changed. Therefore, God is not lying and will not repent or retract what has gone out of His mouth....

b) God is divine, not like humans who lie, change, or go back on their word.

By doing that affirmation, the prophet was also helping the king to understand that because God's decision in the matter of the judgment pronounced upon him was final (Psalm 89:34) and unchangeable, asking him to pardon and worship, was an immensely futile request, like pouring water on a bird's back and expecting the water not to run off, but to settle or absorb on the bird's back instead. But even then, the king didn't quite get it. Oh **when we are sold out to the devil, we just don't seem to understand it, and how it affects our interactions and relations with others**! We just don't seem to know when to stop.

It's like driving in the traffic. We see the red stoplight in front of us because we are physically sighted. But instead of stopping, we drive right through the red light, only to find that we are in a serious collision with an unsuspecting, innocent driver's vehicle coming from the perpendicular direction. It's just like that in the spiritual realm. The traffic lights are like God's commandments. They tell us when to go, do what is right; and when to stop, refrain from breaking God's commandments. When our love and obedience to God are impaired, it means that we are not spiritually sighted as we ought to be. So like that driver, driving through the traffic light when it is on red, we likewise drive through God's commandment when it says, refrain from disobeying Him.

So, Saul in his persistent, hardened heart of self-will and stubbornness, drove again through the stoplight, when he should have stopped, having ignored all the previous warning signs. He repeats to the prophet and further demands: *" I have sinned: yet* **honour me now**, *I pray thee,* **before the elders of my people, and before Israel**, *and turn again with me,* **that I may worship the Lord thy God**.*"* Can you believe it? Yes, you can! The king wants honour in the presence of the elders of the people and before Israel. We get it! We must! You see, Saul's action openly and clearly revealed the condition of his heart for all to see, including the sinless beings in heaven. **He wants honour,**not humility; he wants **the praise of men,** not the surrender to God. Like an impatient, spoilt child, he wants it now! *He wants what is due to God.* He is more concerned about the external, an incessant obsession with ostentation, than with the internal condition of his heart, and love to God and obedience His commandments. What a pity, what a shame! We are not told in 1 Samuel 15 that the prophet ever honoured him according to his request and demand. But the prophet turned and Saul worshipped the Lord. So not all worship of God is true, nor acceptable to God. This part of **the story ended** with statements that the prophet, Samuel:

a) Asked for Agag, then killed him after stating the reason for doing so;
b) Came no more to see Saul until the day of his death.

> *Then said Samuel, Bring ye hither to me Agag the king of the Amalekites. And Agag came unto him delicately. And Agag said, Surely the bitterness of death is past. And Samuel said,* **As thy sword hath made women childless, so shall thy mother be childless among women. And Samuel hewed Agag in pieces before the Lord in Gilgal.**"

Pretended Righteous Used as a Cloak: "*Many who profess to be serving God are in the same position as Saul, - covering over ambitious projects, pride and display, with a garment of pretended righteousness. The Lord's cause is made a cloak to hide the deformity of injustice, but it makes the sin of tenfold greater enormity.*"[286]

---

[286] Manuscript of Ellen G. White, (MS) 1a, 1890.

Self-justification Keeps One in Darkness:

Those whose deeds are evil, will not come to light, lest their deeds should be reproved and their real characters revealed. ***If they continue in the path of transgression, and sever themselves entirely from the Redeemer, stubbornness, and sullenness, and a*** *spirit of revenge will take possession of them, and they will say to their own souls, 'Peace, peace,' when there is every reason that they should be alarmed, for their steps are directed toward destruction. As Saul resisted the reproofs of the servant of the Lord, this spirit took possession of him. He defied the Lord, he defied His servant, and his enmity toward David was the outworking of the murderous spirit that comes into the heart of those who justify themselves in the face of their guilt.*[287]

Saul seeking counsel of the witch of Endor[288]

This third episode with Saul is another very sad and regrettable story that comes just prior to the very end of Saul's life. It is recorded in 1 Samuels 28, among other things, for our learning so that we don't make the same or similar mistake. Again, like the one cited in ii) immediately above, it reveals what can befall anyone who knowingly, willfully and deliberately, decides to act contrary to the commandments of the Lord and refuse His love language. Unlike, the other two stories in Saul's life recorded in this chapter (1 Samuel 15), Satan and his angels enter the picture and they communicate with the living while simultaneously deceiving some to believe that he (Satan) has the power to communicate with the dead. But understand this; ***to communicate with the dead must mean power to resurrect the dead.*** My dear reader, make no mistake on this particular point; **God has not given to the devil and Satan any power to resurrect the dead.**

---

[287] Signs of the Times, page 22, 1888.
[288] See 1 Samuel 28:3-25; Lev. 19:31.

I will try to succinctly outline the major points and messages that are pivotal to having a thorough understanding of the story in the context of the consequence of a refusal to practice God's Love Language.

a) Background and setting:

  i) The Philistines, one of the enemy nations of the Israelites, gathered their armies together for warfare, to fight against the Israelites in Gilboa.

  ii) Recall, the giant, Goliath, that cursed the God of the Israelites, whom David slew in the strength and power of the Lord, was from among the Philistines.

  iii) Israel's chances of winning any battle, including this one against the Philistines, was depended on their relationship with their God, who fought their battles for them, and not so much on their strength or military might. Significant in all of this, was the faithfulness of the king or leader of Israel to the Lord God.

  iv) The faithful prophet and priest of God, Samuel was now dead, and that communication, advice and counsel that Saul had with him while he was alive, no longer existed.

  v) Up to the time prior to this battle with the Philistines, King Saul, during his life time had put away out of the land those that had familiar spirits, and wizards.

  vi) Simply put, he put them to death, consistent with the commandment of the Lord that was given from during the time of Moses, and which states:

"Regard not them that have familiar spirits, neither seek after wizards, to be defiled by them: I am the Lord your God."[289]

vii)   The Israelites were outnumbered by their opponent, the Philistines, such that when Saul saw them he was afraid and his heart greatly trembled. The fearfulness and the trembling of Saul was not so much because he was numerically outnumbered by the opponent, but because he was at an all-time low spiritually with God, whom he had repeatedly disobeyed in order to have his own way.

viii)   Now he needed God more than ever and God's assurance of success. But, by his chosen waywardness and stubbornness, God was not responding tohim, neither by dreams, nor by Urim, nor by prophets. He was,therefore, in "deep waters", a real pickle, and in a prison of loneliness, desperate for a solution as to what to do.

b)   The attempted abominable solution:

It is said that a *"drowning man catches at a straw."* Well, what Saul did was worse than a drowning man catching at a straw. It is like a dog returning to its own vomit. Why? Because he, being living, seeks to get help from among the dead. But if the living can't help you, or if you refused to obey the living while they lived, how in the world are you likely to obtain more success from going to the dead? The wise man Solomon tells us the following:

*"For to him that is joined to **all** the living there is hope: for **a living dog is better** than **a dead lion.**"*[290]

---

289   *Leviticus 19:31.*
290   *Ecclesiastes 9:4.*

381

The fact that Saul tried this option, going to the dead, speaks volume about the low spiritual depth to which he had sunken.

But how was he going about this despicable solution?

He asked his servants to seek out a woman with a familiar spirit, one that he could go and see, visit, and inquire of, about the possible outcome of the imminent military battle. But, what he did not seem to realize, was that while he was asking for the assistance of his servants, he seemingly was unaware that he needed divine help to win the internal spiritual battle between the forces of good and evil, that were waging for the ultimate conquest of his heart. But the dye was cast! The outcome was determined. He had slipped too far on the downward path of stubbornness and self-destruct to retract and retrace his steps. Little did he seem to grapple with the reality that his chosen path would lead him face to face with the foe that he thought was his friend and ally, who was coaching and mentoring him, but to an untested and untried path to his own tragedy.

   c)   The problem and a way out

His servants found a woman with a familiar spirit located at Endor. But there is a problem! How is he going to see her? This must be carefully crafted and executed because it could set *"tongues to wagging"* and *"prating parrots to talk"* out of turn and ruin his plan. Any last mistake would be worse than the first. Imagine, some would proclaim: *"the high and mighty king of Israel is on his way to see a witch in a secluded village for a secret meeting, the living with the dead!"* This would make prime time news on all the top cable news network and TV channels.

"I must find a way out", he must have mused to himself. He must have discussed the trip and journey with his servants and top advisers. Imagine the possible response of his top advisor and communication specialist: *"you can't risk such a journey in the light of day. You have to do it in the night. But again, you cannot embark on*

such an external affairs mission in your regular royal regalia." Because this king has had such a long record of stubbornness, it must have taken much persuasion before he agreed to the strategy. He didn't seem to have any alternatives, so he agreed to comply (which was very unlike him), and using disguised raiment he went to Endor, accompanied by two men. As he went, he must have had a flash forward to Nicodemus' nocturnal journey.

Like Nicodemus, he came by night. But unlike Nicodemus, he disguised himself. Like Nicodemus, he was in search for answers to his questions. But unlike Nicodemus, hesought the wrong master and the wrong place. Both had moments of doubts and uncertainty. But the content of the information they both were seeking were materially different. Nicodemus would find the Master of all masters and gain eternal life. Saul would come in close contact with the Master of all deceivers, and the general of all the disobedient, and guarantee for himself eternal death.

    d)   The nocturnal arrival and meeting

Fortunately, for Saul the journey went "smoothly" as he travelled under the radar. He is at the destination with no fanfare. He meets with the witch, and without any procrastination, he presents his request.

> *"I pray thee, divine unto me by the familiar spirit,*
> *and bring me him up, whom I shall name unto thee."*

If you are a keen observer, you will or should notice a few important things right away:

    i)   This witch (like all the others) cannot truthfully tell the future as they have no connection with God. She was unable to discern that Saul would disguise himself and come to see her by night. This is very unlike what happened when Saul was to be anointed and when he had returned from the battle with the Amalekites. On both these occasions God revealed to his prophet,

Samuel, where Saul was and what he hath done, what he would say or ask of the prophet, and what he should say to him; and this was before and without him asking a single question of the prophet.

ii)   The woman recognized that she was deceived and was in fear of her life. Imagine that! Someone who works for the master deceiver does not recognize deception from one of her own master deceiver allies! *But why is this witch in fear of her life?* She is in fear of her life, because she knows that her witchcraft business is immoral and illegal and that she had been operating in a world of iniquity and witchcraft which God declared as being abominable to Him and that offenders are punishable by death. She declared that Saul put them to death! This she knew, so she was not in ignorance. But even at this point of making her disclosure, she did not recognize that it was the same king that was in her very presence.

iii) The outplaying of the drama of all dramas.
Saul used to put offenders to death. Now Saul seeks council from the offender in the abominable business. And of course, Saul is not operating as an undercover agent, as the plot in the story clearly reveals. What a drama! The upholder of the Law of God now cooperates with a known offender to break the law for personal and selfish motive. Oh, what travesty of spiritual responsibility, accountability, integrity! How much worse can it get? But the plot thickens!
Consider a parallel scenario. A pastor who chairs the church board attends the board meeting. At board meetings from time to time are presented the names of members who commit adultery, which is violation of the seventh commandment. At this particular meeting the name of one woman is presented for action. What is the

proposed action? Disfellowshipping from membership! The church board votes that the action be recommended to the next Church members' meeting. The members' meeting is called and the recommended action is voted and is recorded by the church clerk. One week later the pastor goes to visit his disfellowshipped female member. But instead of counseling with her, he offers her $10,000.00 to sleep (have sex) with him. She consents and they have a one night stand. This is repeated for a number of months over a two to three year period.

How much different is this from the story of Saul? This pastor "upholder" of the Law of God now just cooperated with a convicted breaker of the seventh commandment law for personal and selfish motive. Oh, what travesty of spiritual responsibility, accountability, integrity? What duplicity? Will he return to chair another board meeting? Should he? What should be done to him? How Saul-like can we be?

iv)   Amnesty guarantee and indemnity

Because the woman was not sure as to who it was that was requesting her to knowingly break the law,she sought for assurance of preservation of her life. She didn't know whether she was dealing with the police, who may have come to set a snare for her life, or whether she was dealing with an undercover agent. And of course you must be asking, "what kind of witch is this?" For if she is not sure as to who she is dealing with, how then can she be sure that he has any authority to provide the indemnity and guarantee of life that she is seeking? But Saul gives her assurance, even swearing by the name of the Lord that he has disobeyed, and the Lord who has already rejected him from being king of Israel. This is his response:

"And Saul sware to her by the Lord, saying, As the Lord liveth, there shall no punishment happen to thee for this thing."

Having obtained the assurance of protection of her life, she is ready to deal with Saul's request. Follow the conversation.

The woman: "Whom shall I bring up unto thee?"

Saul: "Bring me up Samuel."

Author: "Can the living wicked bring up or resurrect the righteous dead (or any dead) to life?"

Of course not! Here is the evidence from Solomon, the Apostle Paul, and John respectively.[291]

> *"The living know that they shall die, but the **dead know not anything**, neither have **they** any more a reward; for **the memory of them is forgotten.**"*

> *"The righteous await their resurrection at the second coming of Jesus."*

> ***"All that are in the grave will hear will hear the voice of the Son of God,** and NOT the voice of a witch, an imposter, nor the master deceiver, the devil and Satan."*

See the full contexts herein below from Paul who addressed believers in Thessalonica:

> *"For if we believe that Jesus died and rose again, even so them also which sleep in Jesus will God bring with him. For this we say unto you by the word of the Lord, that we which are alive and remain unto the*

---

291   Ecclesiastes 5:5; 1 Thessalonians 4:14-18; John 5:28-29.

coming of the Lord shall not prevent them which are asleep.

*For the **Lord himself shall descend from heaven** with a shout, with the voice of the archangel, and with the trump of God: **and the dead in Christ shall rise first**: Then we which are alive and remain shall be caught up together with them in the clouds, to meet the Lord in the air: and so shall we ever be with the Lord. Wherefore comfort one another with these words."[292]*

*"28Marvel not at this: for the hour is coming, in the which **all that are in the graves shall hear his voice**, 29And shall come forth; they that have done good, unto the resurrection of life; and they that have done evil, unto the resurrection of damnation."*

*"Behold, I shew you a mystery; We shall not all sleep, but we shall all be changed, In a moment, in the twinkling of an eye, **at the last trump**: for **the trumpet shall sound, and the dead shall be raised incorruptible,** and we shall be changed."[293]*

Author: So, if the living wicked cannot resurrect the dead, what kind of impossible question is the king asking, and who or what will appear?

The question may not be so impossible after all, when certain known facts are taken into account. Note that up to this point the woman has been deceived by Saul, because she did not realize that her visitor was Saul until verse 12 of 1 Samuel 28. *Now the woman, who is in conjunction with the devil, is about to pull off a masterpiece*

---

[292]   1 Thessalonians 4:14-18.

[293]   *John 5:28-29; 1 Corinthians 15:51-52.*

of a deception that fooled Saul and even millions around the world. Saul is so anxious to relieve his fear that anything will suffice to allay his spirit. He is, therefore, sufficiently primed (as prime or first coat of painting in readiness for the final coat of paint) and ripe to swallow up the deception: lot, stock and barrel. As you already know or shall discover shortly, something appeared. But what was it?

Author: *Does the devil have the power to resurrect anyone?*

Author: Again the answer is ***absolutely not*!** We have seen from above that only God can do that, or only through His power can the dead be resurrected. *"Jesus can limit the power of Satan"*[294] And He does limit the power of Satan as it relates to the resurrection, among other things. *If in fact, the devil could resurrect the dead, then there would be no need for weeping of family members of the deceased and hired mourners at thanksgiving services of the wicked who have been used by the devil during their lifetime.* Unless their bodies were cremated, they would have been resurrected, and of course cremation should not reduce his powers to resurrect, if he truly had such powers. But the reality is that he has no such powers. Based on the creation story, the earth is some 6,000 years old. Well, 6,000 years is a long time for the devil not to have utilized that assumed power to resurrect any one, and thereby spare families of his allies' unnecessary pain by resurrecting his deceased allies. *The picture gets much more bleak when you consider the evolutionary alternative.* If as evolutionists claim, the earth is billions of years old, then if we have not seen any resurrection of the devil's best deceased allies, how much hope should you have after all this time, that he is still able to pull it off? And how much more time would he need? Let's not choose to deceive ourselves. The devil was not gifted with that capability or core competence of resurrecting the dead.

---

[294]   Ellen G. White, Counsels on Health, p. 330.

Author: Does the devil have the power to deceive, to transform, and to impersonate?

Author: Most definitely.

Author: How do I know and how can I be so sure?

Author: I know because of what he has done and what has been revealed about his power in the Word of God. Recall the Genesis account of creation and the fall of Adam and Eve. What form did the devil use in deceiving Eve? Answer: the form of a serpent! What does this tell you, or what should it tell you? He has the power to transform or to impersonate. Have you ever heard the word **"duppy."**? In other places it goes by other names. Mark the following quotations[295] below sequentially, write them down and make a special note of them. They refer to the very same one text, but are from different translations to enhance our understanding of the subject content.

> *"For such are **false apostles, deceitful workers**, **transforming** themselves into the apostles of Christ. And no marvel; for **Satan himself is transformed** into an angel of light.* [15]*Therefore it **is no great thing if his ministers also be transformed** as the ministers of righteousness; whose end shall be according to their works."KJV*

> *"For such men are **false** apostles, deceitful workmen, **masquerading** as apostles of Christ.* [14]*And no wonder, for **Satan himself masquerades as an angel of light**.* [15]*It is not surprising, then, if **his servants masquerade as servants of righteousness**. Their end will be what their actions deserve." NIV1984*

---

[295]   *2 Corinthians 11:13-15(KJV, NIV 1984, CEV).*

[13] *"Anyway, they are no more than false apostles and* **dishonest** *workers. They only pretend to be apostles of Christ.* [14]*And it is no wonder. Even* **Satan tries to make himself look like an angel of light.** [15]*So why does it seem strange for Satan's servants to* **pretend** *to do what is right? Someday they will get exactly what they deserve." CEV.*

Comparing the three translations above, we discover that Satan is "transformed into", "masquerades as", and "tries to make himself look like, an angel of light". So too will his "false apostles", "deceitful, dishonest workers/workmen" and "his ministers/servants". And don't forget that Satan has an army of angels (1/3 that fell away from heaven in the uprising which they lost against God) whom he marshals at his beck and call.

It is for this reason that the apostles Peter, Matthew, and John, the revelator, counsel us in **1 Peter 5:8**, Matthew 24:24, and John 8:44 and Revelations 12:9 respectively, cited below as follows:

"Be sober, be vigilant; because your adversary the **devil**, *as a* **roaring lion**, *walketh about,* **seeking whom he may devour:"**

"For there shall arise **false** *Christs, and* **false** *prophets, and shall shew great signs and wonders; insomuch that, if it were possible, they shall* **deceive the very elect."**

"Ye are of your father **the devil**, *and the lusts of your father ye will do. He was a murderer from the beginning, and abode not in the truth, because there is no truth in him. When* **he speaketh a lie**, *he* **speaketh of his own:** *for* **he is a liar**, *and the* **father of it."**

*"And the **great dragon was cast out**, that old serpent, **called the Devil**, and Satan, which **deceiveth the whole world: he was cast out into the earth, and his angels** were cast out with him."*

We must always remember this very important principle cited below:

*"For we **wrestle not against flesh and blood, but against principalities, against powers, against the** rulers of the darkness of this world, **against spiritual** wickedness in high places."*[296]

Having outlined the big picture, and unmasked the devil's character of tricks, deception, lies, falsehood, pretending, masquerading, scary roaring lion and dragon-like disposition and devouring nature, and that heal so operates at the (invisible) supernatural level of principalities, powers, rulers of the darkness of this world and spiritual wickedness in high places, we can better appreciate the nature of this cunning creature called the devil and his involvement in what was about to take place at the meeting with Saul and the witch of Endor that ghastly night.

What happens immediately after the above in this diabolical plot is unique,interesting, and calls for a mind of understanding and a desire to know and understand truth, if we are to better understand aspects of God's Love Language. Notice carefully that the woman's mixed response was a marriage of emotion, sensation, deception, pretension, vagueness and indecisiveness. Saul is left to figure out and interpret the masquerading illusion that was unfolding at the super natural level.

The woman/witch: *"And when the woman saw Samuel, she cried with a loud voice: and the woman spake to Saul, saying, Why thou hast deceived me? for thou art Saul."*

---

[296] *Ephesians 6:12.*

This is high diabolical drama! But you ask, "why do I say that?" But the answer is simple and clear to the spiritually discerned. Double deception is present! First: Saul deceives the witch as to his identity. Second: The woman is about to deceive Saul by crying with a loud voice and pretending that she resurrected Samuel.

Notice carefully, there is no mention that the woman spoke to anyone. There is some communication taking place, but clearly not between the woman and the dead Samuel, who has no memory and cannot communicate with anyone. Neither is it between Saul and the deceased Samuel. *Who told her that it was Samuel? Why did she cry with a loud voice? How did she discover that her visitor was Saul?* Here is the answer. A spirit medium is in communication with her at the supernatural level. This is a case of impersonation. Factually, Samuel is dead. He cannot hear or respond to anyone except the Son of God at the second coming of Jesus, and neither Satan nor his angels have any power of resurrection. So, Samuel is undisturbed in his death bed in the grave in the earth. At the supernatural level the devil or his angel communicates with the woman who is alarmed and emotional over what is taking place. As a result of the revelation by the spirit medium she learns and concludes that it is Saul. So, she exclaims with consternation to Saul with an open-ended question: "Why has thou deceived me?"

Then the dialogue between the woman and Saul resumes with Saul responding to allay her fear of death from the king.

Saul: "Be not afraid: for what sawest thou?"

The woman: "I saw gods ascending out of the earth."

Notice again the woman's response to Saul direct question. *"I saw gods (plural) ascending out of the earth"*. So, what are these *"gods ascending out of the earth?"* Obviously not Samuel (singular). These are gods that are not approved, who do not have the approbation of the Lord God, creator of heaven and earth as the text below helps us to understand.

"The Lord will be terrible unto them: for he will famish all the gods of the earth."[297]

They can only be Satan's falling angels, which were once in heaven, impersonating an earthly being, Samuel. But Saul doesn't appear to be convinced that it is Samuel, so he poses another direct question, trying to get some assurance to soothe his aching soul. But notice that his question simply ignores the *"gods"* the woman spoke of. You see he wants something to hold onto, anything relating to Samuel. So, follow the plot as it outlines a play upon Saul's perception and stubbornness.

Saul: "And he said unto her, What form is he of?"

The woman: "And she said, An old man cometh up; and he is covered with a mantle."

Her response is clearly in conflict with her earlier revelation about the gods of the earth. Clearly she is being influenced by the beings of the underworld, and not by Samuel, and not by God. She is playing up to Saul's tune. He wants to hear about Samuel, not about gods of the earth. Then notice how the plot of deceptions takes a new twist and turn as the intrigue heightens. Saul *perceives* that it was Samuel. Then Saul stooped with his face to the ground, bowed himself, and begins communication with the demon that is doing the impersonation. Imagine the man from humble beginnings, promoted by God to be king of Israel, and from whom God expected high moral compass,probity, and high standard of integrity, now descends to the depths to communicate with sinful angel spirit medium, and workers of iniquity, whom God had cast from heaven. When we transgress God's commandments, there is no depth too low that we will not fall into.

Spirit medium communicator: "And Samuel said to Saul, Why hast thou disquieted me, to bring me up?"

---

[297] *Zephaniah 2:10-12.*

Saul: And Saul answered, I am sore distressed; for the Philistines make war against me, and **God is departed from me, and answereth me no more**, neither by prophets, nor by dreams: therefore I have called thee, that thou mayest make known unto me what I shall do.

Saul's response is a serious indictment on his credibility, reputation and character. He admits to the communication breakdown between him and God. Again, how foolish to expect that God would resurrect His dead saint to permit a discussion with a rebellious, stubborn king, whom He had rejected from being king during Samuel's lifetime. So, the devil simply seized the moment to drive home the nail into Saul's casket.

Spirit medium communicator: *Then said Samuel, Wherefore then dost thou ask of me, seeing the Lord is departed from thee, and is become thine enemy? And the Lord hath done to him, as he spake by me: for the **Lord hath rent the kingdom out of thine hand**, and given it to thy neighbour, even to David: **Because thou obeyedst not the voice of the Lord, nor executedst his fierce wrath upon Amalek**, therefore hath the Lord done this thing unto thee this day.*

> *"Moreover the Lord will also deliver Israel with thee into the hand of the Philistines: and tomorrow shalt thou and thy sons be with me: the Lord also shall deliver the host of Israel into the hand of the Philistines."*

The devil medium is quoting Scripture! Imagine that! But this shouldn't alarm nor surprise you. He did that when he tempted Jesus in the wilderness. He is trying to pull off a masterpiece deception when he does that, as he tried with Jesus!

So, here we see that what the devil medium disclosed to Saul was not new information. The devil and his entourage had been following the journey of Saul's life all along and were being kept a breast of all developments, just like he follows our life story. This is because he was determined to destroy Saul by taking a mile where

Saul yielded to him a yard. This is the lion nature of the devil. He was skillfully and cunningly strategizing and waiting for the opportunity to set-up Saul for his destruction. As Saul had rejected the Lord by his repeated disobedience, aided and abetted by the devil, the Lord had become his enemy, and now in desperation and distress at the lowest point of his career and reign in the corridors of power, he, Saul turns fully to the devil. Yes, I repeat for emphasis, "Saul turns fully to the devil", while in the corridors of power, while still being king of God's people, Israel. Isn't this truly amazing? The devil had been prompting, wooing him all along, and gained successes. This is because Saul had been little by little yielding to the devil over time, who by now had become his ally to the point where he believed the devil more for telling him the same truths that he had rejected to embrace when it was communicated to him through God's prophet, Samuel.

The last part of the text mentioned above speaks to Saul's defeat at the battle with the Philistines. (How ironic an ending when contrasted with his beginning! A quick review of Overview and Background under Subsection 6.3 Case Story 2, states that God had requested Samuel to anoint Saul as captain over His people, Israel, that he, Saul, may save His people out of the hands of the Philistines.) But this ironic defeat was not difficult to foresee because the writing was on the wall. Any analyst could draw the same correct conclusion. *Why is this so?* It's simple.

* God had stated categorically His rejection of Saul and the selection of David as his replacement.
* God had ceased communication with him: no vision, no priests and no Urims.
* He was at an all-time low spiritually and with God.
* He knew that God would not be with him in the battle to fight the Philistines.
* Plus, he was numerically outnumbered in the impending battle with the Philistines.
* He trembled when he saw the numbers of Philistines soldiers.

* His chances of winning the literal, physical military battle were extremely low.

This was compounded by the fact that he had already lost the internal spiritual battle for the conquest of self to the devil. And the devil would do everything possible to ensure the outcome of death for Saul.

Upon hearing the poor military prognosis from the spirit medium communicator, his heart sank further. The body of the once physically fit, strong and empowering being, that was shoulder and head above all the others in Israel, gave way under the weight of predicted imminent defeat, loss of the internal spiritual battle, and fear and discouragement. He fell straightway to the earth. He had already internally conceded defeat. It was, therefore, not the time for war when he was in that shape.

But, to compound his problems, he was also hungry. The woman tried to revive him but to no avail. She persuaded him to have something to eat to gain strength for his journey. But he refused. In his usual stubbornness, he defied the request to eat. But his servants and the woman compelled him and he eventually had the meal that was hastily prepared. After the meal, he along with his servants rose up and went away in the night.

He came to the woman by night and now he departs in the night. What a way for an end to his nocturnal meeting! But it was not only physical night for Saul. It was also a nightmare and spiritual night for him.

e)   Comments from The Spirit of Prophet:

In commenting on Saul's encounter with the witch of Endor, Ellen G. White, made to following comments, quoted below.

The Witch and Satan had an Agreement:

> "The witch of Endor had made agreement with Satan to follow his directions in all things, and he would

perform wonders and miracles for her and would reveal to her, the most secret things if she would yield herself unreservedly to be controlled by his Satanic majesty. This she had done."[298]

It's important to note that anyone who is controlled by, or has given himself/herself over to, the devil and Satan will not embrace God's Love Language, as he or she cannot serve two diametrically opposed masters at the same time.

Saul's Final Step:

*When Saul inquired for Samuel, the Lord did not cause Samuel to appear to Saul. He saw nothing. Satan was not allowed to disturb the rest of Samuel in the grave and bring him up in reality to the witch of Endor. **God does not give Satan power to resurrect the dead.** But **Satan's angels assumed the form of dead friends, and speak act like them, that through professed dead friends, he can better carry on his work of deception.** Satan knew Samuel well, and he knew how to represent him before the witch of Endor, and to utter correctly the fate of Saul and his sons.*

Satan will come in a very plausible manner to such as he can deceive,** and will insinuate himself into their favor, and lead them almost imperceptibly from God. He wins them under his control, cautiously at first, until their perceptibilities become blunted. Then he will make bolder suggestions, until he can lead them to commit almost any degree of crime. When he has led them fully into his snare, he is then willing that they should see where they are, and he exults in their confusion, as in the case of Saul. **He

---

[298]   Spirit of Prophecy, Volume 1, *page 375, 376.*

had suffered Satan to lead him as a willing captive and now Satan spreads before Saul a correct description of his fate. By giving Saul a correct statement of his end, through the woman at Endor, Satan opens a way for Israel to be instructed by his satanic cunning, that they may in their rebellion against God, Lean on him, and by thus doing, sever the last link which would hold them to God.

Saul knew that in this last act of consulting with the witch of Endor, he cut the last shred which held him to God. He knew that if he had not before willfully separated himself from God, this act sealed that separation, and made it final. He had made an agreement with death, and a covenant with hell. The cup of his iniquity was full.[299]

iv) Divine Judgment on Saul and the reasons for his death

a) The final battle and death of the king

The appointment had come for the last military battle between the Israelites and the Philistines with Saul as king of the Israelites. Because of Saul's continual 'runnings' (disobedience) with God and His law, **the presence of God in this battle was absent**. Plus, there was no Samuel to give counsel. The witch would only add to his woes. Satan would only work behind the scenes to ensure the king's failure and destruction, all unknown to Saul. Even if the king wanted to take a leave of absence for this battle, he could not. The cards were all stacked against him. Precedence had already been set. Before the king's anointing and introduction to Israel, it was clearly outlined by the high priest and prophet, Samuel, that the king would fight the battles for

---

[299]   Spirit of Prophecy, Volume 1, *page 376, 377.*

the people. That's how the other nations did it. Now time was running out.

Both armies were drawn into the battle. The Philistines fought hard against the Israelites. The men of Israel fled before the Philistines and many were slain in the mount Gilboa. But the Philistines war leaders were not satisfied with that measure of success. They wanted Saul, the king, and his three sons: Jonathan, and Abinadab, and Melchishua, dead. So they pressed the battle to the gates. The fighting was intense and the Philistines war generals and archers pressed the battle against them. Saul was seriously injured and his three sons were killed in the battle. Recognizing the gravity of his injury, but not wanting to be killed by his opponents, the uncircumcised Philistines, Saul asked his armour-bearer to slay him on site with his sword. But his armour-bearer refused, because he was afraid. Then Saul took a sword and fell upon it, thereby taking his own life. Imagine that, the king commits suicide! Afterwards, the Philistines came and beheaded him.

b) Reasons for Saul's death[300]

What a way to end a life that started with so much promise! What an anticlimax! But to the ordinary man or woman on the street, void of an understanding of God's Word, there is a strong possibility that Saul's death in battle might be seen and viewed as just another death of a king in battle. But to make that conclusion would be to miss the entire essence and purpose of the title of this book and this chapter, as well as to misunderstand that there are divine consequences (and divine judgments) for knowingly going contrary to the God's explicit commandments (law of cause and effect). It would also signal a lack of understanding that an appreciation and acceptance of the salvific love gift of Jesus on the cross carries requirements on the part of the believer, and consequences on those who reject God's love offer of salvation.

On the other hand, we must point out that ignorance of the

---

[300]   Read 1 Chronicles 10:13-14.

law is no excuse for sin. The sin of omission is still a sin. So too is the sin of commission. It is no longer true (if it ever was) that what you don't know won't hurt you. The reality is that what you don't know will hurt you, and may even kill you, as God is not a God of excuses. Some people who were not aware of the tsunami were still swept away by the tide.

Therefore, to avoid any misunderstanding and misinterpretation, I have listed the three (3) main reasons provided in Scripture for the judgment of God upon Saul that led to his death. These are outlined in 1 Chronicles 10:13-14.

i) Saul died for his transgression which he committed against the Lord, even against the word of the Lord which he kept not.

   a) First was when he rashly offered sacrifices and burnt offerings which was the prerogative of the priests of the Lord, he himself not being a priest.

   b) For disobeying the commandment of the Lord to destroy all the Amalekites and their possessions.

ii) Saul died for his transgression which he committed against the Lord, for asking counsel of one that had a familiar spirit, to enquire of it.

iii) Saul died for his transgression for enquiring not of the Lord.

Therefore, He slew him (or rather permitted him to be killed by suicide), and turned the kingdom unto David, the son of Jesse.

v) Lessons for us to learn

There are at least three (3) important lessons God would have us learn from the experience of Saul in the light of God's salvific objective.

a) God is in the business of saving sinners, and He is not desirous that any should perish.[301]

That is why Saul was not destroyed at the occurrence of his first failure. In this regard, the Word of God outlines how God, through His prophet and priest, Samuel, reasoned repeatedly with Saul, just like He does with us, pointing out his sins in the hope that he would choose the path of reason and repentance. This demonstrates the loving, compassionate, forgiving and just nature and character of God.[302] So, Saul received second chances. Hence, he was not removed initially from his position in the kingdom. He received both time and opportunity to fully develop his character for both fallen and unfallen worlds to see. So when God takes the final decision to implement and stamp the justice of His judgment, the entire universe can agree that God is just, and His character of justice will be vindicated. If you know that in your present position, you are doing wrong, breaking God's law, don't feel secure and permanent! If you think that you are smarter than God and others, God is just giving you time to prove your character before the entire universe. You may fool some of the people some of the time, but you can't fool God any of the time.

b) The story demonstrates how seriously God views and values a lifestyle of loving obedience to Him and His commandments.

This underscores the need for us to surrender our self, and our will, to Him. When we do this, we will gain the victory over self, sin, and stubbornness. This, thereby, provides the basis and platform for God to trust us and consider us as trustworthy and faithful followers whom He can trust with heaven and eternal life as we will have the transcript of His character in our mind, heart, soul, and strength. In the end, the summary of Saul's character revealed that he was not trustworthy.

c) The two case stories are recounted herein so that we do not make the same mistakes as Saul and the disobedient prophet.

In this regard, they will help us to understand that God means what He says and that it is a dangerous thing to know what God commands and to disobey, and also that it is a dangerous thing to know what is right and not to do it. The consequences are grave. They include not just the risk of losing our physical lives, but more importantly, eternal life. In Saul's case, he lost both.

6.4 General Consequences

Case stories 1 and 2 as we have seen here in above, recounted the consequences that were meted out to both the prophet of God and to Saul, first king of the Kingdom of Israel. These are two specific cases of cause and effect; the two outcomes of choice: reward and consequence; and the danger of knowing what God's Commandment is and willfully, deliberately choosing to disobey. Like the principles of the law of cause and effect exemplified in those two cases, the Bible clearly and repeatedly outlines similar general consequences of human choosing and action. **It recounts that there are ultimately only two destinations:** heaven and hell, or eternal life and the second death. These outcomes, which are the result of human choices, are remarkably different as day and night, truth and error, saved and lost, or eternal joy and eternal loss. They are so glaringly contrasting and conspicuously recognizable that the earnest and genuine seeker after truth who is led by the Holy Spirit of God, who leads into all truth, will recognize the difference and need not choose the wrong destination.

The Bible also likens the path to hell or the second death as the broad way and the wide gate, but one that leads ultimately to destruction. This path is viewed as easy, accessible, enticing, with little or no rules, where one can do as one pleases, and one where freedom of choice is king. The sister to freedom of choice is tastes, preferences and flexibility. It requires little or no sacrifices and pleasing self is queen. The only rules seem to be "consent to do it" and "right of freedom". Unbelievably, it is a path that seems right unto a man (mankind). So, many find it, and many enter there.

By contrast, the path to heaven and eternal life of joy and happiness is the strait gate and the narrow way or road. To enter and remain on this path requires much thought, thinking, reasoning, and decision making. Consequently, few tend to find and enter there, because it has rules, requirements and guidelines, and therefore, appears to be uninviting and difficult. It places limits on the degree of freedom of choice, tastes, preferences, while it emphasizes that this sacrificial path yields super-handsome dividends. But this is the gate and way that all are encouraged to enter, and this is the journey which all who start, are encouraged to complete. Angels of God and Jesus, the Pearl of Righteousness, the Lord, can help us find and stay in this right way.

The Bible writers: Matthew, Solomon (Proverbs), Moses (Numbers), David (King and Psalmist), and Jeremiah (the prophet), give us an insight into this matter as follows.

*"Enter ye in at the strait **gate**: for wide is the **gate**, and broad is the **way**, that leadeth to destruction, and many there be which go in there at: Because strait is the gate, and narrow is the **way**, which leadeth unto life, and few there be that find it."*

*"There is a **way which seemeth right unto a man**, but the end thereof are the **ways** of death.*

*And the **ass saw the angel of the LORD standing in the way**, and his sword drawn in **his hand: and** the **ass turned aside out of** the way, and went into the **field: and** Balaam smote the **ass, to turn her*** *into the way. Then the **LORD** opened the **eyes** of Balaam, and he saw the **angel of** the **LORD** standing in the way, and his sword drawn in **his hand: and he bowed down his head, and fell flat** on his face.*

*Blessed is the man that walketh not in the counsel of the ungodly, nor standeth in the way of sinners, nor sitteth in the seat of the scornful. But **his delight is in the law of the Lord;** and in his law doth he meditate day and night. And he shall be like a tree planted by the rivers of water, that bringeth forth his fruit in his season; his leaf also shall not wither; and whatsoever he doeth shall prosper.*

*"Thus saith the **LORD, Stand ye in the ways,** and see, and **ask for the old paths, where is the good way**, and walk therein, and ye **shall find rest for your souls.** But they said, we will not walk therein."*

*⁵ "Thomas saith unto him, Lord, we know not whither thou goest; and **how can we know the way? 6 Jesus saith unto him, I am the way, the truth, and the life**: no man cometh unto the Father, but by me."*[303]

Some of the applicable general consequences that apply to those who knowingly refuse God's Love Language are outlined below in three different categories, viz: "During one's life time on earth", "at the second coming of Jesus," and "at the end of the millennium".

---

[303] *Matthew 7:13-14; Proverbs 14:12, 16:2; Numbers 22:23, 31; Psalm 1:1-3; Jeremiah 6:16; John 14:5-6.*

i) During one's life time on earth

Those who knowingly, intelligently, willfully and deliberately, reject God's Love Language will face certain consequences while on earth, and unless they repent before their probation is closed, they will not be translated nor be in the first resurrection. Some of these consequences are cited hereinbelow.

a)   Classified as liars void of truth.

> *"He that saith, I know him, and* **keepeth not his commandments**, *is a* **liar, and the truth** *is not in him."*[304]

When we persistently refuse to love God and embrace His love language, or use our position, or office, of influence to take advantage of the confidence that people place in us, and lead souls to ruin, we are choosing to ward-off His wooing and drawing of the Holy Spirit and to be guiltier than the common sinner. By continuing on that path of lying and deception, we will cross the line of no return, where spiritual truths and error will be indistinguishable, and because all those who fall into this category received not the love of the truth that they might be saved, God sends them strong delusion, that they should believe a lie.[305]

E. G. White has a word for ministers, recorded in Counsels of Health, on this particular matter quoted herein below.

When ministers thus take advantage of the confidence the people place in them and lead souls to ruin, they make themselves as much more guilty than the common sinner as their profession is higher. In the day of God, when the great Ledger of Heaven is opened, it will be found to contain the names of many ministers who have made pretensions to purity of heart and life and professed to be entrusted with the gospel of Christ, but who have taken advantage of their position to allure souls to transgress the law of God...

---

[304]   *1 John 2:4*
[305]   *See 2 Thessalonians 2:8-12.*

*If the society of a man of impure mind and licentious habits is chosen in preference to that of the virtuous and pure, it is a sure indication that the tastes and inclinations harmonize, that a low level of morals is reached. This level is called by these deceived, infatuated souls, a high and holy affinity of spirit--a spiritual harmony. But the apostle terms it '**spiritual wickedness in high places,**' against which we are to institute a vigorous warfare.*

When the deceiver commences his work of deception, he frequently finds dissimilarity of tastes and habits, but by great pretensions to godliness he gains the confidence, and when this is done, his wily, deceptive power is exercised in his own way, to carry out his devices. By associating with this dangerous element, women become accustomed to breathe the atmosphere of impurity and almost insensibly become permeated with the same spirit. Their identity is lost; they become the shadow of their seducer.[306]

b) Their father is the devil.

*"**Ye are of your father the devil,** and the **lusts of your father ye will do. He was a liar from the beginning, and abode not in the truth,** because there is no truth **in** him. When he speaketh a lie, he speaketh of his own: for he is a liar, and the **father** of it."*

c) Their prayers are an abomination.

---

[306] Ellen G. White, *Counsels on Health, page 624, 625.*

*"He that turneth away his **ear** from hearing the law,
even his prayer shall be abomination. "*

d) Their hearts are as an adamant stone and God does not hear them.

> *But they refused to hearken, and pulled away the shoulder, and stopped their ears that they should not hear. [12] Yea, **they made their hearts as an adamant stone**, lest they should hear the law, and the words which the Lord of hosts hath sent in his spirit by the former prophets: therefore came a great wrath from the Lord of hosts. **13** Therefore it is come to pass, that as he cried, and they would not hear; so they cried, and I would not hear, saith the Lord of hosts:[307]*

e) They are cursed by God

> *Even from the days of your fathers ye are gone away from mine ordinances, and have not kept them. Return unto me, and I will return unto you, saith the Lord of hosts. But ye said, Wherein shall we return? [8] Will a man rob God? Yet ye have me. But ye say, Wherein have we robbed thee? In tithes and offerings. [9] **Ye are cursed with a curse: for ye have robbed me,** even this whole nation.[308]*

ii) At the second coming of Jesus

When Jesus returns to earth at His second coming, He comes for His people to take them to heaven. But sadly, those who during their lifetime rejected God and His love language, will not be

---

[307] *Zechariah 7:11-13.*
[308] *Malachi 3:7-9.*

included in that sinless throng that is heaven bound. Shown below are some of the things the Bible states that will happen to those who didn't make it to heaven.

a) The mighty shall cry bitterly, and their silver and gold shall be meaningless.

> [14] *The great day of the Lord is near, it is near, and hasteth greatly, even the voice of the day of the Lord:* **the mighty man shall cry there bitterly.** [15] *That day is a day of wrath, a day of trouble and distress, a day of wasteness and desolation, a day of darkness and gloominess, a day of clouds and thick darkness,* [16] *A day of the trumpet and alarm against the fenced cities, and against the high towers.* [17] *And I will bring distress upon men that they shall walk like blind men,* **because they have sinned against the Lord:** *and their blood shall be poured out as dust, and their flesh as the dung.* [18] *Neither their silver nor their gold shall be able to deliver them in the day of the Lord's wrath; but the whole land shall be devoured by the fire of his jealousy: for he shall make even a speedy riddance of all them that dwell in the land.*[309]

b) The tribes of the earth will mourn.

> *"And then shall appear the sign of the Son of man in heaven: and then shall all the* **tribes of the earth mourn,** *and they shall see the Son of man coming in the clouds of heaven with power and great glory."*

c) Slain with the brightness of His coming.

---

[309] *Zephaniah 1:14-18.*

*"And then shall that Wicked be revealed, whom the Lord shall consume with the spirit of his mouth, and shall **destroy with the brightness of his coming**: Even him, whose coming is after the working of Satan with all power and signs and lying wonders.*[310]

d) They remain dead on earth during the millennium (while the saints are in heaven).

⁵ *"But the rest of the dead **lived not again until the thousand years were finished**."*

They remain dead during the 1,000 years (while the resurrected and translated loving and obedience commandment keeping saints are in heaven) to await their final annihilation and eradication at the end of the millennium. Satan is bound by a chain of circumstances in a bottomless prison pit during the millennial period.

---

[310] *2 Thessalonians 2:7-9.*

THE GOLDEN MORNING IS FAST APPROACHING[311]

The golden morning is fast approaching;
Jesus soon will come
To take His faithful and happy children
To their promised home.

iii) At the end of the millennium

At the end of the 1,000 years vacation, the devil is loosed from his prison abyss and, true to form, in one last final assault, he deceives the lawless, wicked lost, to believe that together they can overthrow God and capture His beautiful city, the new Jerusalem. This concludes Satan's struggle in the great controversy which he started in heaven and brought to earth. It culminates the conflict of the ages, as well as the great controversy of the forces of good and evil, Christ and Satan. Now the final phase of God's executive judgment must be implemented and the unrepentant sinners receive their just reward.

a) They (unrepentant sinners) are resurrected for a short time, only to once again display their sinful, fighting, traits of character they had on earth that disqualified them from heaven and eternal life.

> *And when the thousand years are expired, Satan shall be loosed out of his prison, And shall go out to deceive the nations which are in the four quarters of the earth, Gog, and Magog, to gather them together to battle: the number of whom is as the sand of the sea. And they went up on the breadth of the earth,*

---

[311] Source: http://www.hymnlyrics.org/newlyrics_g/
golden_morning_is_fast_approching.php

and compassed the camp of the saints about, and the beloved city........: Revelation 20:7-9.

b) Hiding and seeking for cover in the dens, in the rocks and in the mountains.

> *And the kings of the earth, and the great men, and the rich men, and the chief captains, and the mighty men, and every bondman, and every free man, hid themselves in the dens and in the rocks of the mountains; And said to the mountains and rocks, Fall on us, and hide us from the face of him that sitteth on the throne, and from the wrath of the Lamb: For the great day of his wrath is come; and who shall be able to stand? Revelation 6:15-17.*

The lost will be found in all the various sectors and strata of earth, viz: socio-economical, financial, educational, political and religious. What a way to end a life of humble beginning wrapped up in robes of opportunities and potentialities. Isn't this very reminiscent of King Saul?

c) Fire comes down from God devours them.

> *"And they went up on the breadth of the earth, and compassed the camp of the saints about, and the beloved city: and fire came down from God out of heaven, and devoured them." Revelation 20:9.*

Look at these categories of people who partake of the second death. Do you know any of them? How did your life influence them?

> *"**But** the fearful, and unbelieving, and the abominable, and murderers, and whoremongers, and sorcerers, and idolaters, and all liars, shall have*

their part in the lake which burneth with fire and brimstone: which is the second death." Revelations 21:8.

d) They shall be stubble, and ashes under the soles of the feet of the saved.

> *For, behold, the day cometh, that shall burn as an oven; and **all the proud**, yea, and all **that do wickedly, shall be stubble:** and the day that cometh shall burn them up, saith the Lord of hosts, that it shall leave them neither root nor branch. And ye shall tread down the wicked; for they shall be ashes under the soles of your feet in the day that I shall do this, saith the Lord of hosts. Malachi 3:1,3.*

But **what about the devil, the imposter**, that masquerader, who has power to transform, deceive, allure, people into sin? **What will happen to him and his angels**; what will be their fate? Well, the Bible is likewise crystal clear on this point, as is cited below.[312]

> *And I saw an angel come down from heaven, having the key of the bottomless pit and a great chain in his hand. And he laid hold on the dragon, that old serpent, which is the Devil, and Satan, and bound him a thousand years, And cast him into the bottomless pit, and shut him up, and set a seal upon him, that he should deceive the nations no more, till the thousand years should be fulfilled: and after that he must be loosed a little season.*

> *And shall go out to deceive the nations which are in the four quarters of the earth, Gog, and Magog, to gather them together to battle: the number of whom*

---

[312] *Revelation 20:1-3, 7-9, Matthew 25:40-42.*

*is as the sand of the sea. And they went up on the breadth of the earth, and compassed the camp of the saints about, and the beloved city: and fire came down from God out of heaven, and devoured them. And **the devil that deceived them was cast into the lake of fire and brimstone,** where the beast and the false prophet are, and shall be tormented day and night forever and ever.*

*And the King shall answer and say unto them, Verily I say unto you, Inasmuch as ye have done it unto one of the least of these my brethren, ye have done it unto me. Then shall he say also unto them on the left hand, **Depart from me, ye cursed, into everlasting fire, prepared for the devil and his angels:** [42] For I was an hungered, and ye gave me no meat: I was thirsty, and ye gave me no drink:*

Conclusion

The lake of fire was not prepared for human beings, like you and me. Neither was the second death! They are not for us. They were prepared for the devil/Satan and his angels who fell away from heaven through sin. God's power is stronger than that of the devil. One-third of the angels sinned and sided with Satan, but God has two-thirds of the angels which excel in strength on His side. God has showed the power of His love for humanity when He died on Calvary. His power is available to us today. Examine the following powerful texts of hope and opportunity.[313]

"But as many as received him, to them gave the power to become the sons of God, even to them that believe on his name:"

Wherefore let him that thinketh he standeth take heed lest he fall. There hath no temptation taken you but

---

[313]   John 1:12; *1 Corinthians 10:12-14.*

such as is common to man: but God is faithful, who will not suffer you to be tempted above that ye are able; but will with the temptation also make a way to escape, that ye may be able to bear it. Wherefore, my dearly beloved, flee from idolatry.

God has no pleasure in the death of any one, including the wicked. But we must choose to love God, and embrace a lifestyle of loving obedience to His commandments, to avoid the sin of self-centered stubbornness, which is as iniquity and idolatry. We must be passionately resolved to choose for the right motive to be on God's side, which is always the winning side.

"The soul that sinneth, it shall die. The son shall not bear the iniquity of the father, neither shall the father bear the iniquity of the son: the righteousness of the righteous shall be upon him, and the wickedness of the wicked shall be upon him.

*But **if the wicked will turn from all his sins** that he hath committed, and keep all my statutes, and **do that which is lawful and right, he shall surely live**, he shall not die. [22]All his transgressions that he hath committed, they shall not be mentioned unto him: in his righteousness that he hath done he shall live. Have I any pleasure at all that the wicked should die? Saith the Lord God: and not that he should return from his ways, and live?*

But when the righteous turneth away from his righteousness, and committeth iniquity, and doeth according to allthe abominations that the wicked man doeth, shall he live? All his righteousness that he hath done shall not be mentioned: in his trespass that he hath trespassed, and in his sin that he hath sinned, in them shall he die".[314]

---

[314] *Ezekiel 18:20-24.*

The critical question is: what will be your response to all of God's goodness and loveliness? Stop, think, and count the cost of your response! For if He doesn't want you to die in your sins, why should you choose to do so? You are of much greater value that two sparrows. Not one of them falls from the skies without God noticing. Well, you are of more value than many sparrows!

HAVE YOU COUNTED THE COST?[315]

There's a line that is drawn by rejecting our Lord
Where the call of His Spirit is lost
And you hurry along with the pleasure-mad throng
Have you counted, have you counted the cost?

---

[315] Accessed at http://www.godlikeproductions. com/forum1/message301651/pg1

CHAPTER 7

OUR RESPONSE TO GOD'S LOVE LANGUAGE

7.1 The most important response:

THAT OUGHT TO be our most important response to God's love? The *most important response is to be **willingly loving and obedient*** to God. This is a broad, yet specific and comprehensive response, because this *requires us to put away the evil of our doings that God knows and sees, and to cease to do evil.* But, to do this, we need the help of the Holy Spirit. It is only with His help that we can learn to do well; to seek judgment, relieve the oppressed, judge the fatherless, and plead for the widow. This is what God expects of one and all, because this is part of the second great commandment of love (second or Table B) which requires us to love one another. This is how the prophet, Isaiah, sums it up including the conditional reward that is inextricably linked to it.

> *"If ye be **willing and obedient, ye shall eat the good of the land**:" Isaiah 1:19*

But he also adds the following:

> *"Wash you, make you clean; put away the evil of your doings from before mine eyes; cease to do evil; Learn to do well; seek judgment, relieve the oppressed, judge the fatherless, plead for the widow."*

> ***"Come now, and let us reason together, saith the Lord:*** *though your sins be as scarlet, they shall be as*

white as snow; though they be red like crimson, they shall be as wool."[316]

The truth is, God is a loving, reasonable, and condescending God. He is willing to reason with us. Let us grasp such a heart-warming opportunity to enter into a covenant relationship with God,the covenant maker and keeper. God is willing to do for us what we cannot do for ourselves. We make a mess of situation when we choose to refuse and rebel against God, which is a path that causes us to be devoured with the sword as the Lord declares. The Law of cause and effect still operates.

7.2 True basis for willing obedience

The Apostle and physician, Dr. Luke, captures for us what should be the true basis for our loving and willing obedience to God's love. By disclosing the encounter with Jesus and a lawyer,the gospel of Luke helps us to understand that we should not be half-hearted in our attitude, aptitude, and obedience for God and His love language. Rather, we are to be true, faithful, genuine, and holistic in our praise response to Him. So, our true basis for willing obedience is that which is centered on love, and this love has two components: first is to be our love for God, and second to it, is to be our love for our neighbours. We may call this double love.

Let us use our imagination to join Dr. Luke as he captures the scene.[317] This scenic development outlines the tenets of the true basis for our willing obedience to God and how it should be always. As he views and observes the setting in the vicinity of Jesus, he notices that a bright, young, lawyer confidently emerges and asks Jesus a billion dollar question:

"Master, what shall I do to inherit eternal life?"

---

[316] *Isaiah 1: 16-18, 19.*
[317] Luke 10.

Dr. Luke's heart may have skipped a beat, as he wondered whether this emergent legal luminary was going to trip and trap Jesus as so many before had tried to do. But in quick reflection, he remembered that Jesus put them all to shame. So, he reassures himself, knowing that Jesus was going to set him thinking by asking him a follow-up question. May be, he was testing Jesus to see how much Jesus, who attended no law school, knew about law. But Jesus was about to test him to see how well he knew the law, the area of his core competence. Here come Jesus' question.

> *"He said unto him, What is written in the law? how readest thou?"*

The lawyer would be disgraced if he failed to answer. So, he had to put up a good showing, and to well represent all those called to the bar. But little did he know that in answering Jesus' question, he, would be answering what turned out to be his own rhetorical question. And did he do well? Read his response as covered by Dr. Luke, the physician, our reporter on location.

> *"And he answering said, Thou shalt **love** (agape) the Lord thy God with **all** thy **heart**, and with **all** thy **soul**, and with **all** thy **strength**, and with **all** thy **mind**; and thy neighbour as thyself."*[318]

"Wow!" "A brilliant answer", you must have exclaimed as you stood beside Dr. Luke and observed the calmness in Jesus' countenance! This is indeed a summary of all of God's Ten Commandments moral law written with the finger of God. That is (agape) love to God for the first four, and (phileo) love to thy neighbour for the last six. It's a combination of love (better yet, double love) and obedience, which summarizes God's Love Language. And this (obedience) is the same idea communicated

---

[318] *Luke 10:27.*

by the prophet Isaiah in Chapter 1 of his book by the same name, and quoted above.

The lawyer knows about the ten commandment law of God. He volunteers the answer as Jesus did not ask him anything about the Ten Commandments. He must have been led by the Holy Spirit to give that answer. He explains also for us, what our response should be to God's Love Language, and this response gets to the heart of the true basis of our response to God.

But what does all of this mean? What are the meanings of such words: "heart", "soul", "strength", and "mind?" Here is the meaning.

The Heart = Social relations and citadel of our emotions and affections.

In all of these social/emotions/affections (or horizontal), we must put God first, in rank, in priority (i.e. in importance and urgency).

The Soul = Spiritual (or vertical) relations. Likewise, I must place God first in all my relations and relationships.

Strength = Using my physical being or prowess to glorify God first and to help one another.

Mind = That part of the brain in which is the seat of intelligence in man, where our ideas and thoughts are formed and decisions are made.

Let us centre our mind on God. Also in all our mental/ educational pursuits, let us make God the central theme of our study.

Philippians 2:5 states: *"Let this mind be in you, which was also in Christ Jesus:"*

It is clear that this love for God must unite all the faculties of heart, soul, strength and mind. But there is more to the meaning of the text and response of the lawyer.

Note the word "**all**" is used before each faculty/part of our being: **all** thy heart, **all** thy soul, **all** thy strength, and **all** thy mind. This means that in our response to God, we must be undivided in our relationship and affection to Him. He desires our ALL or none of us. He is not in competition with anyone else. So it must be ALL of me in response to ALL of God. So,as a lifestyle, Jesus ought to be Lord of all, because He gave ALL of Himself when He died for our sins; He who knew no sin. In our response, we, by of our own volition, must choose to make Him Lord of our language, worship, leadership, relationships, possessions, finances and communication. Simply put, this must be my response to ALL of God or my total and full commitment to God. The Weymouth New Testament puts it nicely by using the word **"whole"** in place of the word **"all"** before each faculty to emphasize the uniting of the total and completeness of each faculty as follows:

> *"'Thou shalt love the Lord thy God,'" he replied, "'with thy **whole** heart, thy **whole** soul, thy **whole** strength, and thy **whole** mind; and thy fellow man as much as thyself.'"*

It is not by might that we will reach this place; it is by the Spirit of God, who guides us into all truth and to glorify Jesus. At this point, **at this place in our yielding and dying to self,we will be ready to accept that the commandments of God must determine my values, your values, and our values.** So when our values are right our behaviour will be right. This results, because we will *allow the rule of Jesus to control all of us, by operating at the deep leve*l. This is the only true basis for willing obedience and love response to God and His love language. Another word to use for it is 'surrender'. *Only then can we love our neighbours as ourselves.*

In continuing the story, we see that Jesus commended our lawyer friend publicly. But in commending him, Jesus highlighted the need for compliance with the same law. Head knowledge alone will not grant any one eternal life. It was true for our lawyer friend, but it is also true for us today. This is Jesus' answer to him:

> *"And he said unto him, Thou hast answered **right: this do, and thou shalt live.**"*

But our emergent and curious lawyer friend was not satisfied. Like so many of us, he wanted to justify himself publicly. As a Jewish young man growing up, he had a very good head knowledge of the law. He would pay tithe to the last farthing and he thought that he was an excellent steward. But, now gaps were appearing in his answer. He mentioned 'neighbour' in his answer. *Now he wanted to know the meaning of his own spoken answer.* So here is his second question to Jesus.

> [29] *"But he, willing to justify himself, said unto Jesus,* ***And who is my neighbour?"***

Jesus was very happy to respond to his question as He loved him. Jesus told him the story of the good Samaritan who helped the man that was robbed and wounded. In His answer, Jesus pointed out that a priest and a Levite offered the victim no help. But that a Samaritan, the same lawyer would not associate or mingle with, had compassion on him and did the unthinkable, helped the victim, who from all appearances was a Jew.

In concluding the story, Jesus said to our lawyer friend: "***Go, and do thou likewise.***" What an opportunity Jesus gave the lawyer; yes, an open invitation to get the blessings which James and John among others have said, is in the doing, the implementation or the execution of knowledge of truth! Sad to say, the lawyer turned away in sadness, as he failed on the all-important area of the phileo love in the commandments of the second table. This means that he really didn't truly love God with his (whole) being. So, because he didn't love Jesus, he would not be able to carry out His command to go and do, to sell all that he had and give to the poor, then to come and follow Jesus. It is only when we satisfy the agape love of the first table commandments that we can love our neighbours as ourselves. Mammon was his God. He wasn't fully surrendered to God.

7.3 Other important responses

An **additional response** to God's Love Language is to be **filled with the Holy Spirit** who guides us into all truth. And God is more willing to give us His Holy Spirit than good parents are willing to give good gifts to their children. We have to make sure that we constantly have the oil of the Holy Spirit so that we will not be like the five foolish virgins; but rather like the five wise virgins who had the right preparation and response to the invitation to the wedding by having oil in their lamps plus the extra oil and were able to go into the marriage with the Bridegroom.

A motor car needs engine oil to keep it running. When the oil light in the car comes on, it is a warning that the oil is getting low or that something is wrong with the engine. Once we see that oil light flashing, then staying on, we know that we ought to stop and check our car. Usually the light comes on more than one time before the car will come to a complete stop, if unattended or ignored. So we must watch for the signs in our spiritual lives when the oil of our Holy Spirit Guide is getting low.

The following are useful reminder signs to help us know if the oil of the Holy Spirit is getting low in our lives.

> *"But ye are not in the flesh, but in the Spirit, if so be that the Spirit of God dwell in you. Now if any man have not the Spirit of Christ, he is none of his."*

> *"This I say then, Walk in the Spirit, and ye shall not fulfill the lust of the flesh. For the flesh lusteth against the Spirit, and the Spirit against the flesh: and these are contrary the one to the other: so that ye cannot do the things that ye would.*

> *Now the works of the flesh are manifest, which are these; Adultery, fornication, uncleanness, lasciviousness, Idolatry, witchcraft, hatred, variance, emulations,*

*wrath, strife, seditions, heresies, Envyings, murders, drunkenness, revellings, and such like: of the which I tell you before, as I have also told you in time past, that **they which do such things shall not inherit the kingdom of God.***

*But **the fruit of the Spirit is love,** joy, peace, long suffering, gentleness, goodness, faith, Meekness, temperance: against such there is no law. And they that are Christ's have crucified the flesh with the affections and lusts.*[319]

When we have the required level of oil of the Holy Spirit in our lives we willfully embrace God's Love Language as it is an outworking and expression of the fruit of the Spirit. When that oil is low or below the required minimum level, we will have difficulty embracing God's Love Language. This is because the fruit of the Spirit will be either absent or consistently sparse such that fleshy lusts and worldly desires come to the core and manifest themselves because there is no love for God nor one another which is what serves as a constraint to bad and wrong behaviour.

Our **final response** is to *acknowledge our weaknesses to God and ask Him to supply all our needs* so that we may remain in Him. The Apostle Paul and John the beloved disciple sum up the picture for us very beautifully as outlined below.[320]

[24] ***What a wretched** man I am! Who will rescue me from this body that is subject to death?* [25] ***Thanks** be to God, who delivers me through Jesus Christ our Lord! So then, I myself in my mind am a slave to God's law, but in my sinful nature a slave to the law of sin."*

---

[319]   Romans 8:9; *Galatians 5:16-17,19-24.*
[320]   *Romans 7:24, 25; Phil 4:19; John 15:1, 4.*

"But my God shall supply all your need according to his riches in glory by Christ Jesus."

"I am the true vine, and my Father is the gardener. **Remain in me**, *as I also remain in you. No branch can bear fruit by itself; it must remain in the vine. Neither can you bear fruit unless you remain in me."*

The story of the Apostle Paul (whose name and character were changed from the persecuting Saul) as cited above is an excellent case of one who was truly converted, as a result of the Holy Spirit working in his life. Hence, he could speak as he did about God's commandments in Romans chapter 7. The Holy Spirit helped him to be honest and to identify and verbalise his own weakness and wretchedness.

But some of us, including those who are very insecure, have not reached that place yet, so we may need others who are around us who have strong characters and will to point out to us (like barometers) our own weaknesses in order to help us on our continuum of character building. But then we should not turn and rail on them, when they are simply trying to help us. Those of us who are quite self-assured will usually not have any difficulty listening to, and positively responding to, those who are close to us, who are thus seeking to help us build better characters for God's Kingdom. And don't forget that God can and does work through others to help us in character building. I can recall an important work related life changing experience some years ago, that changed my life for the better. I was working at a particular company. My supervisor at the time had what I considered to be a peculiar way of stating some truths. I do not remember all the circumstances and the details; but he said something to me which, up to this present time, I still remember. He said: "My greatest strength is my greatest weakness." That to me at the time was like a knock out punch to the head. I just did not understand that apparent paradoxical statement. I wondered then: "How could my greatest strength be my greatest weakness?" It took me a longtime to recognize the profundity of the statement. But thank God that gratefully, I did eventually grasp the significance and the profoundness of the statement. When you are very good at something or very strong, there is the temptation, to which many yield, to lower our guards. It is at that point of lowering the guards that the devil often assails us, and does so successfully.

You have, no doubt often heard it said that too much confidence or overconfidence can be one's downfall. And the wise man Solomon correctly states it this way for us:

> *"**Pride** goeth before destruction, and a **haughty spirit before a fall.**"*

You may recall from the Bible the story of that proud and arrogant, Philistines champion, Goliath, who, although armed with armour and shield, lost the battle with the young and ruddy, David, when he removed his helmet. He removed his helmet protection just in time and long enough for the stone from his opponent's sling to lodge right in his forehead and the towering giant of over nine feet[321] came crashing down to the earth. David with only a sling and staff, but with help from God who promises to fight our battles, then removed and used Goliath's own sword to slay him. What a fascinating story of contrasts and paradoxes? The tall, proud and arrogant, giant, who cursed the God of Heaven was shamefully defeated by an ally of that same God. His opponent, a young, unassuming youth much shorter in stature, who trusted in the God of Heaven was an astounding victor as his God, whom Goliath defied, helped him to defeat the giant.

The truth is that, if we (you and I) are not careful, self may become our/my greatest enemy, as was in the case of Goliath, King Saul, Pharaoh, Nebuchadnezzar (before his conversion) and Lucifer. Ironically, and like many of us, these significant figures refused to acknowledge that their greatest strength was also their

---

[321] See 1 Samuel 17:4.

greatest weaknesses. Leaders generally, especially those first in rank or have the highest position, as well as professionals, including sport celebrities, indeed all who think and convince themselves that they are not only good in their fields, but are brighter and better than everyone else, who love to throw their weight around or wield power, who are controlling, and who believe that they are always right and that everyone else is wrong, are persons at great risk for special targeting and attacks by the devil, and therefore need to be very careful that they rely on the strong arms of Jesus, rather than on self, and pseudo sense of security.

Similarly, church membership, church attendance, and position in church as well as no church connection can be a major hindrance to surrendering ourselves to God, because they can feed the ego. Too much praise and individual attention can inflate the ego to the point where love for ego becomes the preeminent thing and greater than our/my love for God.

We all just have to be careful and ensure that we give the glory to Jesus and not to ourselves. We should remember that our mission and desire is to lift Him up before others. The Apostle Paul understood this conflict very well and writes the following,[322] after having personally won the battle on the matter of ego:

> *"For I say, through the grace given unto me, to every man that is among you, **not to think** of himself **more highly than he** ought to think; but to **think soberly**, according as God hath dealt to every man the measure of faith."*

> *"I am **crucified with Christ**: nevertheless I live; yet not I, but **Christ** liveth in me: and the life which I now live in the flesh **I live by the faith of the Son of God, who loved me, and gave himself for me.**"*

---

[322] *Romans 12:3; Galatians 2:20, 5:24.*

*"And they that are **Christ's** have **crucified the flesh with the affections and lusts.** "*

We need God to supply all our needs and to give us His power through the help of the Holy Spirit to help us to caress His Love Language, because of the ongoing battle waging and competing values between ourselves and Jesus as outlined below. Shown below is a diagrammatic representation of these competing values which was discussed by Dr. Erica Puni[323] at a Stewardship Seminar held at Northern Caribbean University in Jamaica in 2012.

COMPETING VALUE

Values determined by SELF	(We need the cross of Jesus)>>	JESUS (determined values)
1. Self-serving		Service
2. Self-indulgence		Simplicity
3. Self-gratification		Sacrifice
4. Self-seeking		Surrender
5. Self-centeredness		Submission

Only when Jesus reigns supremely in our lives, can the values of self be replaced by the Jesus determined values, so that we will become home sick for heaven and eternal life.

7.4 Right response, behaviour, and living in anticipation of heaven

In the story of the two contrasting fighters in battle, related above, only David's response and behaviour was right, and that was because He depended on God. So, too it must be for all of us who will embrace God's Love Language. Although we are living on earth, we will and must demonstrate by our lifestyle: right response and behaviour, the principles and values of heaven and the new earth as if we were actually living there. The type of living required is like, but in many ways more than what happens in simulation exercises. One of the good things about simulation is that it prepares the simulator for the real thing. Even though we have not seen the real (as in Heaven and Paradise) as Paul describes it in the citation below, we through the eyes of faith will embrace the reality though living on earth.

> *"But as it is written, Eye hath not seen, nor ear heard, neither have entered into the heart of man, the things which God hath prepared for them that love him."*[324]

Nevertheless, against this background, stretch your imagination with me to a time and a world in which we will live in anticipation of all of the following as if they were taking place in our lifetime.

i)   One perfect world with one true God where all worships this one true God.

ii) There is no image made, neither is there any image and heathen worship.

iii) No one takes the name of the Lord God in vain, neither by word nor by a life of misrepresentation.

iv) The entire universe is in unison and one accord, and all rests on, and keeps, the Sabbath day holy throughout the vast limitless space, and there is no commercial activity, as all businesses are closed, and all reflects every week on the Sabbath, in joyful adoration and gratitude in honour of, and as a memorial of, God's wonderful works of creation.

v)   There will be no debate, argument and counter-argument about who is a parent, and what is a family, plus no dysfunctional homes and families, no broken homes and families, no divorce, no trial family, no

---

[324]   *1 Corinthians 2:9.*

concubinage, as all things return to God's original plan for the family.

vi) There are no thoughts, talks, planning, scheming and plotting to take the life of anyone, and no one will be stressed or overworked. Plus, there is nothing that directly or indirectly, leads to or contributes to the shortening of life or the erosion of the quality of life and longevity.

vii) Can you imagine a scene where there is always faithfulness and trustworthiness all around, and no irregular love nor affection?

viii) Property and property rights are always respected, as no one will want to, or need to, "con" any one, no "three-card" persons, no gambling dens and allies, and no stealing.

ix) Imagine only true witnesses all around and fair play. What a sight; what a picture to be hold!

x) Then of course, to put the icing on the cake, there is real joy and contentment, no need to trick or decoy your neighbour or God or His cause to get personal gain. God will be our God, and all who make it there, will be His people.

Is this all a figment of idlers' wildest imagination or is it for real? Where is such a place, if there is such a place? **Yes, it is for real,** and there is such a place! It's all the result of the kind of response God desires of us. This place is called heaven, utopia, and paradise. Paradise Island in the Bahamas in the Caribbean cannot come close to it. **This paradise is located in the third heaven and the earth made new in the realm of time called eternity.**

Enoch, Moses and Elijah are there. Enoch and Elijah represent those who will not taste of death, but will be alive when Jesus comes from there, for His people who will be **translated.** Moses represents those who have tasted of death, but will be **resurrected** when Jesus comes with myriads of angels. Most of all, the triune

God of love: God the Father, the Holy Spirit of Truth; and Jesus, the only begotten Son of God; the central beings of God's Love Language will be there.

What is the requirement for getting there? It is a requirement that can stand the test of time and scrutiny. It is embracing, caressing God's Love Language: A lifestyle of loving obedience to God and His commandments. It involves more and more about Jesus.

I am looking forward to see you in that utopia where eternal life of bliss and eternal joys will be realized. Plan to meet me there!

MORE ABOUT JESUS I WOULD KNOW[325]

More about Jesus I would know,
More of His grace to others show;
More of His saving fullness see,
More of His love who died for me.

◇◇

If your life has been touched, changed, by
reading this book and you would like to share
your experience, Contact the Author by email:
GodsLoveLanguageMinistry@gmail.com

◇◇

BIBLIOGRAPHY

"Achieving Balance in an Unbalanced World, Time Elapsed Since Adam." Accessed August 19, 2012. http://achievebalance. com/data/timeline/

Blackaby, Henry, Richard Blackaby and Claude King. *Experiencing God: Knowing and Doing the Will of God.* USA: Life Way Press, 1990.

Brace, Shawn. "Speaking God's Love Language," *Adventist Review Online.* Accessed May 12, 2012. http://www.adventistreview. org/

Chapman, Gary D. *The Five Love Languages.* USA: North field Publishers, 2010.

"Choice." Accessed August 5, 2012. http://oxforddictionaries. com/definition/english/choose.

General Conference of Seventh-day Adventists. *Cornerstone Connections.* USA: Pacific Press Publishing Association, 1997.

Johnsen, Carsten. *The Maligned God.* Mezien: The Untold Story Publishers, 1980.

Lewis, Larry. "The Beginner's Guide To A Healthy Lifestyle." Accessed August 8, 2020. https://www.slideshare.net/ LarryLewis21/the-beginners-guide-to-a-healthy-lifestyle.

Osherow, Neal. *"Making Sense of the Nonsensical: An Analysis of Jonestown."* Accessed August 12, 2012. http://www.guyana. org/features/jonestown.html

Schwertley, Brian. *God's Law For Modern Man.* Lansing, MI: Brian Schwertley, 2000. Accessed August 26, 2012. http:// www. reformedonline.com/view/reformedonline/law.htm

Seventh-day Adventist Church Inter-American Division. *What We Believe: Being Mindful of His Word.* USA: Inter- American Division Publishing Association, 2012.

_____. *Sabbath School Bible Study Guide.* Florida, USA: Inter-American Division Publishing Association, 2012.

White, Ellen G. *Christian Service.* Hagerstown, MD: Review and Herald Publishing Association,1925.

_____. *Counsels on Health.* Mountain View, CA: Pacific Press Publishing Association, 1923.

_____. *Education.* Mountain View, CA: Pacific Press Publishing Association, 1903.

_____. *Spirit of Prophecy*, Vol. 1. Battle Creek, MI: Seventh-day Adventist Association, 1870.

_____. Testimonies for the Church, Vol. 1. Mountain View, CA; Pacific Press Publishing Association, 1923.

_____. *The Great Controversy.* Mountain View, CA: Pacific Press Publishing Association, 1911.

Lightning Source UK Ltd.
Milton Keynes UK
UKHW010624060821
388402UK00001B/44